The People's Chef

ALEXIS SOYER

PORTRAYED BY HIS WIFE, EMMA SOYER

The People's Chef

The Culinary Revolutions of Alexis Soyer

RUTH BRANDON

WALKER & COMPANY
NEW YORK

Originally published in 2004 in Great Britain by John Wiley & Sons, Ltd.
This edition published in the United States of America in 2004 by
Walker Publishing Company, Inc.

For information about permission to reproduce selections from
this book, write to Permissions, Walker & Company,
104 Fifth Avenue, New York, New York 10011.

Art credits: Frontispiece, and pages 66, 69, and 94 from *The Gastronomic
Regenerator* by Alexis Soyer. Pages 28 and 289 from *The Modern Housewife* by
Alexis Soyer. Page 38 courtesy of W. M. Griffiths Esq. Pages 111, 112, 195, 198,
and 199 courtesy of the Guildhall Library. Pages 137 and 201 courtesy of Punch
Ltd. Page 163 from the Mary Evans Picture Library. Pages 203 and 241 courtesy
of the Wellcome Trust. Page 236 from *Punchinello*. Page 256 courtesy of the
National Library of Jamaica. Pages 245, 253, 269, and 279 from *A Culinary
Campaign* by Alexis Soyer. Pages 285, 300, and 301 courtesy of Frank Clement-
Lorford. Page 302 from the author's collection.

Library of Congress Cataloging-in-Publication Data
available upon request
ISBN 0-8027-1452-8

Book design by Maura Fadden Rosenthal
Book composition by Coghill Composition Company

Visit Walker & Company's Web site at www.walkerbooks.com

Printed in the United States of America

2 4 6 8 10 9 7 5 3 1

For Frank Clement-Lorford
with thanks for all his kindness

Contents

ACKNOWLEDGMENTS

I should like to thank everyone who helped with this book, in particular Vanessa Bell at the Wellcome Trust Library; Simon Blundell at the Reform Club; Dr. Alastair Massie at the National Army Museum; staff at the British Consulate, Istanbul; staff at the Essex County Archive, Chelmsford; staff at the RIBA Drawings Collection; Philip Steadman; James Marshall, Hounslow Library; Robert Thorne; and my panel of tasters: Howard Brenton, Jane Brenton, Veronica Dare Bryan, John Hare, Bill Hillier, Sheila Hillier, Carl Isakson, Lisa Jardine, Howard Nelson, Jinty Nelson, Philip Steadman, and Lily Steadman.

Thanks, too, to my agent, Clare Alexander, whose suggestion that I should pull the recipes up to the front of the chapters was the key to the book's shape, to my editor, Sally Smith, and to all at John Wiley.

Above all, I must thank Frank Clement-Lorford, who knows everything about Alexis Soyer, and who has been so generous in sharing the fruits of his researches. This book is for him. I hope he enjoys it.

The People's Chef

The Menu

Tell me what you eat: I will tell you what you are.
— Jean-Anthelme Brillat-Savarin

If we knew nothing else about this *mot*, we might guess that its author must have been French; and it is to a Frenchman—albeit a different Frenchman—that I propose to apply it.

Some people, in their selves and their doings, seem particularly to embody their time; Alexis Soyer was one such. In 1841, *The Globe* newspaper said of him, without irony, "The impression grows on us that the man of his age is neither Sir Robert Peel, nor Lord John Russell, or even Ibrahim Pasha, but Alexis Soyer." This was of course hyperbole. But it is nonetheless an extraordinary description of a thirty-year-old French cook.

Soyer started out as an unusually talented chef to the upper crust, experiencing in that capacity the 1830 Revolution in Paris, the riot-torn English countryside, and the cavernous luxury of the Reform Club, where he held court in kitchens he had himself designed. He might have confined himself, as did most grand cooks, to the comfortable milieu of the rich who so eagerly sought his services: an easy life, and one of comparatively little interest, at least to future generations. But his restless curiosity and democratic spirit impelled him constantly to explore new possibilities. He entered the world of the starving and destitute, running soup kitchens during the Irish famine and in London's teeming rookeries. He became a man of business, marketing an endless stream of kitchen gadgets and patent drinks and sauces. Through his wife, and after her death his lover, he maintained a foothold in London's artistic life. He wrote three popular and influential recipe books—*The Gastronomic Regenerator, The Modern Housewife, or Ménagère*, and *Soyer's Shilling Cookery for the People*, each of which sold hundreds of thousands of copies. He entered a scheme for the competition to design the 1851 Great Exhibition, and when this failed to win declined the official catering contract, preferring instead to open the first truly universal restaurant in Britain, in Kensington Gore just opposite Paxton's Crystal Palace.

Unlike his employers he had grown up in hardship and knew all about poverty. But, perhaps for this very reason, financial risk held no fears for him. Time and again, having accumulated some cash, he laid it out and lost it, often on ventures designed to improve the lot of the unfortunate. He personally subsidized his model soup kitchens, even when his own finances were far from healthy. And in 1855, after reading W. H. Russell's horrific dispatches to *The Times*, he volunteered his services in the Crimean War, revolutionizing cooking in the hospitals and army camps (and not missing the opportunity to sample exotic oriental dishes) while establishing one of the world's most improbable friendships, with Florence Nightingale. He recounted those strange, interesting, and horrendous months with characteristic idiosyncrasy in a memoir, *Soyer's Culinary Campaign*, written on his return to London; at the time of his death he was collaborating with Miss Nightingale in the reform of British army catering. He died before their plans could be implemented, his health fatally undermined by Crimean hardships.

It is an extraordinary life, and one that offers a unique snapshot of its time; but it is not easy to access, at least by conventional means. Of course, such a well-known figure leaves tracks. There are squibs, stories, and letters in the public prints, and vignettes in other people's memoirs. Soyer's own account of the Crimea and the biography that appeared the year after he died are full of anecdotes. But all these give us only the view from outside. Even Thackeray, who was a friend and in whose novels he appears, presents only an affectionate caricature.

There is little of a more intimate nature. Like most poor children, Soyer had little formal education. He left school at eleven and spent most of his time thereafter in the kitchen. He could read and write French, though his spelling was shaky and his orthography laborious. But he never learned to write English, though he spoke it, and may have been able to read it. He kept a daily "tablet" in which he recorded his doings and possibly his feelings, but this, along with all his other papers, disappeared on his death. The few letters that survive are business correspondence, mostly written for him by others.

This uneasy semiliteracy was neither unusual nor, in many cases, particularly disabling. Soyer was only a cook, and lived at a time when more than half the inhabitants of both England and

France could neither read nor write. But his adult life took him into sophisticated circles, where he keenly wished to be considered an equal and where most communication was by letter. And he ended up producing books in English: a situation in which difficulty with writing might be thought the ultimate inconvenience. He was therefore forced to rely upon amanuenses, in both English (for obvious reasons) and (for convenience, if not absolute necessity) French. While she lived, this role was filled by his wife, who, although she was English, spoke good French, and after her death, by a series of secretaries—Soyer preferred, when he could afford it, to employ one for each language. Most of his surviving correspondence is therefore written in a variety of hands, the labored signature being its one common feature.

This was an expensive and cumbersome situation—and, from the biographer's standpoint, highly inconvenient. You don't dictate intimate letters to a secretary; indeed, given Soyer's uncomfortable relationship with the pen, it is unlikely that even his daily "tablet" was more than a bare note of meetings and expenditures. However, for someone as creative, intelligent, and energetic as he was, this verbal awkwardness simply meant that he must find other channels to express himself. As a result, cookery became not just his living but his medium: his natural means of communication, whether emotional, artistic, or political.

In this situation, the biographer's course is clear. Where the subject leads, she must follow. Directly and indirectly, it is his recipe books that contain the essence of Soyer's world; and it is there that I have not only sought it, but cooked it. In this *diner à la Soyer*, each dish—taken, of course, from one of Soyer's recipes—is appropriate both to its position in the meal and to the topics raised by that particular stage of the story. Here is history, quite literally, on a plate: the first half of the nineteenth century as viewed through the bottom of a saucepan. "Tell me what you eat: I will tell you what you are."

As it happens, Soyer and Brillat-Savarin were Parisian contemporaries, and Soyer in every molecule a product of the civilization Brillat-Savarin expounded. When Brillat-Savarin's great work, *The Philosopher in the Kitchen,* was published in 1825, Soyer, then fifteen, was learning cookery, and much else, in the city's restaurants. Gastronomy, for both the Philosopher and his acolyte, includes conversation, flirtation, jokes, anecdotes: everything that transforms a meal into a long-remembered pleasure—some might say, everything that makes life worth living. Brillat-Savarin points out, not without pride, that certain French words—*la gourmandise, la coquetterie*—express concepts so particularly Gallic as to be virtually untranslatable: Other languages, possessing no direct equivalent, simply adopt them. He might have added *la gastronomie.* This was the sensibility Soyer brought to his life in England.

By the time he arrived there, the shape of the day's main meal had acquired a ritual fixity. The hour of dinner had moved, as the eighteenth century gave place to the nineteenth, from midafternoon to evening, and the table was no longer loaded with different and disparate dishes all offered simultaneously. Instead, one course followed another in the French manner: soup, then fish, hors d'oeuvres, meat, fowl, game or savory, dessert. For a grand dinner this was the minimum; it might be expanded by removes, flancs, relevés, entremets—words could be conjured up to legitimize an almost infinite number of dishes—but at least the diner's taste buds faced only one assault at a time. Our dinner comprises only the basic seven courses: short as lives go, but densely packed.

With one obvious exception, this is a menu Soyer's paying clients might have consumed at any time during his career. In their lives, famine was a rarity. One of the things that made Soyer unusual was that he also turned his attention to those for whom it was the rule.

MENU

———⌒∿⌒———

New Spring and Autumn Soup

———⌒∿⌒———

Fish: Salmon with Shrimp Sauce

———⌒∿⌒———

Hors d'Oeuvres Variés

———⌒∿⌒———

Relevé: Mutton Cutlets Reform

———⌒∿⌒———

Entrée Chaude: Famine Soup

———⌒∿⌒———

Roast: Quail à la Symposium

———⌒∿⌒———

Entremets: Turkish Delights

———⌒∿⌒———

Coffee

Bon appétit!

The Soup

Our *diner* begins with soup, partly because this was the invariable start to all nineteenth-century dinners, but also because this first course is about Frenchness, and soup, avers the Philosopher, is the essence of France. "Nowhere can such good *potage* be obtained as in France," he observes. Soup "is the basis of the French national diet, and the experience of centuries has inevitably brought it to perfection."[1]

And if soup is generically the French national dish, then this rather oddly named New Spring and Autumn Soup—so much more spring than autumn, and thereby doubly appropriate to this account of our hero's early years—is even more unmistakably Gallic, both in its delicate combination of vegetables (lettuce cooked

[1]Brillat-Savarin, *The Philosopher in the Kitchen,* pp. 72–3.

with peas), and in its delightful transformation of a little garden produce into an unexpected culinary treat. It is the simplest kind of home cooking, particularly useful for those who grow their own vegetables. Then as now, this was far commoner in land-rich, agricultural France than in the industrial society England had already become. In the provinces, where Soyer spent his childhood, most families still keep a *potager*; and this is the kind of recipe you need when you find, as every kitchen gardener inevitably does, an entire row of lettuces ready to bolt and the next row coming on fast.

New Spring and Autumn Soup

A most refreshing and exquisite soup. At the end of the London season, when the markets are full of everything and few to partake of them, this soup can be made as a bonne bouche:

Wash, dry and cut up four cabbage lettuces and one cos ditto, a handful of sorrel, a little tarragon and chervil, and two or three small cucumbers, peeled and sliced; put into a saucepan a quarter of a pound of butter, then set in the vegetables; put upon a slow fire and stir often, until there is no liquid remaining; add two tablespoons of flour, mix well, and moisten with two quarts of broth or water and set it to boil; when boiling add a pint of green peas, two teaspoonfuls of powdered sugar, a little pepper and salt; when the peas are tender, serve.

I took this from the *Shilling Cookery for the People*. Soyer gives the same recipe in his more upmarket recipe book for the middle classes,

The Modern Housewife, the main difference being that there water is not mentioned, stock, "as directed," being taken for granted. Since he himself would always have used stock, so did I.

Stock for All Kinds of Soup

Procure a knuckle of veal about 6lb, cut into pieces about the size of an egg, and half a pound of ham or bacon; rub a quarter of a pound of butter upon the bottom of a stewpan, into which put the meat and bacon with half a pint of water, 2oz salt, 3 middle-sized onions with 2 cloves in each, 1 turnip, a carrot, half a leek, half a head of celery; place over a sharp fire, occasionally stirring with a wooden spoon, until the bottom is covered with white thickish glaze, which will lightly adhere to the spoon; fill up the stewpan with cold water, and when upon the point of boiling lower the heat and simmer for three hours; carefully skim off every particle of grease or scum; strain; it is ready to use. (*The Modern Housewife*)

Soyer gives many variants on the theme of stock, consommé, brown sauce, and gravy, but all use more or less the same ingredients. This one may sound extravagant, but everything is comparative: In *The Gastronomic Regenerator,* the first and grandest of his cookbooks, the basis of his stock is 20 lb. of beef, as well as veal and ham, while charity soups for the starving make do with ¼ lb. meat and a few vegetables per two gallons of water. In the latter case, the meat and vegetables form part of the soup, but in the stocks and consommés they are always strained out. Not having an army to feed, I made half quantities of this stock; and since knuckle of veal was not available at my butcher's except to order (and I didn't wish to be landed with a whole knuckle), I used leg of beef—about 4 lb., including bones.

Bones! The very mention of such a thing brings to mind my mother's continually simmering stockpot and the ever-steamy windows of our kitchen. Something always seemed to be boiling then—if not soup then laundry, as often as not both at once. She used to boast of nurturing my infant teeth on bone broth—something few mothers in the post-BSE generation would consider. But in the interests of historical accuracy I risked the prions, trusting to the sanity of the cows supplied by my reassuringly organic butcher. And now here I was, back with the steam. I had intended to use a pressure cooker, but it was far too small for beef bones, especially since everything had to be stirred around at the start. Fortunately, however, I was in no hurry. And since, after the first few minutes, it just simmers, nothing could have been simpler, except the skimming, which was finicky; if I'd had the patience to wait until the stock was cool, this would have been easier.

The taste was excellent—a rich, deep flavor, as one would expect from such ingredients. Not, however, what one would choose for such a soup today. Chicken or vegetable stock would be more to our taste now, a lighter flavor for this subtle combination of summer vegetables. But nowhere in Soyer could I find any mention of such lightweight concoctions; on the contrary, he uses this beef or veal stock as a foundation for all sauces, soups, and gravies—even some of his sauces for fish, such as matelote of salmon or turbot, use it. And this reliance on beef or veal as the foundation of all cookery was not confined to Soyer. Eliza Acton, a contemporary of Soyer's with a subtler, more modern style, also makes no mention of chicken or vegetable stock, basing even her chicken soup on a veal broth—and this despite the fact that she identifies several of her recipes as Jewish. These, however, were obtained long before the influx of east European Jews in the 1880s, for whom chicken soup, as everyone knows, represented the cure for all ills. So we must perhaps conclude that chicken stock arrived with them.

When the stock was ready and all the meat and vegetables had been strained out, the question arose: what to do with them? It seemed almost immoral to throw them all away. Certainly, Soyer would never have done so. These ingredients, covered with new water and boiled for another few hours, will (he assures the reader) make an excellent secondary stock. Or, simmered a little longer and not separated, they become *pot au feu,* the "truly national soup of France," as *Shilling Cookery* describes it (more luxurious versions use more meats: ham, beef, veal, and ox-liver may all go in). This may be eaten as one meal, broth, meat, and vegetables together, or separately as *bouillon,* the broth, poured over *croûtons* of bread, followed by *bouilli,* the meat, with the veg arranged around.

Brillat-Savarin hated *bouilli:* He called it "meat without its juice."[2] He divided persons who ate it into four categories: "victims of habit, who eat it because their parents ate it before them . . . impatient persons, who detest inactivity at table and have accordingly contracted the habit of falling upon the first foodstuff that comes to hand . . . Careless persons, who . . . regard meals as just part of the day's work . . . greedy persons." But Soyer loved it: When he ate at home, this was a favorite dish. The bacon, with greens, he said, was particularly delicious.

[2]Brillat-Savarin, *The Philosopher in the Kitchen,* pp. 72–3.

In this respect, I vote with Brillat-Savarin. The meat seemed to me utterly flavorless—not surprising, since all the taste, after three hours' boiling, had gone into the broth. Only copious added condiments could have made it palatable. Perhaps it is his devotion to *bouilli* that explains Soyer's predilection for the piquant sauces that bore his name, whether specially created for members of the Reform Club or marketed, bottled, to the general public. This pepping-up of dull or indifferent food is, of course, precisely the role of their direct descendants—Daddies Sauce, HP Sauce, tomato ketchup. An Italian friend, captured by the British in Egypt during World War II and set to cooking, liked to recount, in tones of horror, the daily preparation, in the western desert, of "boiled meat with *salsa piccante*"—a combination Soyer would undoubtedly have recognized. In fact, all the classic boiled meat dishes—Italian *bollito misto,* German boiled beef, English boiled leg of mutton—are accompanied by a piquant sauce, which perhaps tells us all we need to know about meat and boiling (cured and pickled meat honorably excepted). Who could possibly face a *bollito misto* without a generous bowl of *salsa verde,* or boiled mutton without its capers? And what are they if not boiled meat and *salsa piccante?* Perhaps it's simply a question of Terry Pratchett's distinction between "meat" and "named meat."

Bouillon, however, makes a truly excellent stock; and once it was ready, the soup itself was simple to prepare. Surprisingly, the *Modern Housewife* version recommends cooking it for half an hour after the peas are added (I used frozen peas, a luxury unavailable to Soyer's readers). But whether your peas are fresh or frozen, this seems excessive. If you follow *Shilling Cookery*'s recommendation to cook only until the peas are ready, about ten minutes would be more than enough. Perhaps this seemingly unnecessary length of cooking was a result of using flour as thickening. This gives a slightly heavy flavor, which evidently appealed to the Victorians—for Soyer, flour is the invariable thickening agent. To thicken such a soup today, or even a sauce, one would use a little cream, giving a lighter, subtler and richer result.

Soyer adds, in *The Modern Housewife,* that "the flavor of the vegetables will be fully preserved" in this recipe, and he's right: Despite all the cooking, it is. I would have added a little lemon juice, though more sorrel, with its sour piquancy, would probably have had the same effect; and for my taste it needed more salt than Soyer puts in. But this is a cheap, simple, fresh, and delicious soup—one that it is easy to imagine a provincial family, like the Soyers, enjoying for lunch on a fine June day.

Soyer left no memoir of his early life. He might have produced one had he lived to a serene old age; but his life, action-packed to the last, ended before he was fifty—a time when most people still look to the future rather than the past. For his secretaries, however, this early death deprived them of both a friend and an income. They therefore set about filling these gaps by setting down the details of Soyer's life, recounting both the stories he had often told them and those episodes in which they had personally participated. Hence the *Memoirs of Alexis Soyer,* published in 1859 by Francis Volant, his onetime secretary (though not, by the time of his death, any longer a friend) and J. R. Warren and James Lomax, also old friends and colleagues.

These were people who had known Soyer for many years, and theirs is an account visibly true to life in many respects. Its claim to accuracy, however, is undermined in the very first sentence: "Alexis Soyer was born in October 1809 at Meaux-en-Brie, a small town in France noted for its famous cheese."[3] Meaux was undoubtedly his birthplace (and this being a gastronomic tale, we should not forget that the town is also known for its mustard, a condiment introduced by Charlemagne to monastic foundations such as that of Meaux, which is built around its cathedral, and used, like *salsa piccante,* to mask unpalatable flavors, especially that of decay). But his birth certificate gives the date not as October 1809 but as February 4, 1810. Thus, at the very start of our tale we see the advantages of soup over mere words as a means of conveying the truth. Words can mislead: soup, at the very most, may disappoint.

Mistaken facts, however, have their own story to tell. Often it is a tale of *parti pris*—but that is unlikely to be true in this instance. Neither Volant nor Warren could possibly have been present at this or any of the incidents described in the book's early pages, nor had they anything to gain from misrepresenting them. So the error can only have been Soyer's own. Of course, there may have been some reason for him deliberately to alter his date of birth (as, for instance, Louis B. Mayer altered his to July 4, in order to prove himself truly all-American). But if so, it is not apparent; and if he simply got it wrong, a fairly chaotic family life is indicated—one in which birthdays were of little account amid the general struggle.

From what we can deduce of the Soyer family's circumstances, this would not be surprising. The *Memoirs* state that Alexis's parents, Emery and Madeleine Soyer, were small shopkeepers. But once again this is not quite correct. Emery and Madeleine certainly began

[3]Volant and Warren, *Memoirs of Alexis Soyer,* p. 1.

married life keeping a shop—on the birth certificate of their eldest son, Philippe, in 1799, Emery describes himself as a *maître épicier,* with an address in the rue du Tan, an area of dingy respectability just south of the cathedral. But the business failed in 1804, six years before Alexis was born, and the family's descent from respectability to poverty can be traced on the map. Meaux at that time divided into three economic sections: the bourgeois district adjacent to the cathedral; the area of small shops immediately to its south; and yet farther south, on the farther bank of the Marne, the cramped dwellings of the poor. At the time of Alexis's birth the family was living in the rue Cornillon, in the poorest part of town, while Emery Soyer took what work he could get, which chiefly meant digging canals.

The pattern of births and deaths in the Soyer family mirrors these ups and downs. There were two sons, Philippe, born in 1799, and Louis, born in 1801, during the *épicerie* years. Then life got harder: There were two more babies in the eight-year gap between Louis and Alexis, but both died in infancy. Alexis, however, survived. Perhaps life had got a little easier; at the very least, the two older children were no longer babies themselves, and would have been able to help rather than adding to the burden. Or maybe the new arrival was sturdier than the two who had died; or Madeleine might simply have learned how to cope. Even so, the sheer day-to-day effort of supporting three children on a laborer's irregular wages can hardly have allowed for much celebration of birthdays. No wonder Alexis, when he grew up, laid such store by thrift and good management in the culinary department. Such an upbringing would certainly explain his devotion to a treat like *pot-au-feu*—the *bouilli* as well as the *bouillon.*

Such were the bald facts. But bald facts never held much attraction for Soyer. If he had stayed in Meaux it would have been another matter: In a small town, everyone knows everything about everyone else. But he did not stay in Meaux. He made his life in another country, on terms with the richest and most powerful in the land. And although everything we know about Soyer shows that he considered himself anyone's equal, which as a proud French citizen he indeed was, it cannot be denied that in the social struggle every little bit helps. So if he preferred to think (and speak) of his parents in their more respectable incarnation as shopkeepers, rather than in their fallen state as members of the laboring classes, who can blame him? It was almost true.

The *Memoirs* go on to tell how Alexis, aged nine, was presented to those in charge of Meaux cathedral as the first step in a career intended to lead to the priesthood, a fate he escaped by exhibiting such extreme naughtiness (ringing the Cathedral bells one night and bringing out the garrison) that he was thrown out of the choir school, this being the only way he could devise of forcing his parents to abandon their ecclesiastical ambitions. But this, too, seems improbable. Soyer is not a common name, in France or anywhere else; so unusual is it, indeed, that Elizabeth Ray, who wrote a short book about him, wondered whether our Soyer might not have been Russian-Jewish in origin, Russian Jews being the only other Soyers she could identify. This, however, is (to say the least) unlikely. What is more probable is that he was a Protestant. Meaux was historically a center of Protestantism; indeed, the history of Meaux is the history of the Reformation in France. Guillaume Briconnet, Bishop of Meaux, was one of its leaders; in the wars of religion, the town was a Huguenot stronghold. And when the position of the Protestants became impossible following the revocation of the Edict of Nantes in 1685, a Soyer appears in a list of French and Swiss Protestants, including some families from Meaux, who left France in the hope of taking English nationality.

Our Soyer was certainly not a religious man. But this provenance would chime with the instinct for practical charity and public spirit that came increasingly to dominate his life. French Protestants were *ipso facto* liberals; they had too often been the victims of reaction for anything else to be possible. It is notable that Soyer's first venture into charity was on behalf of the Spitalfields weavers, descendants of Huguenot refugees. And he, his wife, Emma, and his brother Philippe's daughter are all buried in the Protestant part of Kensal Green cemetery, which in the mid–nineteenth century strictly segregated its different consecrated grounds: surprising, had the family really been Catholic enough to consider the priesthood.

Why, then, does the story appear? Again, it can only have originated with Soyer himself. But why should he make up such a tale? Perhaps because—as with the statement about his parents being shopkeepers—it was not so much untrue as a slight alteration of the truth. Perhaps Emery and Madeleine Soyer did hope their youngest son, the unlooked-for blessing of their later years, would enter the ministry as a Protestant pastor—a prospect he would certainly have detested: It is hard to imagine anyone more unsuited to the religious life, of whatever denomination, than the careless, flirtatious, showy, epicurean Alexis. Perhaps he really did attend the choir school—he had a notably good singing voice, and this might have been a way of getting a free education—and really was thrown out. At any rate, by 1821 his schooling, such as it was, had ceased, and he left Meaux for Paris. Emery Soyer might have fallen on hard times, but he was evidently determined to make sure that his sons, unlike himself, would have a trade to follow. The eldest son, Philippe, was a cook, the second, Louis, a cabinetmaker. When Alexis left Meaux for Paris, it was to join Philippe, who was already there. He, too, would learn to cook.

The *Memoirs* tell us that, to begin with, Alexis showed little enthusiasm for his designated career. He much preferred the theater to the kitchen; he was a natural show-off, good-looking, with a pleasant singing voice, and his ambition was to become a comic actor, like his heroes Brunet, Odry, and Levasseur at the Théâtre des Variétés, where he spent much of his time. Understandably, however, the family did not encourage him in this risky ambition. Most theatrical careers end in failure, and they knew only too well what failure felt like. There was certainly no chance of their supporting him while he made his way. Quite the contrary: He was in Paris to find paid employment, the sooner the better. Philippe (he later told his children) had not been enthusiastic about taking his little brother under his wing. He did not find him easy to work with, and certainly had no intention of having him permanently in his own kitchen. Nevertheless, he finally persuaded Alexis to concentrate on cooking, and apprenticed him at Georges Rignon's famous restaurant, where the boy evidently showed great natural aptitude. At the age of seventeen he was engaged by another well-known restaurateur, D'Ouix, whose establishment was situated in the Boulevard des Italiens, near all the fashionable theaters, and popular with the actors among whom Alexis had once so much wished to spend his working life.

Here, despite his youth, he was put in charge of the kitchen, with twelve cooks under him. He had found his métier. He had also found what he needed—a stage. For he never renounced his love of performing: It was merely displaced. If he could not be an actual actor, he would become the first thespian of the kitchen. And fortunately for Soyer, he lived in the one city in the world where such ambitions might then be realized.

Today the notion of the chef as performer is a commonplace, the combined product of the lifestyle industry and television. But culinary theater, like any other branch of the art, requires a public platform. And a hundred and fifty years before the advent of the television cook, this very particular relationship between a chef and his public was something unique to France—and, within France, to Paris. This was partly because performing implies art, and only in France was gastronomy taken seriously as an art form. But there was also another reason. The cook's real stage, the arena within which he performs and makes his name, is of course the restaurant. And the restaurant as we know it, a place of gastronomic entertainment rather than hurried nourishment, where the public gathers at separate tables to choose a meal and spend a pleasant evening with friends or family, was at that time a wholly Parisian institution.

Of course, France was not the only country where people ate out. Anyone who reads (for example) Samuel Pepys's diary will know how frequently Londoners, both men and women, dined out in the seventeenth century, whether at an "ordinary" or at some more fashionable and expensive haunt—a practice that continued into the eighteenth century. However, these places did not provide a menu from which to choose one's dinner: One simply ate what was offered by the host or hostess, different houses specializing in different dishes.

By the time the nineteenth century got into its stride, many gentlemen preferred (as we shall see) to eat at a private club. But London still had many public eating-houses, and these still offered only the one or two dishes for which they were known. Thus, George

Augustus Sala, recalling the London of the 1840s and "50s, remembered an eating house on Holborn Hill whose placard read "A devilish good dinner for threepence halfpenny": It offered stewed beef with plenty of bread—"a most satisfying meal." And at a higher level there were the *alamode* beef shops (whose product, Sala was at pains to point out, bore no resemblance to the classic French dish of *boeuf à la mode*). He favored one called the Thirteen Cantons off Drury Lane, where for fourpence you got a pewter plate of *alamode* and for sixpence a rather larger portion served on earthenware. "Why it was called *alamode* puzzled me; but it was a distinctly characteristic dish, deriving its peculiarity from the remarkably luscious and tasty sauce, or rather soup, with which it was accompanied."[4]

The notion that diners should be able to choose the dishes they would prefer was not entertained until 1770. That year, the first restaurant, as we would understand the term, opened—not in London but in Paris: the Champ d'Oiseau in the rue Poulies. Paradoxically, its establishment resulted from the rage for English fashions then prevalent in France. Hitherto, the French had preferred to eat at home, while "the English, as is well-known, always take their meals in taverns."[5] Visitors to Paris, if they were fortunate, might be invited to dine at private houses, where the cooking was usually wonderful. But such invitations were not easily come by: According to the English traveler Philip Thicknesse, it was "extremely difficult" for even the most important foreigners to gain admittance to the best French homes. Most therefore had had no choice but to eat at their inn or at the *table d'hôte* offered by their hotel—an uninviting ambience for

[4]Sala, *Things I Have Seen and People I Have Known,* vol. 1, pp. 202–3.
[5]Hayward, *The Art of Dining.*

those who were not regular customers, the quality of the local gossip generally outstripping that of the food, which was dull, basic, and taken at a fixed hour. If the visitor wished to entertain, the only possibility was to order complete meals from a *traiteur,* well in advance.

The Champ d'Oiseau thus fulfilled a clear need. But it differed from an English tavern in one very significant way. Instead of the customer having to eat whatever the cook happened to have prepared that night, it offered a choice: a bill of fare written on a large placard, or *escriteau,* with a list of dishes from which meals might be chosen in permutation, was posted at its door. Henceforth the highest flights of French cooking, hitherto confined to the homes of the well-to-do, might be sampled by anyone with enough money to buy a restaurant meal. The customer would decide how much he wished to spend, and choose a meal to suit both his stomach and his purse.

The success of this new concept was beyond its originator's wildest dreams. He was "a genius," observed Brillat-Savarin, "endowed with profound insight into human nature."[6] Restaurants became the rage. By the time the Revolution broke out in 1789, there were a hundred restaurants in Paris. And the number went on growing. It might have been expected that the Revolution would put an end to such open luxury; in fact, quite the contrary happened. People preferred not to dine too well at home, for fear their servants might report them to the dread Committee of Public Safety. There was, paradoxically, less danger of being spied on or arrested at a restaurant, with the added advantage that one could meet other people there and find out the latest news—essential in a pretelephonic city where the political scene, upon which everyone's lives depended,

[6]Brillat-Savarin, *The Philosopher in the Kitchen,* p. 267.

changed daily if not hourly. The culture of communal meals also re-inforced the habit of eating out—literally so, since these *repas communaux* took place at tables laid in the streets. Meanwhile grand cooks, hitherto employed privately, either fled to England or opened up their own establishments. By the time the first restaurant guide, the *Almanach des Gourmands,* was published in 1803, Paris boasted between five and six hundred restaurants—"a hundred restaurateurs for every bookseller," observed the *Almanach:* "the Revolution, so bad for all the other arts, has increased gastronomic activity." As the old fortunes dispersed, new ones had been made, and "in most of these newly opulent Parisians the heart has been wholly replaced by the gizzard."[7] The new constitution had also brought an influx of legis-lators from the provinces (such as Brillat-Savarin himself, whom the Directory appointed government commissioner at the Versailles Court of Criminal Justice). These were people who needed to eat and wished to eat well, but whose domestic establishments were else-where. For them, restaurants were a godsend—as Brillat-Savarin's ascription of genius makes plain. And where they led everyone else followed, setting a style that endures to this day. Social life took place outside the home—in the theaters, the cafés, and the restaurants. If you wanted to entertain or meet your friends, that was where you did so. As an English journalist observed, "What exists in Paris to a degree which seems to English people astonishing is . . . café life with *appartements* which frequently extend but little beyond the solitary sleeping rooms."[8] He was writing in 1873, but the same observation might have been made fifty years earlier, or fifty years later.

Brillat-Savarin enumerated the different types of restaurant

[7]*Almanach des Gourmands,* 2nd edition, 1803.
[8]*The Architect,* quoted in Olsen, *The Growth of Victorian London,* p. 107.

eaters: the hurried throng of solitary diners, who eat quickly, pay, and depart; the country visitors, careful not to spend too much but enjoying their novel experience (and a few new dishes); the old married couples with nothing much left to talk about, on their way to the theater; the lovers, flirting and enjoying the delicious food; the regular *prix fixe* habitués; a few foreigners, usually English, who ordered the most expensive food and wine and drank (as the English did) far too much; and finally, "those individuals . . . who belong to a type only met with in Paris, which has neither property, capital nor employment, but spends freely for all that."[9] In short, exactly the people one might see in a Parisian restaurant today.

The *Almanach des Gourmands* catered to this new public, telling its buyers where to find "those Artistes most celebrated for their good food." It also indicated who was coming up and who on the slide. For instance, Véry, who had once dominated the scene, was by 1803 on his way down—"sumptuous rooms, but not as good as he was, so no-one goes there any more." Evidently, the allied monarchs did not read the *Almanach:* When they arrived in Paris after the defeat of Napoleon in 1814, it was Véry who received the contract to supply their table—a contract that earned him 3,000 francs a day, not including wine.[10] In 1825, he was still occupying his sumptuous rooms (and still not what he once had been).

Young Soyer plunged happily into this sociable and food-conscious way of life, quickly becoming known in the city. The *Memoirs* recount (clearly not for the first time) how, not long after his move to D'Ouix, he was deputed to carry the dessert to a rich

[9]Brillat-Savarin, *The Philosopher in the Kitchen,* p. 270.
[10]Hayward, *The Art of Dining.*

banker's house whose ball his master was catering. D'Ouix himself had overseen the majority of the refreshments, but the dessert had been left to young Alexis, now promoted from apprentice to second cook. Then as now the caterer also supplied china and glasses, these being carried there and back in wooden trays by the apprentices and second cooks. Once arrived at the house, Alexis was asked ("being a jovial fellow") for a song, and treated to large amounts of food and drink. When he eventually left the house, laden with his tray of used crockery, he passed out in a building site, finally returning in the small hours minus both the tray and his pants. (The wooden tray had D'Ouix's name painted on it, and was soon restored, together with the missing garments.) This exploit made the local press: Henceforth young Soyer became known as "the *enfant terrible* of Montmartre."

It seems that this was not the only occasion on which he abandoned his pants. Many years later a young man, one Jean Alexis Lamain, whose birth certificate showed him to have been born in 1830, visited Soyer in London. He was the son of a dressmaker, Adélaïde Angélique Lamain, and (he claimed) Alexis Soyer. Soyer did not dispute this claim but (after an initial shocked recoil) welcomed the young man as his long-lost son. Jean Alexis subsequently changed his name to Soyer.

Soyer left a set of doggerel verses from this time, which give a vivid picture of his life in Paris:

> The cafés are crowded with eaters and smokers,
> Theatres are bulging with joyous onlookers,
> The alleys are swarming with strollers and jokers,
> And ne'er-do-wells tread on the heels of the loafers.

The husbands are watchful, the lovers in bed;
Respectable folk, let it clearly be said;
On the streets there are nothing but drunkards and playboys,
And the cops pick up bodies passed out in the laybys.

Now even the rich call a cab homeward bound,
And the boulevards are filled with a silence profound;
Behind a blue curtain the shadows advance
Of a late-running group in a wine-fuelled dance.

But hark! In the city the matins bell tolls
And workmen grab coffee and hot buttered rolls,
The hammer and tongs start their daily tattoo
But I hurry bedwards—there's sleeping to do.[11]

---

[11]   *Les cafés se garnissent de gourmands, de fumeurs,*
Les théâtres se remplissent de joyeux spectateurs,
Les passages fourmillent de badauds, d'amateurs,
Et les filous frétillent derrière les flaneurs.

Les maris sont de garde, les amants au logis;
Mais chût! Ça ne regarde que les gens établis;
*On ne vois [*sic*] dans les rues qu'ivrognes et viveurs,*
Et la patrouille grise ramasse les buveurs.

Bientôt donnant l'exemple, les riches rentrent chez eux,
Jusqu'au Boulevard du Temple tout devient silencieux;
La silhouette n'est bien vu que derrière les rideaux bleus
D'une noce en goguette qui danse du merveilleux.

Mais j'entends à la ville sonner l'heure des matines,
Et l'ouvrier agile s'empresse de gagner la tartine,
Le marteau, la tenaille commencent à marcher,
On se lève, on travaille—vite, allons nous coucher.

(Volant and Warren, *Memoirs of Alexis Soyer,* p. 5. My translation.)

In 1830, however, this carefree existence came to an end. Following the fall of Napoleon, the Bourbon monarchy had been reinstated in the person of Louis XVIII, soon followed by Charles X. But this was a very different monarchy from that which had been overthrown by the Revolution: The state remained secular, and there was an elected Chamber of Deputies and a free press. During the years 1826–27, however, France's economic situation deteriorated, and there was a surge of public unrest. Charles, seeing an opportunity to reclaim the monarchy's lost powers, appointed a new prime minister, the ultra-right-wing, ultra-Catholic Prince de Polignac, with a brief to restore public order. But this move received the thumbs-down in the elections of July 3, 1830, which sent a large liberal majority to the Chamber of Deputies. Determined to restore his authority, and egged on by his extremist supporters, Charles now announced four *ordonnances,* ending the freedom of the press, dissolving the Chamber of Deputies, changing the electoral system, and decreeing new elections to be held in September. That was on July 25; on the twenty-sixth, the people learned what had happened and began to organize, while the journalists, financed by the banker Jacques Laffitte, braved the new laws and issued a protesting freesheet. On the twenty-seventh, the first of the three days known as the *trois glorieuses,* the police and army occupied the printshops and put down a number of protests; on the twenty-eighth, the Parisian workers built barricades of cobblestones to protect themselves in the coming struggle. Charles still refused to withdraw his hated *ordonnances;* popular feeling was for the reinstatement of the Republic. However, on the twenty-ninth, the statesman Adolphe Thiers pushed through the idea of a constitutional monarchy on the English model. On August 2 Charles X abdicated, to be replaced by his brother, the liberal Duc d'Orleans, who would reign as Louis-Philippe.

After which life went on as before; not, however, for Alexis Soyer. Unfortunately for him, he had moved that June from his job at D'Ouix to one at the Foreign Office, as deputy to one of the grandest cooks in Paris. On July 26, they had been detailed to prepare a grand banquet for the Prince de Polignac in celebration of the hated *ordonnances*. The banquet, however, was destined never to be eaten. While it was in preparation a revolutionary mob burst into the kitchens, shooting indiscriminately, killing a good many of those they found working there, and pausing only to tuck in to the goodies so abruptly liberated from the rapacious maws of their oppressors. Two of Soyer's colleagues were shot before his eyes; he himself escaped only by bursting into song, beginning with the *La Marseillaise* and concluding with *La Parisienne,* at which the mob carried him from the kitchens shoulder-high (or so he always said).

Despite this momentary triumph, however, Soyer's association with the discredited old regime was not so easily discounted, and he found himself a good deal less popular than hitherto. In 1831, therefore, he left the pleasures and friendships of Paris and once again followed his brother Philippe, this time across the Channel to England, where French cooks had become a necessary adornment in fashionable houses.

Soyer would never again live in France. But although he had everything to learn about the society in which he would henceforth make his home, in one very important way his education—what in France would be called his *formation*—was complete. On the professional level, only in France could he have learned to cook as he did; culturally, only a Frenchman would take food as seriously as he did. And emotionally he remained throughout his life quint-essentially a Frenchman of the postrevolutionary generation, democratic, taking serious things lightly and light things seriously, and with a very particular view of public life and his place therein—a view that would shape the whole of his future existence.

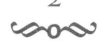

2

The Fish

Up to this point, Soyer's life had been entirely urban. Meaux, though not large, is nevertheless a town, not a village, while Paris is of course one of the world's great cities. But now he not only left France for England but the city for the country. His employers between 1831 and 1835 were the English aristocracy, a class whose chief interests were the legendary hunting, shooting, and fishing; and between 1832 and 1835, he lived as deeply rural a life as it was possible to imagine.

In this world, game ruled supreme. It gave the rich something to do, provided jobs for the poor, officially as keepers, beaters, and huntsmen, unofficially as poachers, and provided free excitement and amusement for even the most ground-down agricultural laborers. The radical journalist Alexander Somerville, who toured rural Britain during the 1830s and "40s, found laborers always ready to

down tools and abandon their hard and ill-paid work for the diversion of a day following the hunt.[1] But as well as an excuse for pleasure, game was an important source of food. Its strong flavors titillated the jaded palates of the well-to-do, and it offered the delicious chance of much-needed free protein for any poor man bold or foolhardy enough to poach.

For this course, then, game is indicated; but since it is also the fish course, the options are limited. Game fish are freshwater fish—pike, trout, and salmon. However, few fishmongers today stock pike, while trout play little part in Soyer's grander repertoire. And since this was his society chef period, something more elaborate than fried trout fillets seems called for. Which leaves only one choice: salmon.

This recipe is taken from *The Gastronomic Regenerator,* where we find his expansive (and expensive) instructions for elaborate dinner-party dishes. Salmon are discussed in some detail. Like oysters, which Dr. Johnson used as cat food, they had once been so cheap and common as to provoke riots on the part of poor apprentices tired of being fed the same thing day after day. But by the 1830s, in-

---

[1]Somerville, *The Whistler at the Plough, passim.*

dustrialization and pollution were beginning to have their effects. "The Thames salmon used to be reckoned the most recherché; but since so many steam-boats have been introduced upon the surface of that noble river, and the tunnel has been built, introducing their greatest enemies, human beings, both above and below their liquid habitation, they have fled to the ocean for protection, and are now no longer discernible from their once commoner brethren," Soyer remarks. Indeed, by 1846, when his book was published, Thames salmon had altogether vanished. During the eighteenth century, flushing water-closets had become increasingly popular, but public sewerage had not yet caught up with private convenience. The new WCs emptied into the old cesspits; these overflowed into drains intended for surface runoff, and thence, via London's tributary streams—the Fleet, the West Bourne, the Ravensbourne, the Tyburn—into the Thames, from which most of London's drinking water was drawn. The results were lethal to more than salmon. Typhoid became endemic, and in 1832, the year Soyer, perhaps thankfully, left the noisome city for the countryside, there were 14,000 cases of cholera. Consequently, "the Severn salmon is now esteemed the best. . . ."[2]

These days, of course, such nice distinctions pale in the face of the great divide between the wild and the farmed; and farmed salmon has once again become one of the cheapest fish available. But as salmon, whatever their provenance, are very large, and I wanted to cook a whole fish for a party of only six, I cheated slightly and bought a salmon trout.

[2]Soyer, *The Gastronomic Regenerator.*

Saumon au Naturel

Put your fish in cold water (using 1lb salt to every 6 quarts water), let it be well covered with water, and set it over a moderate fire; when it begins to simmer, set it out on the side of the fire. If the fish weighs 4lb, let it simmer half an hour, if 8lb three quarters of an hour, and so in proportion; dish it on a napkin and serve lobster or shrimp sauce in a boat. (*The Gastronomic Regenerator*)

My salmon trout weighed a mere 2.2 kg (a little less than 5 lb.), but that's still a big fish, and was clearly going to need a fish kettle. Fortunately, I was able to borrow one. And now I am determined to buy one for myself. Quite simply, I can imagine no better way of cooking large fish.

At first I was dubious: boiling the fish from cold, in brine? Could it possibly work? Nobody these days boils anything. If you must use water (rather than wine or stock) as a cooking medium, the b-word is generally replaced by *poach,* which in the culinary sense of course means placing your material in boiling water and then simmering. But we should abandon our prejudices. Soyer's method works excellently, not only for salmon but for any large fish (I have since cooked a turbot in the same way, using a large, deep frying pan rather than a purpose-built *turbotière,* with similarly delicious results). I used three quarts of water to cover my fish, added ½ lb. salt, brought it to the boil, and simmered it for twenty minutes. The purpose of the napkin is simply to blot up any remaining cooking water, "for the liquor would spoil your sauce and cause it to lose that creamy substance that it ought to retain," but I preferred to let the fish drain, lifting it out of the fish kettle on the kettle's inbuilt colander and standing this on the serving dish. My fish emerged perfectly cooked, firm and juicy but without excess liquor, and excellently flavored by the brine.

Left to myself, I would serve a fish of this sort with either a hollandaise or (easier, less rich, and even more delicious) a light sorrel sauce—shredded sorrel melted in a little butter, then mixed with single cream or *crème fraiche*. For Soyer, however, lobster or shrimp sauce is invariably the first choice for any large fish—recommended for turbot and brill, as well as salmon.

Shrimp Sauce

Melted butter

Mix ¼lb butter in a stewpan, with two tablespoons of flour, without putting it upon the fire; then add a pint and a half of cold water, place it upon the fire, keep stirring until upon the point of boiling, but do not let it boil; season with a tablespoon of vinegar, and a teaspoon of salt, and one-eighth teaspoon of pepper; pass it through a tammie into a basin, then add 2oz more of fresh butter; keep stirring till the butter is melted; it is then ready to use when required.

Make the melted butter but finish with 3 tablespoons of essence of shrimps, and serve half a pint of picked shrimps in a boat with it. If no essence of shrimps, the anchovy sauce may be served with shrimps in it as a substitute.

Anchovy Sauce

There should be no salt in the melted butter. Finish with 4 good tablespoons essence of anchovies.

I began with the shrimps. In England few fishmongers now seem to stock anything smaller than prawns, but I happened to be in France when I cooked this recipe, a country where every fish stall still fronts its display with a mound of little gray shrimps. So obtaining them presented no problem. "Picking" them, however, was another matter. Picked shrimps are shelled shrimps; and shelling shrimps is a slow and messy business—the kind of thing the scullery maid did, in the days when scullery maids still existed. I bought 125 grams—even with their shells still on, rather less than the prescribed mugful—and shelling them took almost forty minutes. Still, you can't have a shrimp sauce without shrimps.

Soyer's wording seems to imply that even in 1846 shrimp essence was not easy to find; in the twenty-first century, the only reference to it I could locate was in a hunting stockist's Web site, where shrimp essence oil was advertised for use as a lure to attract raccoon, fox, mink, and "most furbearers." This may have been the same mixture Soyer had in mind, but it did not sound promising. Anchovy essence, however, is still widely available in grocery stores, so I used that, making my shrimp sauce the "anchovy sauce with shrimps in it" variant.

After I'd finished picking the shrimps, it was time for the melted butter. In his *Shilling Cookery for the People* Soyer quotes "the great diplomatist, Talleyrand," as saying "that England had 120 religions but only one sauce, and that melted butter," adding:

"He was very near the truth, but, at the same time, he should have told how to engraft 119 sauces to the original one, the same as the various sects he mentions, have been offshoots from the primitive one which was first established in this country."[3] Indeed, almost any English sauce recipe from this period seems to begin with melted butter. The preparation sounded bizarre and complicated on the page, but in practice was quick and easy—as it were, a béchamel made with water instead of milk, and with more butter added at the end. The result is glass-smooth, and very rich indeed. The vinegar cuts this slightly, and gives a rather unexpected flavor, quite unlike anything I'd tasted before, but very much in the Victorian sweet-and-sour style that informs much of Soyer's food. Sugar, sparingly used, is a favorite general condiment of his (though it does not appear in this recipe), as is vinegar; and he often garnishes with vinegar-preserved pickles such as capers and gherkins.

Surprisingly, even with four tablespoons of anchovy essence, the anchovy flavor was not overpowering—there was too much else going on, with all that butter and vinegar. The shrimps, however, were quite lost. They became little unrecognizable floating lumps, and (after all that work!) you couldn't really taste them. My mistake was to stir them into the sauce instead of serving them separately, as I realized (too late) Soyer recommends. This would have been much better. The prescribed quantity of sauce was far more than we needed, and if the shrimps had been served separately people could have taken more of them, adding a more recognizably shrimp quality to the dish.

Such an abundant and highly flavored mixture implies a very

[3]*Soyer's Shilling Cookery for the People,* p. 149.

particular view of what sauce is supposed to do. It is not used sparingly, in the French manner, to enhance the flavor of the dish's main
ingredient; rather, sauce and matrix are equal partners. Indeed, the
sauce is almost the main element of the dish, its function, one can't
help suspecting, more often than not to dress up something dull. If
we must have salmon, let's at least give it a decent sauce . . .

Shrimp sauce was a standard dish in England at this time, served
with all fish. It was the kind of thing Soyer's English employers
would have ordered as a matter of course, and he probably picked up
this recipe following his arrival in England, rather than bringing it
with him from France. It figures prominently in the hunt dinners described by Surtees; it appears, exiguously, at a celebratory dinner at
Mrs. Tibbs's boardinghouse, in Boz's sketch *The Boarding House,*
written at this time. Here the salmon accompanies the soup (in more
straitened households, though both might appear, it seems that one
ate soup or fish, not soup and fish) and precedes the imaginary sirloin
and real roast fowl and haunch of mutton. The descendants of this
dish were still to be found on the menus of provincial hotels a hundred years after *The Gastronomic Regenerator* was published, pre-
ceded by brown windsor soup and followed by sponge pudding with
custard, though by then the all-blanketing sauce was flourier, and its
function—as often, one imagines, during its heyday—disguise.

By the time Soyer, now twenty-one, arrived in England, there was
quite a community of French cooks working there. The famous
Louis-Eustache Ude, once cook to the unfortunate Louis XVI, would
become a close friend; his career demonstrated the excellent career

prospects England held for a first-class chef. Ude was now steward and chef at Crockford's, had published a successful cookery book in English—*The French Cook*—and was noisily established with his quarrelsome wife and vocal collection of small dogs in a fine house in Albemarle Street, where Lord Alvanley was their lodger. (The dogs, evidently an ill-trained and overindulged rabble, were in the habit of licking the sugary varnish off male guests' boots at dinner.)

Philippe Soyer had found a good job as head chef to George III's youngest son, the Duke of Cambridge, and when Alexis arrived in London, he worked in Philippe's kitchen. Cambridge was one of the royal dukes Wellington collectively dismissed as "the damnedest millstones that were ever hanged around the neck of any government," but for his young sous-chef he was and would remain a sort of demigod. However, the Soyer brothers still did not get on, and Alexis soon found a job of his own, first at the Duke of Sutherland's London house, then at the Marquis of Waterford's.

When the Duke died in 1833, Alexis moved to Aston Hall near Oswestry in Shropshire, a substantial mansion set in a landscaped park, to work for Mr. William Lloyd, a wealthy country squire (he also owned Upper Brook Street in Mayfair) with an extremely well-connected wife. The Lloyds were members of the Duke of Cambridge's set (which may be how Soyer had come to their attention) and Mrs. Lloyd, a fashionable beauty whose father had been one of Lord Nelson's pallbearers, knew everybody that was anybody. Mr. Lloyd sounds rather dull, though his money made him a desirable *parti;* and Mrs. Lloyd, having quickly provided the requisite heirs, did not let the insignificant fact of marriage cramp her style. An admiral's daughter, she evidently had a *tendresse* for military men, in particular the Duke of Wellington, with whom she

Aston Hall

conducted a long and notorious love affair. Wellington was a man of many mistresses, but Louisa Lloyd seems to have occupied a very special place in his affections: He personally showed her around the battlefield the day after Waterloo and presented her with numbers of keepsakes, including some hairs from his charger's tail, and a branch pulled from a tree beneath which they paused during that momentous ride. No more prestigious lover could well be imagined; Wellington ruled not only the battlefield but the home front, an all-purpose fount of wisdom comprising military genius, politician (he was a member of Sir Robert Peel's cabinet), and general life-adviser: It was Wellington who recommended the introduction of sparrowhawks when the trees enclosed by Paxton's Crystal Palace at the Great Exhibition turned out to harbor impractical quantities of small birds. Another of Mrs. Lloyd's rumored lovers was the Duke of Buckingham, also a friend and ally of Peel's, who had married her cousin and best friend.

These delicious eddies, however, in no way disturbed the time-
less onward flow of life at Aston Hall. Originally a monastic foundation, the house was very ancient, but it had been modernized in
the previous century and by the time Soyer arrived there presented
a classical Georgian front to its lake and the rolling acres beyond.
Nothing could have been more quintessentially English, nor, in its
rural isolation, more utterly different from anything young Alexis
had hitherto experienced.

"My living in Yorkshire was so far out of the way, that it was
actually twelve miles from a lemon," quipped the immortal Sydney
Smith. But when it came to measuring the distance from lemons,
the north Wales border country could compete with anything
Yorkshire had to offer. Although it was already seven years since
George Stephenson had established the Stockton-to-Darlington
railway, places like Aston, still reliant on stagecoaches, remained
inaccessible in ways that would soon become unimaginable. "Eight
miles an hour, for twenty or four-and-twenty hours, a hard seat, a
gouty tendency, a perpetual change of coachmen grumbling because you did not fee them enough, a fellow passenger partial to
spirits-and-water—who has not borne these evils in the jolly old
times?"[4] Thackeray mused. Guests became fixtures to be treasured
or dreaded; once arrived they did not (given the hardships involved) leave in a hurry. For the rest, country dwellers relied for
company on whoever happened to live in the immediate neighborhood. "How long it is since we saw you!" "How I wish I could join
you!" "How I wish you were here!" are refrains that echo through
Louisa Lloyd's correspondence down the years following her mar-

---

[4]Thackeray, *Pendennis,* ch. VII.

riage, when for much of the year she abandoned the pleasures of
London for the depths of rural Shropshire.

Any new addition to this narrow society was eagerly assessed for
what he or she might have to offer, and young Soyer, cheerful, personable, and sociable as well as being an outstandingly talented cook,
soon became almost as well-known a figure around Shropshire and
Denbighshire as he had been in Paris. Indeed, he was not easily over-
looked. Thackeray, who portrays him as the comic French cook Alcide Mirobolant in *Pendennis,* pokes fun at his flamboyant manner
and outlandish and gaudy taste in clothes (*mirobolant* translates as
"dazzling"). This was a slightly older Soyer—Thackeray met him at
the Reform Club, which is to say after 1837—and it seems unlikely
that the young Alexis of the Aston Hall years would yet have developed his full plumage. However, even at this early stage of his career
it is clear that reticence was not his mode; and his sartorial style, even
when undeveloped, is unlikely to have resembled anything hitherto
encountered around Oswestry.

Everyone who knew Soyer remarked on his easy charm, and he
seems to have settled quickly and happily at Aston, as indeed he did
everywhere he lived. The Volant memoir records that he found two
of his fellow apprentices—whether from Paris or the Duke of Cambridge's we are not told—living near his new home, presumably as
cooks in the kitchens of nearby great houses: Even here in the far recesses of the countryside, no fashionable household was complete
without its French cook, the mere fact of nationality carrying both
cachet and an appreciable premium in wages. He soon became a
great favorite at the Hall and at the nearby Queen's Head hostelry,
where he was the life and soul of the party, entertaining the company
with his songs, his uninhibited stories, and his quaint accent. Neigh-

boring magnates such as Mr. Myddelton Biddulph of Chirk Castle, across the border in Denbighshire, borrowed him for their dinner parties and collected his recipes; Mr. Biddulph's steward, Charles Pierce, would remain a friend and ally for the rest of his life.

However, not all the attention attracted by this uppity young foreigner was benign. Sir Watkin Williams Wynne, a bucolic neighboring squire and lifelong hunting crony of Mr. Lloyd, was in the habit of unbagging a fox for his friends' delectation every March 1—"Taffy's day." On this occasion, he saw the chance for some extra amusement and arranged for his huntsman to set up, for Soyer's benefit, a trick chase in which a dog, not a fox, would be the quarry. To the glee of the local farmers and other onlookers, the young Frenchman swallowed the bait and set off in eager pursuit. In the heat of the chase, he was thrown from his horse and pitched into a hedge, whence he emerged, bedraggled, to find the rest of the field, stout farmers and red-coated huntsmen, splitting their sides with laughter.

One of Soyer's most consistent and admirable characteristics was his capacity to laugh at himself. He loved jokes, and being almost completely without pomposity was unperturbed if, as occasionally happened, he found himself the butt of someone else's humor. On this occasion, however, he was both hurt and upset—so much so that he never forgot the sting of that moment. This reaction was so uncharacteristic that it must have been prompted by more than an apparently harmless jape. Indeed, it seems clear that the incident contained an element of real malice, felt and intended (though doubtless indignantly denied). For Sir Watkin and his friends, any presumptuous newcomer was presumably fair game, to be ritually cut down to size for the general amusement. But the Lloyds' new cook was also a Frenchman; and although Frenchmen were all very well in the kitchen—Sir Watkin vainly tried to induce the young man to come and work for him at his house, Wynnstay Park—France was the traditional enemy, and Frenchmen needed to be taught their place. Indeed, the scene of Soyer's discomfiture—red-faced John Bulls enjoying the unsporting Frenchman's disarray—was an almost mythic enactment of national stereotypes. It might have been drawn by Rowlandson, Gillray, or Cruikshank; indeed, they *had* drawn it, a thousand times, in various political and satirical contexts.

The last material expression of this old enmity had been the combat with Napoleon, concluded in 1815. But although that had comprehensively disposed of the military threat, things French still sent shivers of suspicion down the spines of well-to-do Englishmen. France was Britain's nearest neighbor—only twenty miles distant across the Channel—and over the last half-century, a series of terrifying political dramas had taken place there. The first French revolution had shown only too clearly what might happen to the propertied classes if things got out of hand; and just as it had been finally worked through, Napoleon defeated and the rightful monarch restored, the same thing had happened all over again—albeit the King had not, this time around, actually been beheaded. What was to stop something similar taking place in England? Behind the serene and solid façade of houses such as Aston Hall lay a gnawing nervous awareness of what might be in store. The Lloyds and their circle lived in constant fear of an uprising against what one contemporary commentator, Gibbon Wakefield, termed "the peasant-hated rural aristocracy."[5] "I detest King Philip [Louis-Philippe] and his revolutionary gang,"

[5]E. Gibbon Wakefield, *Swing Unmasked,* quoted in Hobsbawm and Rudé, *Captain Swing,* p. 229.

the Duke of Buckingham confided to Mrs. Lloyd in 1831, the year before Soyer arrived at Aston.[6] In these circles, the new cook's connexion with the Prince de Polignac, and his consequent hurried departure from Paris, would have been wholly a recommendation.

At almost any other moment, such fears, though understandable, would have been misplaced. France and Britain were so different, politically and economically, that the one very rarely influenced the other in a direct way. But in 1831 and 1832, for the first and only time in the nineteenth century, political events in Britain genuinely seemed to be developing in parallel with those in continental Europe. A few months after the French July revolution, the English poor rose against their masters, inspired, so Gibbon Wakefield believed, by the "heroes of the barricades" in Paris, the news of whose exploits inflamed them "against those whom they justly consider as their oppressors." In Blackburn, Middleton, Carlisle, and Kent, in London and Lancashire, workingmen paraded with tricolor flags as spontaneous risings spread across England.[7] In London, the Queen's carriage was stoned and the Duke of Wellington had to be rescued by troopers from the mob, while whole streets of houses had their windows broken. And in the country the situation was even more ominous. Ricks were fired, and some farmhouses set ablaze; threatening letters were sent, often in the name of a mysterious Captain Swing, everywhere sought and never identified. Gaols were breached and prisoners released, agricultural machinery was broken, and seditious speeches led to riots up and down the country. In June 1832, the Reform Bill was finally forced through, and revolution, for the moment, averted.

[6]Harvey papers, Essex County Archive.
[7]Hobsbawm and Rudé, *Captain Swing,* p. 217.

It was hardly surprising that the English rural poor felt inspired to revolt. Before 1789, the contrast between laborers' living conditions in rural France and rural England had been all to England's advantage, sturdy British yokels contrasted with starveling Frenchmen. But since then the conditions of the French had immeasurably improved, while those of the British had deteriorated almost beyond imagining. In France, the Revolution had confirmed smallholders' claim to their land; in some regions, the peasant population even increased. But this was just what those directing British policy did not want.[8] "The possession of a cow or two, with a hog, and a few geese, naturally exalts the peasant, in his own conception, above his brothers in the same rank of society . . . Day labour becomes disgusting; the aversion increases by indulgence; and at length the sale of a half-fed calf, or hog, furnishes the means of adding intemperance to idleness," severely observed the Survey of the Board of Agriculture for Somerset in 1798[9]—disapproving sentiments that remained unchanged thirty years later.

For British policymakers, peasants were undesirable on two counts. First, they are notoriously attached to their bit of land, while the aim of British policy was to detach the rural population from its ancestral lands and send it to the cities to provide labor for the emergent industries that were transforming the country's economy. And second, this was an inefficient form of agriculture, unsuitable for the rapidly expanding urban population of the new industrial age.

The destruction of the English peasantry was conducted with

[8]A position that has not changed down the years: The primacy of the French peasant, as reflected in the Common Agricultural Policy, reviled in Britain, untouchable in France, divides us to this day.
[9]Hobsbawm, *The Age of Revolution,* p. 149.

dispatch and brutality. Enclosures, in which big estates hedged off what had hitherto been common and waste land, created larger and more efficient farms at the expense of the laborers, removing their ancestral grazing rights and their gardens. This now landless proletariat depended for its livelihood on the miserable wages and uncertain employment offered by farmers. But the farmers no longer needed them—or only very few of them. They preferred the new agricultural machines. The bitterness that prompted Captain Swing was largely caused by threshing machines, which performed tasks that had hitherto provided winter work; the breaking of these machines was a central element of the Swing riots. Mechanization also closed down cottage industries such as handloom weaving, which had provided a source of extra cash. In 1795, a handloom weaver earned 33s. a week; by 1829, this had been reduced to 5s. 6d.[10]

On top of all this, agriculture, which had flourished during the Napoleonic wars, was now in a depression. In 1817, the harvest had been so disastrous that famine threatened; in 1829, it threatened again. Meanwhile, the Corn Laws, brought in to protect farmers' incomes following the palmy days of wartime, kept the price of corn artificially high, even in times of plenty. Country bread might not be adulterated with alum as city bread regularly was, but many agricultural workers could not afford it; some even lacked potatoes, the poor man's fallback. When the infamous Millbank Prison opened in 1817, its inmates rioted in an attempt to increase the food allowance; nevertheless, it was labeled "Mr Holford's [the governor's] fattening-house," comparisons being drawn between the gastronomic lot of the "comfortable" convicts and the straits of desperate and hungry

---

[10]Hobsbawm, *The Age of Revolution,* p. 41.

free laborers. An idea of what seemed enviable may be given by the fact that when public opinion forced Holford to decrease rather than increase the prison rations, over half the convict population fell ill with scurvy, and thirty died.[11]

Farmers, caught between their wretched laborers and their rich landlords, who were often interested in their land more for the sport it provided and the rents it produced than for what could be grown upon it, knew that if they reduced wages the parish—using the poor rate that they, the farmers, also paid—would make up the difference. So the poor rate, designed as a minimum resort for the desperate, became the effective working wage, and the distinction between workers and paupers vanished. After 1834, this desperate state of affairs became even worse: A new Poor Law decreed that outdoor relief, which allowed its recipients to continue living at home, be abolished. Henceforth relief would be available only in the local workhouse, where conditions were deliberately designed to be unbearable. The food was uneatable; and what was worse, men and women were segregated, on the pretext of preventing procreation, but in reality to split families and make workhouse life so intolerable that few even among the desperate would subject themselves to it. Only thus—by a policy of attrition that was no less effective for being unstated—could surplus population be induced to move from the country, where it was not needed, to the town, where the new factories required hands to work the machines. By 1851, the English urban population, uniquely in the world, outnumbered rural dwellers[12]—a situation not reached in France until the 1930s.

[11]Robin Evans, *The Fabrication of Virtue: English Prison Architecture 1750–1840,* Cambridge, 1982, p. 249.
[12]Hobsbawm, *The Age of Revolution,* p. 11.

Which brings us back to our recipe; for game such as salmon was central to the near-revolution of the 1830s in several ways. Here was a ubiquitous but forbidden source of free food, constantly visible to a desperately poor and hungry populace that knew it took its life in its hands every time it snared a rabbit, jumped a pheasant, or netted a fish. Of course, such things happened every day. But punishments for poaching were draconian. Salmon and rabbits might be wearisomely plentiful, but they were other people's salmon and rabbits, and only their owners had the right to dispose of them. At best, poachers risked being sent to the penitentiary; at worst, they might even be transported. Only the most daring and insubordinate spirits dared make a habit of so dangerous a pursuit. It was not coincidental that the leaders of the agricultural uprisings were often either poachers or smugglers, an equally lawless race. They were better-fed and less servile—stronger in both body and mind.

Its unavailability to the hungry was not the only grievance concerning game. Few landowners took a personal interest in agriculture; most were more interested in sport. So the preservation of game—a commodity whose name echoes its sporting function—invariably took precedence over agricultural needs. If a hunted fox chose to run through a field of young corn, the hunt followed it regardless, breaking down not only the farmer's crops but his fences. The farmer knew better than to complain—he was probably a member of the hunt, and next time it would be someone else's field. And where a laborer still cultivated his own bit of land, he had two enemies: the hunt and pests such as rabbits—especially if (as sometimes happened) his vegetable plot was one allotted by a farmer in lieu of part of his wages. Alexander Somerville, traveling around rural England at this time, counted "sixty-odd rabbit holes, mostly made by young rabbits learning to excavate, as young rabbits do, among the potatoes," in one such plot. Its hapless allottee had also tried to grow peas, turnips, and greens for the winter: "every blade went to the rabbits." There was nothing the man could do. "The land was rented from Colonel Wyndham of Petworth, and the game was his game."[13] This man had been earning nine shillings a week—not enough to live on. The farmers of the parish had just announced that the wage would be reduced to eight shillings, since everyone now had allotments and could live cheaper.

Since he wrote no letters and kept no diary, we have no record of Soyer's first impressions of his new country. But these differences, and in particular the absence of peasants and the accompanying local produce, were inescapable for anyone familiar with the French countryside. Had Aston Hall been a French château, the local smallholders would have been a source not only of produce but of a regional cookery based on local specialties—the opposite, so to speak, of universal salmon with shrimp sauce. But in England, no such specialized rural culture any longer existed. "If we travel over the country, we feel surprised to find how small a portion of the ground is engaged in agriculture, and much smaller in horticulture," Soyer observed some time later in his career, pondering the puzzle of the British disdain for vegetables. "The consequence is, that in England (excepting in large towns) scarcely any vegetables are to be obtained, and the needy are doomed to exist on bread and cheese, with a very small portion of animal food; while, on the other hand, the ground might be well-stocked with cabbages, broccoli, and other vegetables."[14] To anyone

[13]Somerville, *The Whistler at the Plough,* p. 404.
[14]Volant and Warren, *Memoirs of Alexis Soyer,* p. 289.

unacquainted with British politics, such a lack must indeed have been puzzling.

Of course, these strictures did not apply to an establishment like Aston Hall. Such a place was a community in itself, lavishly provided and almost entirely self-sufficient as to food. It would make its bread from its home farm's corn, eat meat grown on the estate, fish from its own brooks and ponds, pheasants from its own coverts, grow its fruit in its own orchards and vegetables in a walled kitchen garden, with espaliered fruit trees and greenhouses. All this required a small army of retainers, most of whom would live in the house or in tied cottages. And if this sounds like a feudal hangover, that is exactly what it was. The way of life in great houses had altered very little over the centuries, though some modern improvements had begun to appear. By the nineteenth century, there were probably water closets and perhaps even bathrooms with piped hot water (though water for washstands still had to be carried up every morning). Wagon railways might bring coal from the store into the house—though that, too, still had to be carried to individual rooms, and their fires made up and kept going, a never-ending chore in wintertime. But even the most up-to-date houses still depended on a plentiful supply of cheap labor—always, of course, available while starvation reigned in the countryside. To be in service meant long hours fetching and carrying, sweeping and dusting, preparing vegetables, washing dirty dishes, and doing the laundry. There was no escape from the dehumanizing realization that as far as the family was concerned you were invisible, nor from the constant demeaning awareness of being always at someone else's beck and call. But it also meant regular meals in the servants' hall. And although the living conditions were bleak—cold attics or dark back rooms, far removed in every sense from the family's luxurious apartments—and the domestic offices little better, often tucked away in damp basements, they were probably no worse than most cottagers routinely experienced at home.

However, even great houses could not avoid the realization that times were changing. Naturally, everyone around Aston would know Mr. and Mrs. Lloyd, and Mr. and Mrs. Lloyd would know them: These were families that had lived side by side for the past several hundred years. But what had once been a personal, almost familial relationship between landowners, farmers, and laborers was now entirely money-based. And the fact that the rich did not realize what this must mean for their neighbors' lives showed how separate they had become from village reality—as separate, indeed, as their own food supplies from those of the villagers. Eric Hobsbawm and George Rudé observe that "the upper classes probably did not realize, until riot and incendiarism taught them differently, quite how much they had been excluded from the village community by the poor."[15]

As it happens, Aston was not situated in that part of the country most affected by the riots, which had mostly taken place in the south and east, where corn was the main crop. There had been relatively few enclosures in Shropshire, no machine-breaking (perhaps because there were no machines to break, agriculture in those parts being pastoral rather than arable), and only three cases of incendiarism.[16] The rich were nevertheless terrified, wherever they happened to live. The frightening example of France was too close

---

[15]Hobsbawm and Rudé, *Captain Swing,* p. 61.
[16]Hobsbawm and Rudé, *Captain Swing,* p. 202.

in both space and time for that not to be true. "I believe from all I hear that the state of things in your part of the world is very bad," wrote the Duchess of Buckingham to her cousin Mrs. Lloyd in October 1830. "We hear that the colliers are all in league. Are they quiet in your neighbourhood?" "The storm of Insurrection is fast rising and passing westward," wrote her husband the Duke the following month, after successfully quelling a rising on his own estates. ". . . I am very sorry to see how dismally ill the Magistracy and Gentry have in general behaved in giving way to the Mob. A little steadiness and the treating of one's own farm people well are all that is necessary to keep down any English Mob." However, despite this wishful thinking the riots did not quickly subside. In 1835, the harvest failed again, and there was such starvation that the specter of revolution once more stalked the plush-lined corridors of the family seats.

Like many Englishmen, the Duke of Buckingham refused to countenance the unnerving possibility that revolutionary feelings might be a native product. Only the wicked influence of foreigners could possibly explain the current happenings. "The Revolution is postponed sine die in town," he wrote in November 1831. ". . . But in the Country things are going on very ill. The burnings are spreading and . . . there is no doubt that they originate with foreigners."[17] In fact this was quite untrue. But it was what people believed; so that a Frenchman in the countryside might find himself in more ways than one an object of suspicion.

Despite all this, the luxurious life of the rich continued unchecked, with its constant round of visits, sports, and entertainments.

[17]Harvey papers.

And not least of their pleasures, in the changeless routine of country life, must have been the constant sense of delightful anticipation afforded by a really good cook. But although the high wages commanded by French chefs would seem to confirm this, English attitudes to food remained very different from those in France, and in many cases their presence in the household seems to have been a matter of status rather than genuine gourmandise. Thus, the Duke of Wellington, England's leading aristocrat, naturally had to employ the best available French chef. His name was Félix; he had once worked for Lord Seaford, but that gentleman could no longer afford him. Some months after Félix left Seaford's employ, however, a guest at his house observed, "You have got the Duke's cook to dress your dinner." This was indeed the case; but, as Seaford explained, Félix was no longer the Duke's cook. "The poor fellow came to me with tears in his eyes and begged me to take him back again, at reduced wages or no wages at all, for he was determined not to remain at Apsley House. 'Has the Duke been finding fault?' I asked. 'Oh, no, my lord; I would stay if he had; he is the kindest and most liberal of masters; but I serve him a dinner that would make Ude or Francatelli burst with envy, and he says nothing; I serve him a dinner dressed, and badly dressed, by the cookmaid, and he says nothing; I cannot live with such a master, if he was a hundred times a hero.'"[18]

That was an extreme case. However, judging by her correspondence, Mrs. Lloyd took little more interest in culinary matters than her lover. Food is never mentioned in the hundreds of family letters; when pleasure is discussed, it takes the form of horses and sport. For instance, Mrs. Lloyd's cousin the future Duchess of Bucking-

---

[18]Hayward, *The Art of Dining*, p. 16.

ham, writing in 1804 when both were still unmarried, tells how sorry she was to miss the Chelmsford races, where all her cousins had gathered to enjoy themselves. And in another letter she comments on her cousin's courtship: "I suppose you will take many a merry gallop with Mr. Lloyd."[19] Of course, one hardly expects fashionable young ladies to concern themselves with matters culinary. But even as the years progressed, punctuated by complaints about the monotony of country life, this lack of interest continued, sport merely being replaced by hypochondria as the favorite topic. Not that French *châtelaines* were often to be found in the actual kitchens. But they took an active interest in food that would have been considered quite unusual—indeed, almost indecent—in England. And if cooking and gardening were strictly matters for servants, what else was there to do in the countryside but hunt, shoot, fish, and contemplate your aches and pains?

In this riven society, the question of one's exact station in life assumed enormous importance. And for Soyer this remained, throughout his career in England, a very vexed question indeed. He himself summed up the dilemma in the introduction to his *Shilling Cookery for the People,* published in 1854, after nearly twenty-five years' doughty combat in this battle of perceptions. "In ancient times"—or, he might have added, in France—"a cook, especially if a man, was looked upon as a distinguished member of society; while now he is, in the opinion of almost every one, a mere menial." Servant or artist? A mere cook or a valued adviser on questions of fundamental importance to humanity? In his own mind, there was never the slightest doubt; and from time to time it seemed that the

[19] 1804. Harvey papers, Essex Record Office.

world was finally coming around to his view of things. However, most of the people, most of the time—and in particular, employers— sadly failed to share it.

Generally speaking, society's iron social gradations obtained as rigidly below stairs as above. Visiting servants' status echoed that of their employers, a Duke's valet taking precedence over a mere baronet's. At the Duke of Chandos's establishment there were four tables in the dining room—the Duke's, the chaplain's, the household officers," and that for the gentleman of the horse; and the servants' hall also held four tables, the musicians ranking highest, the kitchen hands at the bottom.[20] But although the musicians might not earn more than the Duke's steward, who headed the servants' establishment at £100 a year, their status was more ambivalent and the "exclusive" nature of their table reflected this. The steward, though top of his particular domestic tree, was still indisputably a servant. Anyone could learn his job. But musicians were born, not made: They were artists. And artists, if they were talented enough, could leap the social gap. To take two examples from among Soyer's contemporaries, Lord Egremont offered J. M. W. Turner a studio at Petworth, and Edward Lear became a valued friend of the Stanley family. Talent—the one quality no money can buy—transcended social boundaries. And was not a cook like Soyer as talented as any musician? French chefs' high wages reflected (among other things) the fact that they regarded their occupation as an art: No journeyman English cook could ever have conjured up creations comparable to those produced by Ude or Félix. Like musicians and painters, they possessed a very particular talent.

[20]G. E. Mingay, *A Social History of the English Countryside,* London, 1977, p. 227.

Talent still opens all doors to its lucky possessors; and today, cooks form part of this exalted elite, populating the gossip columns and the best parties alongside actors, musicians, painters, and writers. Not, however, in Oswestry in 1832. Thackeray places his M. Mirobolant on a social level with the local small-town milliner. Doubtless Soyer would have been charming to such a lady, especially if (unlike Thackeray's Miss Fribsby) she was young and pretty. But although this had indeed been his social level while in France—a country where, paradoxically, he would have had no trouble gaining the professional and artistic recognition he craved—his career in England was to take him well beyond it. Yet he never really gained acceptance as a member of the professional class—which was certainly how he saw himself. Indeed, the very notion was, quite simply, a joke. For Thackeray—a well-born member of that class as well as a great writer—it was *the* joke as far as Soyer was concerned. Pendennis's first reaction at a local ball, when Mirobolant asks the daughter of the house for a dance, is: "By Jove, it's the cook!" And when the affronted Mirobolant challenges him to a duel, Pendennis retorts, "Confound it, I can't fight a cook!" As for the notion of the cook as artist, this was even more absurd. "I advised myself to send up a little repast suitable to so delicate young palates," Mirobolant burbles. "Her lovely name is Blanche. The veil of the maiden is white; the wreath of roses which she wears is white. I determined that my dinner should be as spotless as the snow. At the accustomed hour, instead of the rude *gigot à l'eau* which was customarily served at her too simple table, I sent her up a little *potage à la Reine* . . . as white as her own tint, and confectioned with the most fragrant cream and almonds . . . the only brown thing which I permitted myself in the entertainment was a little roast of lamb, which I laid in a meadow of spinaches, surrounded with croustillons, representing sheep, and ornamented with daisies and other savage flowers. . . . The blonde misses of Albion," declares M. Mirobolant, "see nothing in the dull inhabitants of their brumous isle, which can compare with the ardour and vivacity of the children of the South."

All this is both very funny (not least because it is by no means untrue to life) and utterly ludicrous. Yet the paradox of Soyer's subsequent career was that, despite his lack of ultimate social acceptance—here so unerringly reflected by Thackeray—many people were prepared to take him at his own valuation. If he thought of himself as an artist, and therefore as a friend rather than a servant, then so too—up to a point—did they. One of his life's aims would be to transcend that point.

By the time Mirobolant made his appearance, Soyer had been working in London for many years. But although his character was less formed in 1832 than in 1849, there is no reason to think he was a fundamentally different person—merely younger. In Oswestry, as previously in Paris and later in London, he was charming, sociable, merry, and popular. However, any notion that this might equate to general social acceptance was clearly misconceived, at least where county folk were concerned.

Soyer's relations with the Lloyds were certainly not of this sort. Mrs. Lloyd had grown up in a family where communication between kitchen and drawing room was strictly impersonal, mediated by butler and housekeeper. The only mention of a cook in the family correspondence occurs in 1840, when Mrs. Lloyd's mother, Lady Louisa Harvey, describes how she had rung for her butler to "give him warning" on account of his getting drunk in a pub the previous evening, then sent him with some orders to her cook: She records that he promptly transmitted these—and then shot himself, presumably in terror of losing his post without a character. "I can't think what upset him so," she wrote, before passing on to other matters.[21]

Such a family could never have considered making a friend of their cook, however entertaining they might find him. Indeed, the one surviving letter from Soyer to Mrs. Lloyd, written in 1844, nine years after he left her service, could not be more formal in character—very definitely the letter of a menial to an employer rather than an artist to a friendly patron. "I should like to express my appreciation of your continuing kindness towards me," he writes, despite the fact that it is he who is doing her a favor (she had asked him to find her a new cook). "Please accept the humble greetings of your faithful servant."[22]

Nevertheless, the fact that they were still in contact after so long indicates an extremely cordial relationship. This was Soyer's first appointment as head cook—until he moved to Aston he had always been second-in-command. He was very young to hold such a responsible position, and it is clear he much enjoyed his years at Aston Hall. However, despite the genial nature of the post, this was not where he wished to spend his life. By 1835, he was back in the orbit of London, working for the Marquis of Ailsa at his luxurious new house in Isleworth, Middlesex.

Aston Hall's main distinctions lay in its imposing bulk and ancient provenance. Ailsa's residence, St. Margaret's House, a recently

[21]Harvey papers, Essex County Archive.
[22]Lloyd papers, National Library of Wales.

built and outstandingly elegant *ferme ornée* situated on the banks of the Thames opposite Richmond Hill, could not have been more different. Soyer's new employer, though the head of one of Scotland's oldest families, declined to spend his time in rugged Ayrshire. An eccentric and hedonistic gourmet, he preferred the milder climate and more cosmopolitan ambience of London's leafy outskirts, where he lived in sophisticated opulence. The elaborate pleasure grounds surrounding his house included a plantation representing a Roman amphitheater, with trees as spectators, and several specially commissioned groups of sculpture in marble taken from the Ailsa estates in Scotland. There was also a walled four-acre kitchen-garden featuring many varieties of espaliered fruit trees, and a glasshouse 108 feet long, heated by hot water and including a vinery and two peach houses.[23] Thames salmon might be scarce, but clearly mere scarcity would mean little when it came to stocking the Marquis of Ailsa's table.

Ailsa was no Duke of Wellington when it came to appreciating a good cook. On the contrary, as Soyer was to find, no one could have valued his talents more highly. And London brought its own advantages. There would be no more xenophobic rural "jokes" to cope with: London teemed with foreigners of all nations, and no one was likely to notice a Frenchman more or less. Soyer had finally arived at the city that he was to make his own, and where he would live for the rest of his life.

[23]*Twicknam Park*, p. 114.

3

The Hors d'Oeuvres

How to translate *hors d'oeuvres*? Soyer himself uses "flying dishes," which certainly conveys their sense of being outside the main meal. However, hors d'oeuvres are not placed among his starters but appear between the Removes, the Entrées, and the Roasts, the third, fourth, and fifth courses. Hence you will not find an hors d'oeuvres section in his *Shilling Cookery for the People*, whose intended audience would rarely eat so extensively. Nor are the recipes he lists as hors d'oeuvres the ones that would instantly spring to our minds. Hors d'oeuvres, for Soyer, meant rich and crispy savory mouthfuls of this and that, minute crab rissoles and tiny lobster vol-au-vents: the kind of thing more likely to be found these days on the platters of little goodies classy restaurants serve up between courses to keep the eaters happy while the kitchen toils. It is when he talks of salads that we recognize the piquant appetizers of the hors d'oeuvres trolley, intended, as *Shilling Cookery* puts it, "to invigorate the palate and dispose the masticating powers to a much longer duration."[1]

Since, with two courses down and five to go, invigoration is not out of place—and since, too, we shall here be discussing our hero's salad days—I propose to give the hors d'oeuvres their modern form, as salads. But they remain, metaphorically, hors d'oeuvres in Soyer's "flying dishes" sense; for this is a chapter about love—a topic which, although a recurring theme in his life, remained peripheral to it: more of a "flying dish," as things turned out, than he hoped or expected.

Soyer's salads fall into two types. There are green salads of lettuce and (his favorite) endive, then as now used as light summer dishes or to freshen the palate in the middle of a heavy meal. But there are also many vegetable salads, whose ingredients may include "beetroot, onions, potatoes, celery, cucumbers, lentils, haricots, succory, or barbe-de-capucin, winter cress, burnet, tansey, marigold, peas, French beans, relish, cauliflower." And these are all strictly separate dishes. In the pretend correspondence between two lady friends that is the device Soyer uses to link many of his recipes and comment upon them, he says:

> In the foregoing receipts you will perceive that I have used each salad herb separate, only mixing them with the condiments or with vegetable fruit. I have a strong objection to

[1] *Soyer's Shilling Cookery for the People*, p. 155.

the almost diabolical mixture of four or five different sorts of salad in one bowl . . . The freshness as well as the flavour of each is destroyed; they agree about as well together as would brandy and soda water mixed with gin and ginger-beer, for each salad herb has its own particular flavour, and the condiments, which are onions, chives, parsley, chervil, tarragon, celery, eschalot, garlic, cucumber, beetroot, &c, &c, are only to give it piquancy like the oil and vinegar, salt, and pepper.[2]

And if these small, separate salads seem oddly familiar, it is perhaps because we recognize in them the familiar contents of the hors d'oeuvres trolley.

Haricot and Lentil Salad   To a pint of well-boiled haricots add a teaspoon of salt, quarter of pepper, one of chopped onions, two of vinegar, four of oil, two of chopped parsley, stir round, and it is ready; lentils are done the same. A little cold meat, cut in thin slices, may be added as a variety.

Beetroot Salad with Onions   Boil four onions in the skin till tender, also a piece of beetroot; let both get cold, remove the skin, cut them in slices, put them in a plate, one slice on the edge of the other alternately; put into a small basin half a teaspoon of salt, a quarter of pepper, one of good vinegar, three of oil, mix them well; pour over when ready to serve.

[2]*Soyer's Shilling Cookery for the People*, p. 157.

Celery, Young Onions, and Radishes may be used in salad with the above dressing, adding a teaspoonful of mustard.

Cucumbers Cut in thin slices on a plate, with salt, pepper, oil, and vinegar in the above proportions.

Green French Beans When cold put into a bowl, with some tarragon, chervil, and chopped chives, dressed as before.

Brussels Sprouts, the same way.

Potatoes If any remaining, cut them into thin slices, and season as before. A few haricots, or cold meat, or a chopped gherkin, may be added.

Meat and Poultry If there are any of the above left, and you require a relishing dish, and not having any fresh salad herbs, proceed as for the other salads, using a little chopped parsley, onions, or pickles. Some cucumber or celery may be used. The meat or poultry should be cut small.

I prepared my hors d'oeuvres for two, carefully following Soyer's instructions. They took just under an hour to assemble, but with more or less the same expenditure of time and effort you could feed twenty. What was noticeable about all of them was the lively taste: Soyer always insists that the seasoning of dishes should be done in the kitchen rather than at table, and following his instructions in these dishes you can see why. The green beans, in particular, benefited from his herb mixture—tarragon, which I had hitherto associated only with chicken, brings out their flavor wonderfully well.

With the haricots, in place of the endless soaking and simmering described by Soyer, you can use, as I did, cooked cannellini beans from a can (but of course if you *were* cooking for twenty this would be far more expensive). I mistakenly took one can to equal the pint of beans Soyer refers to, with the result that my beans came out much too salty: I realized, too late, that in fact a can is more like half a pint. I was surprised to see that for cooking dried haricots he doesn't recommend even the slightest shortcut, such as using boiling water for the initial soak, which means the beans are ready to cook in two hours rather than having to be left overnight (of course, domestic pressure-cookers, which reduce the subsequent cooking time by three-quarters, were unknown in his day). Using boiling water to soak, and then a pressure cooker, it is possible to cook beans from dry in four hours. But in France, Soyer probably preferred the semi-dried beans still in their pods, *haricots à écorcer*, which need no soaking and only half an hour's cooking. For some reason, I have never seen these unpromising-looking but delicious beans for sale in England, though I know, because I've tried it, that they will grow here.

The real revelation, however, was the beetroot and onion mixture. I was rather dubious about this even though I love beetroot, as boiled onion tends to be slimy and (to my taste) unpleasantly sweet. In fact, though, it was, I thought, the best of all. I used smallish red onions and boiled them for about a quarter of an hour—larger ones would take longer—then sliced them rather roughly, as they tended to fall apart. The only beetroot I could get was ready-cooked in vinegar, so already a little piquant. But the combination was unexpected and delicious. The onion was sweet and crunchy but devoid of its lingering aftertaste, and perfectly complemented the sweet-sour beetroot.

The striking thing about all these little salads, at whatever point
in the meal they appear, is how contemporary they feel. This is the
stuff of healthy eating as recommended in a thousand newspaper
columns, the starting point of every supermarket's ready-packed
takeout salad lunches in our five-portions-of-veg-a-day society. But
the notion of *crudités* must have seemed dangerously exotic in
mid–nineteenth century England, when a simple home dinner
party for eight, if Soyer is to be believed (his menu appears in *The
Gastronomic Regenerator*, complete with engraving of the party
seated around "my table at home"), might consist of soup (he speci-
fies French *pot-au-feu*, replete with varied meats); fish (three slices of
salmon *en matelote*); two removes (braised fowls with spring vegetables, leg of mutton basted with devils' tears); two entrées (lamb cutlets with asparagus and peas, salmi of plovers with mushrooms);
two roasts (two ducklings, four pigeons wrapped in vine leaves);
four entremets (orange jelly, green peas, omelette fines herbes, and
gooseberry tart with cream); and finally an iced cake with fruits.

The notion that he entertained in this manner at home was
probably more cookbook fantasy than reality. But fantasy menus
are as revealing, in their way, as real ones; and even Soyer's fan-
tasies ran mostly to solid muscle. A few vegetables hover around
the edges, but they are a mere garnish. And in this he faithfully reflects the tastes of his adopted country. "It is remarkable," writes
one of Soyer's fictitious ladies, "that though the inhabitants of this
country were for so many centuries (from the nature of the climate)
a salad-eating people, yet they seem the least to know how to season
them."[3] Presumably, (s)he was thinking of the wilted lettuce-leaf,

[3]*Soyer's Shilling Cookery for the People*, p. 158.

two slices of tasteless tomato, and doorstep of unpeeled cucumber that even now tend to represent salad in Britain.

One great disadvantage of the English countryside, from Soyer's point of view, must have been the dearth of amorous possibilities. He loved the company of women; it was yet another aspect of his Frenchness, and doubtless made him even more suspect in the eyes of the rollickingly macho John Bulls. Soyer had grown up in a society one of whose contemporary literary masterpieces was that cool-eyed analysis of the sexual game *Les Liaisons dangereuses*, and where witty *salonnières* exercised real political and cultural power; and although he is unlikely to have read Laclos's novel, or attended a salon (at least as a guest), like most urban Frenchmen he saw women as social equals. The fact of their sex only added to the interest of what they might have to say. No social gathering could be truly complete without them. "A dinner party without ladies is a garden without flowers, the ocean without waves, a fleet without sails," he lyrically captions a picture entitled *My Table at Home*—a view that held true even in the most unlikely circumstances: "We could not help remarking, and feeling at heart, the want of ladies at our board," he remarks of his arrival at Scutari during the Crimean campaign.

This was very different from British attitudes. For Englishmen, the presence of women at a gathering meant, *ipso facto*, that the evening would be fundamentally uninteresting. "The student should listen with profound attention to whatever hostesses may please to acquaint him with in the matter of their domestic economy," writes "The Alderman" in *The Knife and Fork for 1849*, a "guide for enlight-

Soyer's table at home as he liked to imagine it (and as his unexpected visitor hoped to experience it). "A dinner party without ladies is a garden without flowers."

ened epicures." "He will, in all probability, have to endure tedious narratives of the ill-doing of servants, and their ingratitude to their mistress; he must appear interested in long stories of little Malcolm's prodigious precocity."[4] Dull indeed (though not, one imagines, duller than The Alderman): No self-respecting Frenchwoman would broach such topics in polite company. However, given that domestic economy was all respectable British ladies were supposed to think about, it is hard to see quite how they were supposed to discuss anything else. From which we may conclude that this was the way Englishmen liked things.

Tall, handsome, vivacious, flirtatious—and French: Soyer must

[4]"The Alderman," *The Knife and Fork for 1849*, London, p. 80.

have created a sensation in the Aston servants' hall. It seems inconceivable that he can have remained celibate during his three years there. However, these romances, if indeed they took place, were not of any great depth. They certainly failed to efface old memories; for as soon as he returned to the environs of London he set about commissioning a portrait to be sent "we believe to an old love" in Paris, with a view to resuming their relationship.[5]

Although his biographers do not give the name of the Parisienne he had in mind, we know that Soyer had conducted at least one serious affair before he so abruptly left France. But, as so often, it seems clear that both the relationship and its consequences were infinitely more serious for the girl than for her carefree young spark. Her name was Adélaïde Lamain, and like so many of the *soubrettes* and *grisettes* who people the Romantic novels of the period, and whose own lives often turned out (like hers) so very unromantic, she was a seamstress. On June 5, 1830, just as young Alexis was making his fatal move to the Foreign Office, Mlle. Lamain gave birth to a little boy; and although she refused to tell her son who his father had been, she did divulge that name to a friend before, eight years later, dying. It was Alexis Soyer.

Obviously, since he was still in Paris during the first few months of his son's life, Alexis must have known about Adélaïde's pregnancy. Indeed, the boy, who seems to have had unusually vivid recall of his early months, "recollect[ed] confusedly to have seen a person at M. Lequesne's, a friend of my mother's, who seemed to take great interest in me."[6] But this interest, if indeed any such was really displayed,

[5]Volant and Warren, *Memoirs of Alexis Soyer*, p. 10.
[6]Volant and Warren, *Memoirs of Alexis Soyer*, p. 242.

failed to develop into anything more solid before Alexis's precipitate departure for England in 1831. The attachment, in the words of his old friend Volant, "was rather troublesome to him. He was then only twenty years of age, thoughtless, of light and rather timid disposition. He profited by his brother's suggestion to start off to England, and leave his first love to take care of herself and her baby."[7]

It seems probable, then, that he now intended to readdress himself to Adélaïde. We do not know whether he wrote to her during his years at Aston—given his previous behavior and his awkwardness with the pen, it seems unlikely—but now at last he could send an unequivocal token to show that he had not forgotten her. The thoughtless youth had had plenty of opportunity to reflect and mature during the past four years; his son was growing up; and everything we know about him indicates an exceptionally kind and affectionate nature. What more natural, if he now wished to settle down, than to try and get in touch once more? When in 1851 the boy, now a young man of twenty-one, sent a letter introducing himself, and setting out the circumstances of his life, Soyer in no way contested the fact of his paternity. After the first shock, the two met with "mutual affection," and two years later Soyer visited Paris and formally acknowledged his son, conferring his name and all legal rights of inheritance.

However, whatever his intentions or lack of them vis-à-vis Adélaïde, they came to nothing—for the very good reason that before he could put them into effect he met someone else, and fell hopelessly in love.

There can be no portrait without a portraitist, and Soyer knew no one suitable. So he made inquiries; and a curiosity shop in Rath-

---

[7]Volant and Warren, *Memoirs of Alexis Soyer*, p. 242.

Emma Soyer: a self-portrait.

bone Place sent him to a Flemish artist, François Simonau, some of whose paintings it displayed, and who lived five minutes' walk away, in London Street, just off Fitzroy Square. Simonau was rather eccentric, but the two nevertheless hit it off: As Volant put it, his "somewhat peculiar disposition rather pleased than displeased Alexis." However, the portraitist declined to execute the likeness himself, passing the job to his pupil, "Emma Jones, a very clever girl, who had already given so many proofs of her talent, that she was daily besieged by members of the aristocracy, to have sketches of their likenesses in *crayon*."[8]

Emma was not only clever but (as her self-portrait shows) pretty and vivacious. Soyer was instantly dazzled; and being a personable

[8]Volant and Warren, *Memoirs of Alexis Soyer*, p. 10.

fellow, full of gaiety, wit, and charm, he dazzled in his turn. She already had a suitor, but Alexis, undeterred, sent her a bunch of tulips. He received in return a note that read: "Miss Jones is quite astonished at the liberty M. S. has taken, in sending her such a present without her request, and consequently by the next mail, he will receive a box and his flowers back; and it will be useless for him to send any more, as she will return them in the same manner." The promised box duly arrived; glumly, he opened it—to reveal a painting of his bunch of tulips executed by the young lady.[9] A clearer sign of encouragement it would be hard to imagine, and the two were soon deep in love.

It is highly unlikely that Soyer had ever before met anyone like Emma Jones, if only because very few people like her then existed in England. Her straightforward confidence, which offered the possibility of true friendship as well as sex and domesticity, was something he found immediately appealing. Indeed, this confidence, the result in each case of a successful professional career, was a trait of all the three women to whom he became genuinely attached—Emma, the ballerina Fanny Cerrito, and in a quite different way, during his time in the Crimea in 1855 and 1856, his revered colleague Florence Nightingale. They were all very different, but each was independent, talented enough to command attention in a man's world, and determined to use that talent: qualities proper Victorians found shocking and uncomfortable. Soyer, however, found them deeply attractive. Once he had met Emma, he could never have been satisfied with Adélaïde.

Emma Jones was the unconventional daughter of an unconven-

<hr />

[9]Volant and Warren, *Memoirs of Alexis Soyer*, p. 142.

tional mother. Her father, Richard Jones, had died, or so her mother said, in 1817, when she was four years old. At any rate, he had vanished that year; and it may or may not be coincidental that this was the year M. Simonau arrived in London with the intention of opening an academy of drawing and painting. The official story was that Emma's mother visited him with her litle girl, requesting lessons; and although he hesitated to take on so young a pupil, after about six months Emma "showed such decided talent, that her mother proposed to remunerate him for the loss of all his other pupils if he would give his whole time to her daughter's instruction." Whether or not that was the exact sequence of events, or whether other fancies also played their part, the fact remains that within three years Mrs. Jones and M. Simonau were married. So either Mr. Jones really had died, or he and Emma's mother had never been married; for although Volant, in his memoir, always refers to her as Mrs. Jones, on her marriage certificate to Simonau her name is given as Elizabeth Newton, spinster. (The wedding was witnessed by her daughter, Elizabeth Emma Jones, then only seven, and her son, Newton Jones.)

That Emma was an exceptional young woman is not in doubt: Her intelligence, charm, and liveliness shine through everything she did and wrote. Whether her talent for painting was anything out of the ordinary it is hard to say, as little of her work survives; the few pictures Soyer reproduces seem rather uninspired. However, she was undeniably accomplished; and painting, unlike, say, medicine or the law, had the advantage of being a profession open to both men and women, talent being the only qualification. It had the added attraction that to be classified as an artist was, socially speaking, highly convenient. Artists were rather like Soyer's flying dishes: They hovered around the interstices, in this case of society—acceptable anywhere provided they were interesting enough, but nowhere fixed. They were rarely (if female) entirely respectable: hence the Brontës' and George Eliot's assumption of male names. But Emma had grown up in artistic circles, and (having, in that sense, no respectability to lose) was perfectly happy to retain her own identity, both professionally and socially. She was also, of course, half foreign, at least by stepparentage; and it is perhaps not coincidental that the suitor Soyer displaced was another Frenchman, i.e., a person outside the carefully layered confines of British society, and one brought up in a culture that allowed women—especially talented women—to participate fully in all aspects of life.

"Tell a woman now-a-days that she is an angel, and she will laugh at you; pay deference to her opinion, laugh at her jokelets, and . . . she will put you down in the list of 'agreeable gentlemen,'" disapprovingly observed the breathtakingly patronizing but not unrepresentative author of *The Knife and Fork*. He would not have got far with Miss Jones. If all else failed, or even if it didn't, she could make her own way in the world. Her considerable abilities, far from being carefully dissembled for fear of frightening off suitable gentlemen, had on the contrary been nurtured on the assumption that she would use them to make a living. She knew French and Italian, and as well as learning painting with Simonau took piano lessons with a well-known performer called Ancot, a friend of Rossini and Weber, who also taught the Duchess of Kent—like Emma, to professional level.

Unsurprisingly, Emma held trenchant views on the affectation and ignorance then thought proper in young women. She expressed them in a scornful parody:

FASHIONABLE PRECEPTS FOR THE LADIES

🐚 Nothing, in the eye of Fashion, is more amiable than to deviate from Nature.

🐚 To speak naturally, to act naturally, are vulgar and commonplace to the last degree.

🐚 To hear a story and not to express an emotion you do not feel is rude and unmannerly . . .

🐚 To move and think as you feel inclined are offences that no polite person can ever in honour or delicacy forgive . . .

🐚 Nothing is more common than pretensions to science or classical literature; therefore hold such studies and their professors in profound contempt. As to the learning you ought to pursue, you need be very little solicitous: it is unfashionable to put the mind to severe exertion, or to blunt natural sensibility by an over-studious attention to the more dry and abstruse departments of knowledge . . .

🐚 Take your meals invariably later than your vulgar neighbours. Go to bed at two in the morning, and rise at twelve next day.

🐚 You will then become a fashionable lady, and, in the midst of congratulation, will entirely forget the sacrifice of truth and nature by which you have acquired this enviable distinction.[10]

---

[10]Volant and Warren, *Memoirs of Alexis Soyer*, pp. 19–21.

Emma, for one, did not propose to make such a sacrifice in such a cause.

Her talents had shown themselves while she was still very young. Her first picture to be exhibited at the Royal Academy, "Watercress Woman," was shown (if the Academy's list of exhibitors is to be believed) in 1823, when she was only ten. Meanwhile, she had also begun to display decided musical capabilities; however, at the age of twelve a casual sketch drawn while the family was on holiday at Dunkerque produced such an effect that her mother and M. Simonau decided she should specialize in painting, and pursue music simply as a hobby. By the time Soyer met her in 1835 she was sending a picture a year to the Academy, and would continue to exhibit there regularly until her death. Her style may be deduced from her pictures' titles. The "Watercress Woman" was followed by "Study of an old man," "Children with rabbits," "The little masquerader," "Girl going to market," "Willy and his dog," "Childhood," "A Chelsea pensioner in his 104th year," "The escape," "The blind boy"—and many other such. In short, Emma painted sentimental genre pictures of the sort beloved, and eagerly bought, in her day. Almost all have vanished; one of the few to survive is a charming likeness of her husband, executed around the time of their marriage; there is also a frequently reproduced drawing, probably taken from it.

Soyer soon realized that here was a person with whom he could happily spend his life, and proposed marriage. But although Emma loved him, her stepfather hesitated. Even in this unconventional setting, class could not be altogether escaped: M. Simonau "would have had his pupil marry anyone rather than *a cook*."[11] This may have been for purely social reasons—when, in the 1841 census, Soyer gave his occupation as cook, the census taker automatically listed him among the servants, when in fact he was the householder. But there were also practical objections. When Soyer first met Emma he was still working for the Marquess of Ailsa, and although they were (as events would prove) good friends as well as master and servant, a living-in servant he nevertheless was. What would Emma do in Isleworth, as the wife of Lord Ailsa's cook?

Perhaps this was one reason why, in 1837, he left Lord Ailsa's and took a job at the newly established Reform Club. Here he would not be expected to live in, would be based in central London, and would earn an excellent salary. At any rate, the move seems to have done the trick: On April 12, 1837, two years after they first met, Alexis and Emma were married in St. George's, Hanover Square. Their witnesses were a friend of Emma's, Charlotte Amelia Walrow, and Soyer's old friend Ude, who gave away the bride—Simonau's opposition, it would seem, still not having been completely overcome. M. Ude particularly took to Emma; she and Soyer visited him often, and were regular guests at Ude's annual birthday feasts, where she brought him pictures as birthday presents. On the one invitation that survives, she is pointedly mentioned:

[11] Volant and Warren, *Memoirs of Alexis Soyer*, p. 11.

London, August 21, 1841

Dear Sir,

You will oblidge *me to favour with your Company you and your* Wiffe, *on Wednesday next at ½ past five o'clock* been *my birth day.*

The favour of an answer is requested.

Your *truly,*
Louis Eustache Ude.

Mr Soyer and Wife.[12]

Ude lived in grandly overfurnished style in wealthy Albemarle Street; the young Soyers' house at 5 Charing Cross Road, although only ten minutes' walk from Ude's residence, was part of an altogether different world, the raffish square mile that comprised Soho and Covent Garden. This was Soyer's favorite part of London, and would remain his home for most of his life. It was convenient—within walking distance of the Reform Club, the theaters, and the opera—and culturally congenial: so cosmopolitan, indeed, that one magazine described it as "a sort of petty France."[13] And for the next five years it would be bathed in the glow of M. and Mme. Soyer's married bliss.

Bliss, in this context, is of course a cliché; but it also properly describes the wonderful happiness now experienced by Alexis and his Emma. Besottedly in love, each successful and enoying the other's success, comfortably off, friends as well as lovers—it would not have been surprising, or much of an exaggeration, if they thought them-

[12]Volant and Warren, *Memoirs of Alexis Soyer*, p. 28.
[13]*The Builder,* quoted in Olsen, *The Growth of Victorian London*, p. 106.

selves the happiest and most fortunate couple in London. The way of life upon which they embarked feels, even in the twenty-first century, delightfully relaxed. Every morning Alexis would depart for his kitchens at the Reform Club, leaving Emma to her own work of drawing and painting. If she felt like seeing him during the day she simply called by the Club, secure in the certainty that he was never less than overjoyed to see her. A maid took care of the housework, and there was a constant stream of friends and houseguests: For example, on the night of the 1841 census, 5 Charing Cross Road contained, as well as the young couple, Alexis's brother Louis, another Frenchman, Louis Lowil, Simonau (Emma's mother had died in 1839, "happy," as the *Morning Post*'s obituary of Emma put it, "in the knowledge that her daughter had attained eminence by her talents and enjoyed prosperity with the husband of her choice," and leaving her well enough off not to have to worry about selling her paintings), and the maid, Sarah Vaughan, who also acted as an occasional model and confidante. In his search for a portraitist, the fortunate Alexis had chanced upon the one social setting that suited him to perfection: cosmopolitan, classless, creative.

> Melpomene and Terpsichore
> My favourite muses are!!
>> [warbled our hero, who was indeed very fond of the opera and the ballet]
> But painting is the art I love—
> It's Emma I adore!!![14]

[14]*Terpsicore et Melpoméné/Me sont deux favoris!!/Mais le peinture est l'art que j'aime,/Emma seule je chéri* . . . (Volant and Warren, *Memoirs of Alexis Soyer*, p. 13, my translation).

He loved her as a woman; and his pride in her artistic talent was beyond even the power of Soyerian hyperbole to express. On one occasion, after awaiting him fruitlessly for an hour in his office at the Reform Club, she made a crayon sketch of herself on the wall, rang the bell, told the servant that she had waited long enough, and (pointing to the sketch) had left her card. Soyer, on his return, was so delighted at his wife's wit and skill that he set a glass over the likeness and put a frame around it—a story that caused "general merriment" in the Club, and brought a stream of visitors to his office to view the divine artwork.[15]

At home, it sounds as if she rather than he may have done the cooking. His description, in *The Modern Housewife*, of what to eat on limited means in early married life reads as if from experience, and tends to the English rather than the French manner:

Sunday's dinner	Roast beef, potatoes, greens and Yorkshire pudding.
Monday	Hashed beef and potatoes.
Tuesday	Broiled beef and bones, vegetables, and spotted-dick pudding.
Wednesday	Fish, IF CHEAP, chops, and vegetables.
Thursday	Boiled pork, peas-pudding, and greens.
Friday	Peas soup and remains of pork.
Saturday	Stewed steak, with suet dumplings.[16]

[15]Volant and Warren, *Memoirs of Alexis Soyer*, p. 27.
[16]Soyer, *The Modern Housewife*, p. 413.

There is no knowing if this was actually autobiographical. But it is perfectly possible. We have already noted the pleasure Soyer took in *bouilli*. And his friends all remarked with surprise on his fondness for simple food—how, for example, after leaving a post-theater gathering, all dressed up in white tie and tails, he liked to buy a paper twist of fried fish, which he would eat with his fingers as he walked home. A man who spends his days concocting elaborate truffled sauces might well look forward, in the evening, to his wife's simple cooking.

In 1842, Emma found herself pregnant; the baby was due early in September. In August Soyer's friend Volant called on her, and found to his surprise that Alexis had left his heavily pregnant wife to visit Belgium. The Duke of Saxe-Coburg had admired her pictures, some of which adorned the Reform Club kitchens, and had invited the proud husband to return to Brussels with him, bringing two paintings the Duke especially liked. His brother, the King of the Belgians, was a connoisseur of paintings, and would appreciate an opportunity to see, and maybe even buy, the pictures.

It was an invitation Soyer could hardly refuse; and besides, it was an unrivaled opportunity to advance his beloved Emma's career. For her part, she was unworried. Her actions and writings are those of a sturdy and confident young woman; her portrait, gazing serenely from its frame, speaks of unhysterical calm. The baby, as she assured Volant, was not due for a fortnight. Its father would easily be back in time. Of course, every woman knew that childbirth was a dangerous business. But it is evident both from his actions and her tranquil acceptance of them that neither she nor Alexis felt anything but happy expectation.

On September 1, with Alexis still in Brussels, London was hit by a violent thunderstorm. Emma complained that it made her feel unwell, and spent most of the day in bed. In the early evening she reappeared, apparently feeling much better, and began to sketch her maid, Sarah Vaughan. But the continuing thunder disturbed her so much that she returned to bed. Her contractions began, and only two hours later (or so Volant says), both she and the child were dead. She was twenty-eight years old, and had been married five years.

Quite what went wrong it is impossible to know. Conditions such as pre-eclampsia can kill, but no one suffering from such a thing would feel well, and it seems unlikely her husband would have left her, even to see a king, had she seemed at all ill. Exhaustion and blood loss accounted for a good many fatalities, but a mere two hours' labor seems insufficient for that to have been the explanation. It seems more probable that Volant got it wrong, and that the whole business was altogether more drawn out. He hints that it was a miscarriage—a "premature confinement." If that were the case it might explain the speed of events, though this version hardly chimes with his earlier worries about Alexis departing so late in Emma's pregnancy. However, even if she had got her dates right, the fact was that in 1842 childbirth, even at full term, was still perilous. Hemorrhages, breech births—as every woman knew, any routine emergency might prove fatal. Chloroform, which both deadened labor pains and anesthetized if a cesarean was needed, was not discovered until 1847 (when a wag suggested its motto might be "Does your mother know you're out?"). But chloroform, like antisepsis, came too late for poor Emma.

Volant now had the unenviable task of journeying to Brussels, where Soyer was staying with Simonau's brother, to break the awful news. He could not bring himself actually to say the words, but his face spoke for him, and the distraught Alexis's first reaction, when he finally prized the true situation out of his friend, was to try and run himself through with a kitchen knife. For the next two hours he was incoherent with grief and shock. But eventually he calmed down, and, once safely on the Ostend to Dover ferry, it became clear that so long as sufficient distraction could be provided, he would survive. The weather was fine, there were several acquaintances among the passengers, and the voyage passed a great deal less badly than Volant had feared it might. The sight of all his good friends awaiting him, however, once again reduced him to despair, and when they arrived at the house he and Emma had shared he broke down again. He requested one last look at Emma in her coffin, but his friends, for undisclosed reasons—perhaps the effects of the hot weather—would not allow this.

Poor Soyer's feelings can scarcely be imagined. His marriage to Emma had been that Victorian rarity, a true love-match that succeeded on all levels. He had left her happily pregnant, without, it is clear, the least premonition of disaster. Had she or the child lived, his life would probably have been very different—and a good deal less adventurous. Domestic life would have satisfied him as his bachelor existence never wholly did: Much of his subsequent hyperactivity feels like an attempt to fill the void Emma left in his life. Indeed, for him she never wholly died, watching over him through the paintings with which he for the rest of his days took such pleasure in surrounding himself: his tutelary goddess, the woman of his dreams— and, increasingly, with a dream's insubstantiality. Her pictures, which he henceforth made a point of buying back for his own collection whenever the occasion arose, became a sort of shrine, to be carried with him wherever he went and shown off to whoever would listen. They lined his walls and every vertical surface of his rooms; they adorned his kitchens and, later, his soup kitchens. When the time came, one even accompanied him to the Crimea, a constant and comforting reminder of great happiness.

Meanwhile, as can be seen from Volant's account of the voyage back to England, his outgoing personality and the evident pleasure he took in his work probably both masked his grief and made it easier to bear. And soon he was submerged in the thousand and one chores attendant on death. There was the funeral to arrange; and *The Times* ran a gratifyingly extensive obituary ("Her group . . . depicting two boys selling lemons, has been recently engraved by Gerard of Paris, in mezzotinto, and is a fine illustration of the talents of the deceased. It partakes of the style of Murillo; but, though in his manner, it has not the subservience of imitation, nor the stiffness of copy . . ."), which he later reproduced, for the benefit of a wider public, at the back of *The Gastronomic Regenerator*. He sent a few chosen pictures to members of the aristocracy with whom, for various reasons, he felt a particular connection, including the Duke of Saxe-Coburg, at whose behest he had made the unfortunate trip to Brussels, and his old employer the Duke of Cambridge; the polite letters of thanks and condolence sent off by the royal secretaries in response constituted a further proof that his wife really had lived and really had been as talented as he remembered, and were lovingly reproduced alongside Emma's obituaries. Of course, such proof was really superfluous. He knew exactly how wonderful and gifted Emma had been, just as he knew he could cook. But these truths would always lack solidity for him without the written imprimatur of the rich and powerful. In the meantime, his hopeful assumption that class difference need not preclude friendship was borne out by the Marquess of Ailsa. From St. Margaret's House, Ailsa wrote to M. Simonau "deplor[ing] poor M. Soyer's and your loss. If I could render him any service, I should be happy to do so. He is most welcome to come here, and you with him, and stay as long as you please.— Your most obt. Servt.—AILSA."[17]

Emma's disappearance left Soyer bereft in more ways than one. In particular, there was the vexed question of his inability to write English. During their marriage she had acted as her husband's amanuensis; now he decided he really must learn to write for himself. But although he took lessons three or four times a week, he made slow progress, and after a couple of months gave up. From now on he would be forced to employ a secretary; and as his life increasingly involved writing, this soon became a permanent appointment. (Thackeray, describing the arrival of M. Mirobolant at Clavering Park, tells how his "library, pictures, and piano, had arrived previously in charge of the intelligent young Englishman his aide de camp.")

Soyer and Simonau were both now widowers; and whatever Simonau may once have felt about Emma's marriage, it is clear they had become the best of friends. While Emma was alive Simonau had fended off loneliness with frequent visits to 5 Charing Cross Road; now Soyer, though keeping on the Charing Cross Road house, spent much of his time in Simonau's spacious rooms in Leicester Square, where they lived a life of cheerful domestic chaos. A curious lady visitor hoping for a quick sitting with Simonau arrived unannounced one day to find the portraitist ensconced in a large and beautiful room thickly hung with pictures, both Emma's and his own. In one

[17]Volant and Warren, *Memoirs of Alexis Soyer*, p. 42.

corner was an unmade bed; on the floor a feather bed and mattress; on an elaborate drawing-room table sat a heap of meat and vegetables destined for a mutton stew. A maid-of-all-work hung awkwardly around the door, anxious to start cooking but unable to get in and claim the food while the lady was in the room. Simonau, noticing this, and more concerned for his broth than his visitor, excused himself for a moment "on a little culinary business," and snatching up the mutton, and closely followed by the maid carrying the vegetables, dived into the small, untidy back kitchen where she slept, and where the household's washing and cooking were done. To Simonau's astonishment, though not his discomfiture, the visitor followed. "You see, madame, we are very domesticated," he said. "We do everything at home; besides, we foreigners cannot live without good soup and some relishing stews; these are as much the half of our lives, as roast beef and plum pudding are to the English."

No one could have loved his wife more than Soyer had done, nor could anyone have more tenderly cherished her memory. Nevertheless, "It would be absurd," writes Volant, "to imagine that our friend, after the sudden loss he had sustained in 1842, would seriously make a vow of remaining single at the age of thirty-two, endowed, as he was, with a rather handsome countenance, plenty of wit and conversation for the fair sex, and possessed already of the highest reputation in his art."[18] And the conclusion of the surprise visitor's story demonstrates that potential objects of affection were not far to seek—indeed, they positively queued at his door. For as well as the qualities just enumerated he possessed the most potent of all: fame—to which even respectable ladies were not immune.

[18]Volant and Warren, *Memoirs of Alexis Soyer*, p. 59.

"Then do you mean to say that M. Soyer is going to dine with you?" the lady inquired of Simonau, who replied, "Indeed, madame, he does not make it a rule; but I can assure you he enjoys what I cook, particularly my potage."

Highly excited at the prospect of the celebrated Soyer's imminent arrival, the visitor eagerly wondered, when our hero eventually appeared, whether he would not like to show her his famous "kitchen at home." He put her off: "It would afford me great pleasure, madame, to satisfy your curiosity; but my kitchen at home is *out of town*, and, as I am unfortunately a bachelor, I do not see a chance of granting your request." But she was not to be so easily disposed of. During the next few weeks she haunted his office at the Reform Club, and the acquaintance was only ended when Soyer, taking her at her implied word, penned a flowery and rather direct love-poem: *"Quand je t'ai vue, adorable Thalie,/On aurait dit la reine de Paphos/Tu m'éblouis et ta gorge embellie/Eut fait pleurer un marbre de Paros. . . ."*[19] After which she vanished; what else is a respectable lady to do when a gentleman starts writing sonnets to her breasts?

However, we may be sure that there were other ladies less unwilling to carry flirtation to its logical conclusion; and it was in these more relaxed circles—specifically, dress circles, not to mention stalls, galleries, and wings—that Soyer now began to spend his spare time.

Of course, he did not visit the theater only, or even primarily, to meet actresses. The stage was an old passion of his; and it offered an obvious and welcome solution to the problem of empty, Emma-less

[19]Volant and Warren, *Memoirs of Alexis Soyer*, pp. 81–5.

evenings. Soon he was a fixture both in the audience and backstage. He knew all the stage managers and front-of-house men, and could always wangle a pass.

But of course theaters do contain thespians; and it was not surprising that he now looked to the profession, if not for a new Emma—that was unimaginable—then for a new lady friend. Actresses and dancers were real women in the sense that Emma had been a real woman: independent, leading their own creative lives, potential friends and equals outside the stiff and artificial hierarchies of fashion, class and propriety—in short, the kind of women he now knew he liked. And of course they knew how to make themselves attractive, as well as being famously untrammeled by conventional morals—a decided point in their favor.

Within this world, his sights soon fastened on one woman in particular. When the lady visitor had inquired whether M. Soyer was really expected that evening in Leicester Square, Simonau had assured her that he might well arrive, "for we expect the admirable Mademoiselle Cerrito to give her last sitting, and probably he will come."[20]

Fanny Cerrito was a ballerina—one of *the* ballerinas, then at the height of her fame, equaled only by Fanny Elssler and Marie Taglioni. In 1844, the year she met Soyer, she was twenty-eight, a middle-class girl from Naples whose determination to dance, and evident abilities in that direction, had overcome her parents' initial resistance and taken her to the top of her chosen profession. She had arrived in London fresh from a triumph in Milan, where as the *London Morning Herald* reported, "Serenaders by the 'million'

[20]Volant and Warren, *Memoirs of Alexis Soyer*, p. 83.

Fanny Cerrito at the time Soyer first met her.

made the air tuneful under her windows—her carriage was a sort of Juggernaut before which the population bowed—princes feted her—archdukes loaded her with praises and presents."[21]

As this report indicates, dancers mixed with members of the highest society—something that rarely happened to middle-class girls from Naples. Quite on what terms they met was another matter. London's reception was typically equivocal. "Taglioni, of course, was not generally received," reported Lady Dorothy Nevill, "but, nevertheless, I once met her at a party, though I cannot remember where, nor how she got there. Cerrito, however, I perfectly well recollect seeing at Mr Long's, at whose house in Grafton Street one used to meet all sorts of clever and interesting people, for he had the especial gift of collecting together notabilities of every sort. I was introduced to the famous dancer, who

[21]Guest, *Fanny Cerrito*, p. 49.

looked very pretty and demure, and made an excellent impression on everyone."[22]

Fanny's mother accompanied her everywhere, and hoped for the best. That is to say, she hoped to become the mother-in-law of a prince, or at worst a duke or count. Unfortunately, it soon became apparent that these hopes were unlikely to be fulfilled. Fanny met plenty of noblemen who liked her very much, but marriage was another matter. "I am told that in a private drawing room, when *décolletée*, she is a splendid creature, but she is more fully developed than is at her age becoming," observed William Archer Shee, who to his disappointment saw her only when modestly covered by "a large lace shawl"[23]—not the kind of remark one would make about a respectably marriageable young lady. Indeed, as far as matrimony was concerned her choice, as she approached the end of her twenties, lay between two aspirants, each, in the eyes of an ambitious mother, less suitable than the other. One was her leading man, Arthur Saint-Léon; the other was Alexis Soyer.

We do not know exactly when Soyer and Cerrito met. There was a natural professional interchange between ballet dancers, who were frequent subjects for portraits, and the artists who painted them. Perhaps Simonau introduced them following his commission, though it is possible, since Emma had painted Taglioni, that Soyer was already at home in ballet circles. But by September 1844, when Emma's monument was erected at Kensal Green cemetery, the two had almost certainly become lovers.

This monument, a huge and elaborate construction, had cost

[22]Guest, *Fanny Cerrito*, p. 86.
[23]Quoted in Guest, *Fanny Cerrito*, p. 87.

the enormous sum of five hundred pounds. The pedestal was over twelve feet high, surmounted by a colossal figure of Faith, which took the full height to over twenty-one feet. Floating cherubim presented a palm to the deceased, who appeared on a medallion done in white marble by her doting stepfather. One of Soyer's Reform Club acquaintances—Sala, who tells this story, was unsure whether Douglas Jerrold, or Thackeray, or Monckton Milnes, or Bernal Osborne, or Disraeli—suggested that the epitaph should be "Soyer Tranquille,"[24] but this was rejected in favor of the simple dedication "To Her." At the tomb's consecration in 1844, Emma's palette and brushes were placed in a recess at the back of the monument, to be sealed with glass; and to these Cerrito added a wreath of her own, made from a crown recently placed upon her head by an Archduke of Austria (doubtless one of those mentioned by the *Morning Herald*) on the stage of La Scala, Milan—a somewhat bizarre gesture that would surely only have been made if she and the grieving widower were on intimate terms.

By then the affair had probably been going on at least six months. Soyer's first published work, the eccentric ballet scenario *La Fille de l'orage* (Daughter of the Storm), "dedicated without permission to she who is universally *chérie, chérie Cerrito!*," is a sort of extended homage to its intended star from one who was either a hopeful or a grateful *innamorato*. This "revue seria buffa," a skit on the then current melodramatic ballet scenarios, was not published until 1845, but internal evidence indicates that it was almost certainly written in March the previous year. In the introduction, the "amateur," who may be identified by his trousers in

---

[24]Sala, *Things I Have Seen and People I Have Known*, p. 245.

"couleurs mirabolantes" (evidently, Thackeray read the scenario; his M. Mirobolant, however, corrects Soyer's spelling, shaky even in French), begs Mlle. C. to accept his ballet and the name of "La Fille de l'orage." "Turning to the noisy crowd, 'What do you think, sirs?' she asks. 'What, him compose a ballet?' quips one by-stander, 'I think he must have made a mistake, what he means is that he's going to make another soufflé a la Clontarf!'"

Just as mothers place events by reference to the then age of their offspring, so one may date Soyer's productions by their references to his latest culinary feat. On March 9, 1844, "At a very recherché dinner given . . . (by some friends of Mr. O'Connell) at the Reform Club, there was a remarkably dainty dish placed upon the table, entitled 'Le Soufflé Monstre a la Clontarf,' the height of it was twenty-nine inches, and the width seventeen inches; it took four and a quarter hours to bake, and contained thirty-six eggs, with other ingredients in proportion. Fifty very small *soufflez* were seen clinging round this colossal mountain, and an extraordinary good likeness of the Great Agitator (drawn on rice paper, and surrounded by wreaths of shamrock) appeared as if it were rising from the volcanic crater."[25] The reference was to the monster meetings lately conducted throughout Ireland by Daniel O'Connell, in a bid to achieve political reform without violence, following which a grateful British government had imprisoned him.

We may therefore deduce that by March 1844 Soyer and Cerrito were, at the very least, in an advanced state of flirtation. Producing a book is by no means effortless even for the literate; it seems unlikely

---

[25]*The Sun*, March 11, 1844.

Soyer would have put himself to so much trouble without some exceptionally powerful motivation.

In *La Fille de l'orage* we get a rare sense of what Soyer's conversation must have been like, and the social atmosphere in which he moved. This is partly because it is in French, a language in which he was always far more at ease than in English, and partly because it reproduces the back-and-forth of backstage repartee. Throughout, the "amateur" is trying to persuade "Mlle C." to take the leading role in his ballet, against a barrage of jokes, catcalls, and excruciating puns. The scenario involves gods, storms, spirits, and a vast range of special effects. Halfway through, the amateur is carried away by a dream "in which are heard these confused words: Consommé . . . Turtle . . . Supreme . . . Foie Gras . . . Essence . . . Truffles . . . Ortolans . . ." At the end, "The curtain falls . . . The Public, delighted with the evening's entertainment, applauds at the height of its lungs, and cries from the gods: Give us our money back! Out with the authors, the actors, the directors, the singers, the scene shifters and above all the sweepers-up! . . . Meanwhile the Fille de l'orage goes to her dressing-room and asks her *gazeuse* (gassy/not too moral) maid for a lemonade. The maid remarks to her heavenly mistress that she should take care not to drop makeup (*mousse*) on her dawn-coloured costume, since *la mousse tache* (stains)" . . . When the amateur gets up to go, one of the company that has been teasing him throughout murmurs, "Surely you're not angry, my dear fellow, I meant it all as a joke, you know," to which our hero replies, "Who, me? My dear sir, not at all, you were very witty, I couldn't possibly get angry at such good jokes." Then he disappears down the stairs, hails his cab, and drives off into the night; after which "everyone laughed a lot at his expense."

This is not exactly the stuff of literary or terpsichorean classics. Harrison Ford famously remarked of George Lucas's script for *Star Wars* that "you can type this stuff, but you can't speak it." *La Fille de l'orage*, like many of Soyer's written effusions, demonstrates the reverse defect. It is more understandable spoken, puns and all in a flourishing sweep, than written; which since it was undoubtedly dictated is hardly surprising. But it is so jolly, so amusing (despite the puns!), and so good-humored and lacking in self-importance that one can easily imagine how attractive the company of such a fellow must have been amid the crowd of thespian egos and back-stage flatterers.

We are also shown a glimpse of Cerrito's domestic life. While everyone is arguing about their preferred roles in the proposed scenario ("Write something comic for me!" urges a fat man, while "a very small man, though a very great dancer"—Saint-Léon, Soyer's rival—wants "tragique, tragique pour moi"), Madame Cerrito, Fanny's mother, is thinking about Sunday dinner. "Six o'clock, don't be late, it'll be quite informal, I'll do that Italian dish I promised you."

Madame Cerrito was soon to become a good deal less welcoming. It was Saint-Léon whom Fanny in the end preferred, a fact that was made clear to Soyer when he arrived one day in Brighton, where she was then based, to find the two lovers wrapped up in each other and himself clearly unwelcome. Soon she was married; and as far as Fanny and Alexis were concerned, that, according to both his biographer and hers, was that. He was a footnote to her life.

In fact, however, this is far from the truth. Cerrito separated from Saint-Léon in 1851; in June, he signed a three-year contract with the Paris Opera, while she left for London. It was the year of the Great Exhibition, and she is recorded as visiting the Symposium, the restaurant Soyer opened that year just opposite the Crystal Palace. In 1853 she gave birth to a daughter, Mathilde, whose father was not Saint-Léon; on the birth certificate the father's name was left blank. After Soyer's death in 1858, Fanny attributed paternity to a Spanish nobleman, the Marqués de Bedmar y Escaluna—a person far more exalted, and of course far wealthier, than either Saint-Léon or Soyer—who eventually acknowledged Mathilde. But why did she wait so long before identifying the child's father? Was it because she was uncertain of the child's paternity and hoped for another outcome—perhaps marriage?

If so, Soyer may well have been the other man. Between 1850, when he left the Reform Club, and his departure for the Crimea in 1855, he often visited Paris. There was talk of his offering high-class gastronomic tours there, and he ran a business importing French delicacies such as pâté de foie gras for resale to London clients. Having now reestablished his friendship with Cerrito, he would certainly have visited her on these trips at her villa in the rue de l'Observatoire, near the Louvre.

In 1854, when Cerrito was thirty-eight and Mathilde one year old, the *Figaro* flagged the approaching end of her dancing days with the cruel observation that "She had never much style, and today she lacks breath." For the next few years she toured frenetically, determined to earn as much as possible before finally hanging up her shoes. In November 1855, she danced in Moscow, at the Bolshoi, returned to London, and then, in the autumn of 1856, was once again in Russia.

This was the time of the Crimean campaign, which meant that Soyer, too, was then in Russia. It is conceivable that they met; what is certain is that on his return to Europe, he stayed awhile in Paris—

with Cerrito. She was in the habit of lending her villa, when she was away on tour, to her brother Joseph; if he happened still to be in possession when she returned, she used a small hotel in the rue de l'Arc de Triomphe in the fashionable suburb of Passy. We know, because one of Soyer's letters was addressed from there, that he, too, was staying there that year; and when he finally returned to London, it was on the same boat as Cerrito.

Clearly, then, they were once more the closest of friends, though as Cerrito was Catholic and married, and Saint-Léon still very much alive—he did not die until 1870—they could not, officially, be anything more. However, there is some evidence that in 1857, in Paris, Cerrito and Soyer made a public declaration of joint intent, perhaps with Mathilde in mind.

Had he lived they might even, finally, have set up house together. The arrangement—especially if Mathilde were Soyer's daughter rather than Bedmar's—would doubtless have suited them both. However, he died in 1858, as he put it "still unfortunately a bachelor." With Emma, he had come nearer than most to ideal happiness. Not caring to risk an inferior model with a lesser woman, Cerrito had been the only other real possibility. Failing that, he saw to it that, one way or another, his life was full.

4

Relevé: Mutton Cutlets Reform

In moving from Aston Hall to London, Soyer moved into the modern world. If country house life had changed little over the past several hundred years, London was whirling forward into what we now know as the Victorian era, with the Reform Club in its van. Indeed, 1837, when Soyer moved to the Club, was the year of the young Queen's accession. On the occasion of her coronation the following year, he provided two thousand breakfasts for members and their guests: his first taste of catering a great public event.

The classic Victorian dish, the dish of grand municipal dinners and great occasions, was of course turtle soup—Lewis Carroll's "beautiful soup so rich and green." Soyer called it "the delight of civic corporations, the friend of the doctors, and the enemy of the alderman"; for him it "has been, and perhaps ever will be, the leading article of English cookery."[1]

In this prophecy he was of course wrong—the decline of turtles and the rise of cholesterol consciousness have seen to that. I doubt there is an Englishman living who has actually tasted this delicacy. Indeed, it is hard to imagine a dish that runs more wholly counter to every twenty-first-century inclination. Even had I wished to make it, turtles are no longer common culinary currency. Neither is this exactly the stuff of home cooking, as the following extract shows:

> Make choice of a good turtle, weighing from one hundred and forty to one hundred and eighty pounds, hang it up by the hind fins securely, cut off the head and let it hang all night . . . Take out the interior, which throw away, first collecting all the green fat that is upon it, then remove the fins and fleshy parts, leaving nothing but the two large shells, saw the top shell into four and the bottom one in halves; then put the whole of the turtle, including the head, into a large turbot kettle, and cover with cold water, . . . place it upon a sharp fire and let it boil five minutes, . . . then put the pieces into a tub of cold water, and with a pointed knife take off all the scales, which throw away, then take out carefully the whole of the green fat, which reserve, place the remainder back in the turbot kettle, where let it simmer until the meat comes easily from the shells and the fins are tender, then take them out and detach all the glutinous

[1]Soyer, *The Gastronomic Regenerator,* p. 85.

meat from the shells, which cut into square pieces and re-
serve till required . . .

Green fat! And that's just the start. For a turtle of this size (which
is, Soyer assures us, the best, since smaller ones have comparatively
little green fat), the soup will need ten gallons of stock made with
60 lb. veal knuckles, 20 lb. beef, 6 lb. lean ham, four onions and a
carrot; and for the final preparation 3 lb. butter, 4½ lb. flour (no
soup being complete without its flour thickening), and for each
tureen a saltspoonful of cayenne and a quarter of a pint of Madeira.
Aficionados of *Alice in Wonderland* will be delighted to know that
the recipes for turtle soup and clear turtle soup are followed by one
for Mock Turtle Soup, whose main ingredient is a calf's head:
Clearly, I was not the only one to boggle at the mere thought of
tackling the genuine article. Not that a calf's head seemed much
more manageable. But in any case, the soup course was behind us. I
needed to find some other dish to carry our dinner forward.

Fortunately, the choice was easy. Soyer of course cooked, or
oversaw the cooking of, countless dishes while at the Reform Club.
But of all his culinary inventions, by far the most famous was the
one he named for the Club itself: Mutton Cutlets Reform.

"The discovery of a new dish does more for the happiness of
mankind than the discovery of a new star," observed Brillat-
Savarin; and few such discoveries can have spread more happiness
in their day than this. It appeared daily in the dining room; it
graced the grandest dinners; and after 1846 it could even be made
at home, since the recipe appeared in *The Gastronomic Regenerator,*
the best-selling cookbook Soyer published that year (and for which
Brillat-Savarin's aphorism served as epigraph). This was his trade-

mark dish, and for this course in our dinner there could really be no other choice.

Mutton! The very name is redolent of boardinghouses and institutional hash. But although it was once the daily meat of every table high and low, mutton has now all but vanished. When the wave of world food burst over Britain, its place was taken by lamb, the Mediterranean meat. Supermarkets stock exclusively lamb; in most butchers' displays you will search in vain for mutton. However, my butcher, the redoubtable Mr. Portwine, told me he usually stocked mutton and could always get me a haunch if I ordered it a little in advance. As I wanted a rack, not a haunch, I could only hope that he dealt in other cuts as well. They must surely exist— lambs have ribs: ergo, so must sheep.

In the event, when I went to inquire, he happened to have a rack of mutton in his cold room. It came from Ronaldsay in the Orkneys, where the sheep are slender little beasts that live (he assured me) entirely on seaweed. The rack made eleven small, dark-red, almost fatless chops. Since we were to be six at table, I added a lamb chop to make up the dozen. Its pale coloring and healthy layer of fat looked somehow decadent beside the trim little Ronaldsay offerings.

The mountain sheep are sweeter/But the valley sheep are fatter;/I therefore deem it meeter/To feed upon the latter, rhymed Thomas Love Peacock, apropos Welsh mutton. Soyer, though, differed. He thought "the best [Welsh mutton] is brought in direct from its native mountains, the heath upon which it feeds gives a very rich flavour to the meat, which is very dark without much fat; many are fed in the English counties, they are excellent and much fatter, but do not possess the same wild flavour."[2] That was it, my mutton exactly. Clearly, there is something special about sheep from the Celtic fringes.

Having procured the mutton, I set about the sauce.

Sauce à la Reform

Cut up two middling-sized onions in thin slices and put them into a stewpan with two sprigs of parsley, two of thyme, two bay leaves, two ounces of lean uncooked ham, half a clove of garlic, half a blade of mace, and one ounce of fresh butter; stir them ten minutes over a sharp fire, then add two tablespoons of Tarragon vinegar, and one of Chili vinegar, boil it one minute; then add a pint of brown sauce or sauce Espagnole, three tablespoons of preserved tomatas, and eight of consommé; place it over the fire until boiling, then put it on the corner, let it simmer ten minutes, skim it well, then place it again over the fire, keeping it stirred, and reduce until it adheres to the back of a spoon; then add a good tablespoon red currant jelly, and a half ditto of chopped mushrooms; season a little more if required with pepper and salt, stir it until the jelly is melted, then pass it through a tammie into another stewpan. When ready to serve, make it hot, and add the white of a hard-boiled egg cut into strips half an inch long and thick in proportion, one gherkin, two green Indian pickles, and half an ounce of cooked ham, or

[2]Soyer, *The Gastronomic Regenerator.*

tongue, all cut into strips like the white of egg; do not let it boil afterwards. This sauce must be poured on whatever it is served with.

I admit that when I read this my heart sank. This is restaurant food *par excellence,* by which I mean that it assumes you have pinches of this and spoonfuls of that always available (Soyer's Reform Club kitchens included revolving spice and condiment racks fixed around pillars beside the main work surface), as well as basics such as brown sauce ready to hand. It is also a lot of effort, and so hardly worth making in small amounts—which of course in the Reform Club it never was. And if the complication seems somewhat arbitrary, that, too, went with the job. Soyer was not hired by the Reform Club to produce simple home cooking. On the contrary, he was on his mettle as never before. Deeply desiring to make a good impression, he excelled himself in inventiveness—a quality that, in culinary terms, almost demands complication. Modern chefs rack their brains to devise improbable yet delicious combinations; nineteenth-century chefs did the same. The difference lay in the style of combinations they preferred, and the results they desired. Where now the aim is for every ingredient to contribute its own recognizable taste and texture to the whole, the preference then, if Soyer is any guide, was for a smooth (always sieved) yet piquant blend of skillfully combined, individually unrecognizable flavors.

Fortunately, most of the ingredients for Reform Sauce are still easy to find. I did not have chili vinegar, so I substituted a (small) chopped dried chili pepper. And for "preserved tomatas" I substituted tomato puree, though it struck me later that perhaps canned chopped tomatoes might more accurately have reproduced Soyer's preserves. As the puree was probably stronger I reduced the amount, using one and a half tablespoons instead of three. The brown sauce was based on the stock I had already made for the soup; I had frozen what was left over so that, as in Soyer's kitchen, it was conveniently to hand. For the consommé I used a beef stock cube.

To make the brown sauce,

> put one pound of butter into a deep stewpan, (which is best for this purpose,) place it over the fire, stirring it until it melts; then stir in one and a half pounds of best flour, mix it well, and keep stirring it over the fire until it assumes a brownish tinge; then take it from the fire and keep stirring the roux until partly cold, then pour in the stock quickly, still stirring it; place over a sharp fire, and keep it stirred until it adheres to the back of a spoon, when pass it through a tammie into a basin, stirring it occasionally until cold, and use it where required.

Since these are quantities for two quarts of stock and I wanted only a pint of sauce, I quartered the amount.

The Reform Sauce took, in all, two and a half hours to make, not including shopping for all the bits and pieces (gherkins, red currant jelly, Indian pickles, cooked ham, etc.). The result, before adding the garnishes, was a smooth, translucent reddish-brown. Clearly, it was going to be strong—the ancestor of that wartime *salsa piccante* our Italian friend found so distressing, which must have been some relative of HP Sauce or Daddies Sauce. What I found when I tasted it was, however, not quite what I'd expected.

Here, to all intents and purposes, after hours of labor and all those stocks and butters and spoons of this and pinches of that, was— tomato ketchup! The world's favorite sauce! No wonder Reform Sauce was so popular.

Once the sauce was ready, the rest of the meal was quite straightforward.

The Cutlets

Chop a quarter of lean cooked ham very fine and mix it with the same quantity of bread-crumbs, then have ten very nice cotelettes, lay them flat on your table, season lightly with pepper and salt, egg over with a paste-brush, and throw them into the ham and bread-crumbs, then beat them lightly with a knife, put ten spoonfuls of oil in a sauté-pan, place it over the fire, and when quite hot lay in the cotelettes, fry nearly ten minutes (over a moderate fire) till a light brown colour; to ascertain when done, press your knife upon the thick part, if quite done it will feel rather firm, possibly they may not all be done at one time, so take out those that are ready first and lay them on a cloth till the others are done; as they require to be cooked with the gravy in them, dress upon a thin border of mashed potatoes in a crown, with the bones pointing outwards, sauce over with a pint of sauce reform, and serve.

Preparing and frying the chops was a matter of minutes— fewer minutes, indeed, than the recipe prescribed. Despite my resolve to follow Soyer's instructions to the letter, I couldn't bear to cook my tender little chops until they turned rigid and gray. I gave them five minutes rather than ten, on a quite high heat, turning them once, by which time they were perfectly done, crispy on the outside and pink in the middle. I served them up as directed, the chops arranged inside the ring of mashed potato so that their bones stuck up in a crown. The sauce filled the hollow in the middle; as always with Soyer, it was far more copious than would be considered necessary today.

Mashed Potatoes

Plain boil or steam six or eight large mealy potatoes; when well done peel and put them into a stewpan with two ounces of butter, a little salt; then with a prong of a fork whisk them till quite in pureé; then add two tablespoonfuls of milk, work up with a wooden spoon till forming a paste, then roll on a clean cloth, roll it to the circumference of a fourpenny or six-penny piece and form a round with it in your dish according to size of the entreé; alter the proportion according to the size of the flame or remove.

Soyer's method with mashed potato was excellent, smooth and well-flavored, with none of the wateriness you sometimes get if the potatoes are peeled and cut up before boiling. I used great big potatoes, of the sort more usually used for baking, one each and one to spare, and just built them into a ring with a spoon. Every morsel vanished.

The company was charmed by this dish. One of us had sampled its distant cousin at the present-day Reform Club, but in her view their twenty-first-century version is far inferior to the original—assuming that what I produced was what the dish's originator intended. When I asked people what the sauce reminded them of, they did not at once jump to my base conclusion; and when I mooted the tomato ketchup connection, did not altogether agree. The resemblance is undoubtedly there, but Sauce à la Reform, we concluded, is decidedly subtler than what you buy in red bottles. We found its sweet-and-sour tang more than a little Oriental. Its piquancy was just enough to set off the flavor of the meat, even though the Ronaldsay mutton's seaweedy tang was subtle rather than strong. It would have been even more welcome with the more usual, much fattier meat, the vinegar in the sauce cutting the fat, as capers do with boiled leg of mutton, or sorrel or green gooseberries with goose. But mutton of the sort we were fortunate enough to find really needs little if any garnish. It is a true delicacy, just as Soyer described, and I am grateful to him for introducing me to it. By contrast, the one lamb chop—an excellent chop in itself—seemed dull and flavorless.

The Reform Club was founded, as its name suggests, by the group of Whig liberals who had forced through the Reform Act in 1832, and who now wished for a club that would reflect their political leanings. Their first cook, Auguste Rotivan, left after only three weeks, and in 1837, Soyer was appointed in his place. And there he stayed from 1837, the year after the Club was founded, until 1850. It was a transforming symbiosis: The Club made his name, and he put it on the map. "It is well-known," sniffed *The Times* in 1844, "that this concern [the Reform Club] has for some years past . . . lived entirely upon the reputation of its club-house . . . and the supposed reputation of its enormously-puffed culinary department— the produce of which, by the way, though of the most ordinary description, when *Frenchified* or *Italianized,* passes for something *recherché* amongst men whose station in society, by accident of birth, has entitled them, with a fifteen-pence qualification, to the entrées of William's Boiled Beef House in the Old Bailey, Hancock's eating-house in Regent-Street, or Upton's ditto in the Strand."[3] Envy drips from every letter. No better proof of genuine success could possibly be imagined.

Soyer was still only twenty-seven when he took up his Reform Club job—extraordinarily young for a post of such responsibility: on the one hand a single young Frenchman, on the other (as Volant puts it) "some fifteen hundred members of the aristocracy whose appetites were on the *qui vive.*"[4] But he was in a state of mind to rise to any occasion. He had just married a wife he adored; both enjoyed their work; in both cases the prospect of recognition and success beckoned; he was earning a good salary, and there was plenty of money on her side. A better setting for ideal happiness can scarcely be imagined.

Soho, where the Soyers lived, was at that time, George Sala remembered, "almost as French as the rue Montmartre. French *charcutiers,* French restaurants, hotels, barbers and hairdressers, newsvendors, circulating libraries and cigar-shops encompassed [their] dwelling; while the floors over the French shops were ten-

[3]*The Times,* October 14, 1844.
[4]Volant and Warren, *Memoirs of Alexis Soyer,* p. 22.

anted by French tailors, milliners and dressmakers."[5] By contrast, the Reform Club was in its way as outlandishly English as any foxhunting squire in the wilds of Shropshire. Indeed, it is hard to imagine any two institutions more emblematic of their societies' social attitudes than the French restaurant and English gentleman's club. The former were, in their way, as egalitarian as the Revolution that had so enhanced their popularity, their only entry qualification the ability to pay, one of their chief characteristics and attractions the teeming variety of the clientele; the latter, product of a society dedicated to maintaining every fine degree of social distinction, fulfilled precisely the opposite function.

Clubs are about inclusion, but of course they are also, and almost more importantly, about exclusion: keeping the wrong people out. And if you had to ask who those wrong people might be, you were probably one of them. Anyone put up for election at one of the London gentlemen's clubs might be "pilled," or blackballed, without explanation. "There are a whole bushel of reasons, most of them unlooked-for, why a man gets 'pilled' at a London club," Thackeray explained to George Sala. "Fortunately your name is not Smith, as, if it were, all the Smiths in the club would combine against you, through fear that their letters might be misdelivered to you. On the other hand you would probably get two or three black balls because your name is Sala and not Smith. Some people would say that you are a fiddler, or that your father was a hairdresser or a cook, or something foreign and socially ineligible."[6] Members wanted to be absolutely sure that, once safely ensconced in their club, they would

[5]Sala, *Things I Have Seen and People I Have Known*, p. 244.
[6]Sala, *Things I Have Seen and People I Have Known*, p. 35.

meet only thoroughly acceptable fellows, from exactly the same social, political, or professional background as themselves. Almost all the complaints that came before the Reform Club committee during Soyer's time there had to do with disgruntled members having spied strangers in the dining room. And of course it went without saying that all these contentious strangers were chaps. In French restaurants, as in every other aspect of French social life, women were regarded as an essential part of the scene. But Thackeray, in his rundown of the possibly unacceptable, felt no need even to mention—it being so obvious—the most unacceptable feature of all as far as British club membership was concerned: being a woman.

The London gentlemen's clubs had their origins in the coffee houses and gaming establishments of the seventeenth and eighteenth centuries. Nevertheless, they were an essentially nineteenth-century phenomenon, their success firmly rooted in two quintessentially nineteenth-century institutions: the public schools and the railways. And the public school system, which of course was not public at all but extremely private, ensured that every well-connected English boy, from the age of seven, as well as all those not yet in the right class but with upward aspirations, associated the organization of a well-run society with complete sexual and social segregation. In this worldview, public-school life was a kind of ideal state to be perpetuated by all possible means, and institutionalized bachelorhood its natural continuation. Home-based bachelorhood had certain disadvantages—squalor, loneliness, solitary meals. But gentlemen's clubs removed them all. A club offered all the pleasures of public school— the company, the social certainties, the nursery food—but with added comforts: such comforts, indeed, as only the possession of a quite unusually large income could otherwise provide. In the approving words of the author of *The Knife and Fork,* whose views on female company we have already encountered, for "those epicures not yet tethered to conjugal skirts" a modest outlay of £20 a year would buy "a home . . . [at] one of those west-end palaces called clubs, from the contemplation of which the virgin minds of England shrink with instinctive horror." And for those who had fallen into the married state, membership of a club ensured that they need never notice the difference. A story was told of a "very masterful" club member who brought his wife to dine. When challenged he asked for a book of rules, and triumphantly pointed to that which gave permission to invite a friend, making no specific reservation as to sex. "He was no doubt right on the strict letter of the law, but yielded on the question of good taste."[7] Anthony Lejeune recalled being told by an old member of Brooks's that in his grandmother's or great-grandmother's papers was a diary with the entry: "We have now been married exactly a year, in which time my husband has dined with me but once. Every other night he dined at Mr Brooks's Club."[8]

Before the railways, it was mostly London gentlemen who used their clubs to escape the unpalatial drabness and female-infested trivia of home. But the railways made London easy of access from the country. The railway companies, having laid out vast sums, were interested only in profitable customers: They had to be compelled by Act of Parliament to introduce third- and fourth-class carriages and cheaper fares on so-called parliamentary trains. But first- and second-class passengers traveled in great comfort, and many of

[7]A. G. F. Griffiths, *Clubs and Clubmen,* London, 1907, p. 190.
[8]Anthony Lejeune, *The Gentlemen's Clubs of London,* London, 1979, p. 14.

them were gentlemen, hitherto marooned in the country, for whom a short stay in London, and the attendant delights of temporary bachelorhood, had suddenly become a practical proposition. Without railways, the clubs might have languished. And "without Clubs," as Surtees observes, "the railway system would have been incomplete. After such luxurious travelling a man requires something better than the old coaching house . . . The Clubs invite visits. A man feels that he has a real substantial home—a home containing every imaginable luxury, without the trouble of management or forethought."[9]

The first requisite of a club was therefore a suitably commodious clubhouse; and this, when Soyer first came to work there, the Reform Club still lacked. It had begun life at The Westminster Club at 34 George Street, later renamed The Westminster Reform Club. Then the more radical members, led by Edward Ellice, MP, decided to create their own club, which would be called simply the Reform Club. They purchased 104 Pall Mall, for £20,000, and adapted the house for club use. But when the club opened in 1836, although it had 998 members, the dining room seated only fifty. Obviously, a new clubhouse was needed; so the Committee decided to rebuild, moving meanwhile into leased premises. The commission was won by Charles Barry, architect of the new House of Commons. Demolition began in 1839, and in 1841 the new clubhouse was opened.

The vastness of the new Reform Club's proportions and the sumptuousness of its decoration drew general awe and acclaim. But for both the architectural profession and the general public, the kitchens were the real center of interest. Barry had designed

---

[9]Surtees, *Plain or Ringlets,* quoted in Lejeune, *The Gentlemen's Clubs of London.*

them in close consultation with Soyer—as his son observed, "The enthusiasm and knowledge of M. Soyer were allowed full scope"[10]— and his practical experience is everywhere evident: in the general layout, in the gadgets he loved to invent, and in the supremely practical (and terrifically expensive) individual arrangements of the various departments. These were kitchens such as had never before been seen: chef's heaven, with Soyer as presiding deity. Largely on their account the Reform Club, along with the House of Commons and Pentonville Prison, was for a considerable time accounted one of the three most technically advanced buildings in London. (In Pentonville, designed to accommodate the latest theories regarding solitary confinement, each cell had individual ventilation, a wash-basin, and a lavatory—essential if no convict was ever to meet any of his fellow prisoners.)

The kitchens, which were naturally located in the basement, encompassed an entire world of service. There were store cellars, ale cellars, bottle cellars, knife cellars, a still room, a scullery, a brushing room, a steward's dining room, a maid's room, a butler's pantry and plate-room, a servants' hall, a cleaning room, a clerk's office, a housekeeper's room, and a cook's room. There were stoves for stewing, steaming, and broiling, and, the ultimate modernity, gas stoves (gas having been piped to Pall Mall for lighting since 1807). Previously, gas had been used for roasting, but this was the first time this new fuel had ever been employed for stove-top cookery, where its cleanliness and adjustability were (as every cook will testify) a kitchen revolution. The new stoves, Soyer truly observed, "afford the greatest comfort ever introduced in any culinary arrangement; each

[10]Quoted in Morris, *Portrait of a Chef,* p. 11.

A section through the Reform Club kitchens—the poster commissioned by Soyer. He is in the middle, conducting a tour. Notice Madame Soyer's pictures along the back wall under the game rack.

Soyer instructs his minions in the use of the newfangled gas cooker.
He wears, as always, his suit and cap à la zoug-zoug; *other staff are*
confined to regulation white aprons and overalls.

stove is divided into five compartments each having a separate pipe
and brass cock, with a separate main pipe to each stove which supplies sufficient gas to burn the whole five compartments at once, or
if all burning at once the fire may be regulated to any height you
think proper by means of the brass cocks, turning the gas either full
or only partially on. It possesses also the following advantages: you
obtain the same heat as from charcoal the moment it is lit, it is a fire
that never requires making up, it is free of carbonic acid which is so
pernicious, especially in small kitchens, and creates neither dust or
smell . . . With the aid of my new octagonal trivet I can place nine
stewpots over without the fear of upsetting either, some only simmering and others boiling at the same time, which is invaluable . . .

The gas stoves also tend to greater economy as they are not lit till the moment wanted, then only as the quantity required and may be put out the moment it is done with."[11]

There were other marvels. The roasting range was so designed that kitchen inmates were almost wholly shielded from its heat, which was channeled into hot cupboards for keeping joints warm. Steam power, generated by a massive boiler, turned the roasting jacks and worked the dumbwaiters (and also the lifts taking coals to the members' bedrooms), heated the bain maries, steam tables, and a steam closet, with three cast-iron hollow steam-heated shelves for warming delicate dishes. There was a special rack for hanging game. There was a four-feet-by-three-feet marble fish-slab, with a slate surround placed at an angle, at the higher end of which a horizontal shower pipe supplied iced water from a cistern, thus keeping the fish clean and cool. The cooks worked at

a table constructed on an entirely new plan having twelve irregular sides, which afford great facility for working without anyone being in the way of another, with sliding boards immediately under the edge, for the purpose of passing sauces, purees etc (which being lower than the table is much more convenient and preserves it perfectly clean) and drawers underneath. At each end of the table are tinned moveable copper cases with water and sponge to facilitate the cutting up of Meat, Poultry, Fish etc., on the same spot. On the column at each end of the table are tinned copper cases, clasped round and turning on casters, on a fixed frame, with

[11]Soyer, *The Gastronomic Regenerator.*

ten divisions in each, one is used for fish sauces, the other for chopped herbs, spices etc.[12]

There was constant hot water, even when the fire was out, and an ice room in the area beneath the Pall Mall pavement. All this, down to the very saucepans, was meticulously drawn by Barry.

In the normal way of things, this world would have been invisible except to those who toiled within. The Reform Club, like all such institutions, was divided into the two worlds of upstairs and downstairs, intimately interdependent but spatially and psychologically entirely separate. Above ground, in massively pillared halls, libraries, and dining rooms, their elaborate ceilings lost in the upper atmosphere, gentlemen snoozed, read the papers, discussed weighty matters, and prodigiously ate. Below, their needs were catered to with clockwork efficiency. Although the denizens of downstairs inevitably penetrated upstairs in the course of their work—dusting, waiting, bedmaking, fire-tending—there was generally no traffic in the reverse direction, communication between worlds being mediated by the butler, the housekeeper, and the dumbwaiter. But this was not true of the new Reform Club, where under Soyer's direction the kitchen department became one of the sights of London.

His first move was to orchestrate a campaign of press publicity that would both draw people's attention to his empire's hidden wonders and make it quite clear who was responsible for them. Of course, the kitchens, like all the other apartments of the Reform Club, were ultimately Barry's work; and it was the members who

[12]Part of the caption to Soyer's print of the kitchen, 1842.

had so handsomely (too handsomely, some felt)[13] paid for them. Soyer was "happy to have the opportunity of acknowledging" these obligations in *The Gastronomic Regenerator.* But everyone's impression—an impression he was at pains to encourage—was that he, Soyer, was the only true begetter of this new world of marvels. The *Illustrated London News* announced in 1842 that "M. Soyer, the *chef de cuisine,* and husband of the lady whose paintings we recently had occasion to notice, has the chief credit of the improvements which have effected these surprising results, and has been gratified by their transfer in several instances to the corresponding departments of the royal palaces." It claimed that "dinner for six hundred persons can be cooked . . . in something like the time required to roast an ordinary joint of meat." And in the midst of it all stood Soyer. He was where he had always wanted to be—onstage; and he would play his part to the hilt.

He began by dressing the role as it should be dressed. Not for Alexis the plain white linen imposed upon lesser chefs. Thackeray describes M. Mirobolant's "light green frock or paletot, his crimson velvet waistcoat, with blue glass buttons, his pantalon Ecossais, of a very large and decided check pattern, his orange satin neckcloth, and his jean-boots with tips of shiny leather . . . a gold-embroidered cap and a richly-gilt cane . . ." As always this is exaggerated—but only slightly. The figure that appears in Emma's painting is recognizably this same flamboyant fellow, the cap set, as always, at his favorite skew—*à la zoug-zoug,* as he liked to put it. And not just his cap, but everything he wore reflected this passion for the bias—

[13]By its completion the Reform Club building had cost £84,042 plus Barry's bill of £3,393, which was contested. Kitchen accoutrements accounted for £674 of that figure.

even his business card, a diamond-shaped piece of pasteboard that said, simply and slightly surprisingly:

ALEXIS SOYER
LONDON—PARIS

and which he handed to guests as he ushered them into his private room.

There he stands, center stage, cap at the usual angle, in the print of a section through the kitchens commissioned by him in 1842, welcoming a club member and his lady beside the twelve-sided worktable, while various subordinates (plainly clad in white uniforms, alongside which the *chef's* brilliant plumage shines to even greater advantage) scurry around performing menial tasks. On the left game hangs from its special rack, while a selection of Emma's pictures adorn the back wall. Fourteen hundred copies of this print were sold, a guinea colored, half a guinea plain; the list of subscribers included Barry, the Marquis of Ailsa, the Baron de Talleyrand, and Giuseppe Verdi.

A tour of the Reform Club kitchens became all the rage in London. "Into that kitchen," observed the *Illustrated London News,* "some from curiosity, some to explore the mysteries of science, and some to catch fragrant odours upon appetite—have gone peers, princes and nobles beyond compute. There is hardly a person of distinction who has not sought to visit that mansion of good things of the life terrestrial, and departed from it with a due impression of the sublimity of the art that is practised within its walls." And of course this most especial of cook's tours did not proceed unguided. On the contrary, left to themselves there was always the danger that visitors might miss some interesting corner, some especially titillating innovation. Some of the parties were so large that it was necessary to split them into several groups. "It is an actual fact," wrote Volant, who being the secretary in question was in a position to know, "that the gentleman upon whom devolved the duties of secretary to Soyer, had to neglect his business very often to pay attention to Lord This, or Count That, who had called, sent in their cards, and begged permission to see the improvements of the renowned model kitchen."[14]

We may be sure, however, that this task only devolved upon the secretary when the master was otherwise occupied. If there was a lord or lady to be shown around, only *force majeure* would prevent Soyer himself from doing the honors.

> When Soyer himself showed the place [Volant wrote] it was curious to watch him, with his red velvet cap and spoon in hand, explaining to elegantly dressed ladies . . . his various methods of concocting soups of exquisite flavour, or his different styles of producing his dishes of fish, game, poultry, etc., at the same time giving full proof of his power over the art, by handing round either some *properly made* Mulligatawny, or a basin of filleted sole à la maitre d'hotel, sending home his tasters positively rabid for their dinner and wishing Soyer could be divided into as many pieces as the calf's head for his mock-turtle . . . Sometimes he would suddenly plunge his finger, diamond ring and all, into what appeared to be a boiling cauldron of glue, pass it across his tongue, wink his eye, and add either

[14]Volant and Warren, *Memoirs of Alexis Soyer,* p. 69.

a little more salt, pepper, or some mysterious dust, known possibly only to great *artistes,* to make it palatable . . .[15]

As time went on, Soyer spent more of his time delightfully onstage, and correspondingly less at the actual stove. He still added the finishing touch to some particularly important orders, but orchestration, rather than chopping, cleaning, simmering, roasting, and baking, was now his chief role. He reserved his energies for general supervision, for his distinguished tourists, and for the occasional supreme performance. He invented the dishes and instructed his team, and like a well-trained chorus or *corps de ballet* they performed the various maneuvers while he, the tenor lead, the *primo ballerino assoluto,* "the *artiste* who directs by his gestures the subalterns tricked out in white, and whose eye takes in at a glance the most difficult combinations in the culinary art,"[16] led his audience into realms previously unvisited, regaling them with tidbits as he dipped a spoon here, broke off a tasty morsel there. Nothing fazed him, nothing put his nose out of joint. From four until five was supposed to be his rest hour, which he would spend in his room experimenting with new combinations—the kind of experimentation that had, on one particularly fortunate day, resulted in Sauce à la Reform; but someone was sure to drop by, in which case Soyer would regale them with a taste of the most recent creation. All this was accompanied by constant calls for members' dinners, and frequent consultations with the clerk of the kitchen, who received the orders and kept the accounts. Meanwhile, the stream of jokes and

[15]Volant and Warren, *Memoirs of Alexis Soyer,* pp. 69–70.
[16]The Vicomtesse de Malleville, quoted in Soyer, *The Gastronomic Regenerator.*

puns rolled on relentlessly. One day it was Lord Melbourne's turn to take the tour. "How is it you have such a number of pretty female assistants?" he inquired. "My Lord," returned Soyer, quick as a flash, "we do not want plain cooks here."[17]

The high point of this phase was the summer of 1846, when he created two banquets that can rarely have been equaled in the history of human eating. The first, on May 9, was a private dinner commissioned by a rich gourmet, a Mr. Sampayo. Together the two contrived a feast Soyer described as "the most *recherché* dinner I ever dressed."[18]

REFORM CLUB

9 Mai, 1846   Dîner pour 10 Personnes

Potage à la Comte de Paris

Do. à la purée d'Asperges

DEUX POISSONS

Saumon de Severne à la Mazarin   Rougets gratinés à la Montesquieu

DEUX RELEVÉS

Le Chapon farci de Foie gras à la Nelson

Saddleback d'Agneau de Maison à la Sévigné

---

[17]Volant and Warren, *Memoirs of Alexis Soyer,* p. 68.
[18]Volant and Warren, *Memoirs of Alexis Soyer,* p. 92.

QUATRE HORS D'OEUVRES À LA FRANCAISE

Les Olives farcies   Salade d'Anchois historiée

Thon mariné à l'Italienne   Sardines à l'Huile de Noisette

QUATRE ENTRÉES

Sauté de Filets de Volaille à l'Ambassadrice

Petites Croustades de Beurre aux Laitances de Maquereaux

Côtelettes de Mouton Galloise à la Réforme

Turban de Ris de Veau purée de Concombres

(Rissolettes à la Pompadour)

DEUX RÔTS

Les Dotrelles aux Feuilles de Vigne

Le Buisson d'Ecrevisse Pagodatique, au Vin de Champagne à la Sampayo

(Les grosses Asperges vertes, sauce à la Crème)

La Gelée de Dantzic aux Fruits Printaniers

Les Croquantes de'Amandes Pralinées aux Abricots

Les Petits Pois nouveaux à l'Anglo-Français

Les grosses Truffes à l'Essence de Madère

Le Miroton de Homard aux Oeufs de Pluviers

La Crème mousseuse au Curaçao

DEUX RELEVÉS

La Hure de Sanglier demi-glaçée, garnie de Champignons en surprise

Les Diablotins au Fromage de Windsor

The climax of this Lucullan feast was supposed to be a dish of two dozen ortolans, to be eaten with truffles. But as truffled ortolans— i.e., ortolans stuffed with truffles—are an impossibility, the birds being too tiny to stuff, Soyer proposed instead to stuff the truffles with the birds. "Having already procured twelve of the largest and finest truffles I could obtain, it was my intention to have dug a hole in each, into which I should have placed one of the birds, and covered each with a piece of lamb's or calf's caul; then to have braised them half an hour in good stock made from fowl and veal, with half a pint of *Lachryma Christi* added; then to have drained them upon a cloth, placed a border of poached force-meat upon the dish, built the truffles in pyramid, made a purée with the truffle dug from the interior, using the stock reduced to a demi-glace, and poured over; roasted the twelve remaining ortolans before a sharp fire, with which I should have garnished the whole round, and served very hot." Unfortunately, however, bad weather prevented the ortolans arriving from Provence. In their absence, the most extravagant dish in the menu was the *buisson* of crayfish, whose recipe Soyer would never reveal except to say that it involved stewing them in champagne together with two large bottles of Perigord truffles—not, perhaps, the best way to bring out the delicate flavor of crayfish, but undoubtedly as extravagant a combination as could well be devised. This was served in one of Soyer's special culinary inventions, a dish called *pagodatique* for its Chinese inspiration. He was very taken with the Chinese habit of eating in which each person makes his own combinations of meat, vegetables, and sauces from a selection of dishes simultaneously presented. The "pagodatique" dish facilitated this, being equipped not only with recesses that could be filled with hot sand, thus ensuring that no delicacy congealed, but with numerous detachable subdishes, so that "one entrée might have four different sauces, four might have sixteen, or eight"—all of which might now be served simultaneously and selected by the diner as he chose.[19] The *pagodatique* dish thus allowed the cook to demonstrate even more culinary complexity and inventiveness.

Such private feasts would (until Soyer published the good news in *The Gastronomic Regenerator,* where they were discussed at length and their menus given) be known only to club members and their friends. But great public dinners were of course reported in all the newspapers. One such was given by club members that July for Ibrahim Pasha of Egypt, the dashing Arab leader who in 1846 was invited to England to meet Queen Victoria:

DINNER FOR HIS HIGHNESS
IBRAHIM PASHA

SEIZE POTAGES.

Quatre à la Victoria.

Quatre à la Comte de Paris.

Quatre à la Louis Philippe.

Quatre à la Colbert, aux
Légumes Printaniers.

———— ∽ ————

SEIZE POISSONS.

Quatre de turbots, Sauce
à la Mazarin.

Quatre de Buissons de
Filets de Merlans à l'Egyptienne.

Quatre de Saumons de
Severn à la Crème.

Quatre du Truites
Saumonées en Matelote Mariniére.

[19]Soyer, *The Gastronomic Regenerator.*

SEIZE RELEVÉS.

Quatre de Chapons à la Nelson.

Quatre de Saddleback de
Southdown Mouton, rôti à
la Soyer.

Quatre de Poulardes en Diadême.

Quatre de Saddleback d'Agneau,
rôti à la Sévigné.

Baron of Beef à l'Anglaise.

Entrée Pagodatique de riz à la Luxor

CINQUANTE-QUATRE ENTRÉES.

Six de Poussins Printaniers
à l'Ambassadrice.

Six de Côtelettes de
Mouton à la Reform.

Quatre de Ris de Veau
Piqués en Macedonie de
Légumes.

Quatre de Petits Vol-au-
vents aux Laitances de
Maquereaux.

Quatre de Timballes de Riz
aux Queues d'Agneau.

Quatre de Jambonneaux
Braisés au Vin de Madère.

Quatre de Volailles Farcies
à la Russe aux Légumes
Verts.

Quatre de Pâtés Chauds de
Cailles à la Banquiére.

Quatre de Rissolettes à la
Pompadour.

Quatre de Grenadins de
Boeuf à la Beyrout.

Six de Côtelettes d'Agneau
à la Vicomtesse, et

Quatre de Turbans
Epigramme de Levreau au
Fumet.

SEIZE RÔTS.

Quatre de Turkey Poult
Piqués et Bardés.
Quatre de Levreaux au jus
de Groseilles.

Quatre de Gros Chapons
au Cresson, et
Quatre de Canetons au Jus
de Bigarades.

CINQUANTE-QUATRE ENTREMETS.

Six de Gelées Macédoine
de Fruits au Dantzic.
Quatre Turbans de
Meringues Demi-Glacées.
Quatre de Croquantes
d'Amandes aux Cerises.
Quatre de Galantines à laVolière.
Quatre de Mirotons de
Homard à l'Indienne.

Quatre de Salades de
Volaille à la Soyer.
Quatre de Haricots Verts
au Beurre Noisette.
Six de Tartelettes Pralinées
aux Abricots.
Quatre de Pain de Pêches au Noyeau.
Quatre de Petits Pois à
l'Anglo-Français. Et
Quatre de Gelées
Cristallisées à l'Ananas.

RELEVÉS DE RÔTS.

Crème d'Egypte à
l'Ibrahim Pacha.
Gâteau Britannique à
l'Amiral.
Quatre de Jambons Glacés
en Surprise.

Quatre de Côtelettes en
Surprise à la Reform.
Quatre de Manivaux de
Champignons au Curaçao
en Surprise.
Deux de Meringues
Chinoises—Pagoda aux Fraises.

What an odyssey of the human stomach! It is hard to believe that, at the end of this, any of the diners were in a condition to stand up, or indeed that any of them ate again for several weeks following. There were 154 at table, but many other club members turned up to watch the proceedings (and perhaps bet on who might survive until the end). The guest of honor's arrival was marked by the band of the Scots Fusiliers Foot Guards, who played the Sultan's March, followed by light Turkish airs during the course of the dinner. Given that Ibrahim Pasha was Egyptian, this seems an odd choice of music, but it undeniably approached the correct cultural segment—brown, mussulman, fond of belly dancing. . . .

Soyer, in his now habitual presenter's role, had planned to spend the evening in the dining room rather than the kitchen, waiting personally upon the great man, and drinking in the compliments as his creations were unveiled and sampled. But to his chagrin, his supporting cast, doubtless feeling that their hard work had too often gone unappreciated while the *chef* took all the credit, chose this key moment to down tools. Late enough in the day for there to be no choice in the matter, it became clear that if the *chef* did not personally take charge of the cooking, there would be no dinner to serve. Faced with the possibility of unprecedented humiliation rather than the expected triumph, he abandoned his grand plans, doffed his dress suit, and descended to the basement.

All was not lost, however. During the dessert, Ibrahim Pasha was so impressed by the Crème d'Egypte á l'Ibrahim Pasha that he asked to meet the gratified chef, whom he fulsomely complimented through his interpreter. This *crème* was indeed an extraordinary creation: a pyramid about two and half feet tall made of light meringue cake to imitate stones, its three angles represented by sheets of waved sugar through which could be glimpsed a pineapple cream, the whole surrounded by grapes and other fruits, and topped by a portrait of Ibrahim's father, Mehmet Ali Pasha, in a gold frame. Ibrahim Pasha, overcome, took his father's portrait down and showed it to his suite, only to find beneath it—a portrait of himself. He was naturally intrigued and asked Soyer how he had transferred these likenesses to the dessert. Soyer explained that the heads had been traced from a drawing by Horace Vernet onto rice paper, which was placed on the damp jelly representing the glass. The paper was then dissolved so that only the transferred drawings remained. The gilt frame was made of jellied eau-de-vie of Dantzic and *goldwasser,* with added gold leaf. This chef d'œuvre of culinary artifice, although doubtless delicious, was evidently too intimidating to attack. It remained untouched on the table until the end of the feast.

The Ibrahim Pasha banquet was reported at length in all the newspapers, reports in which the banquet's creator figured with gratifying prominence. In the London chefs' chorus he was now unquestionably the leading tenor. Ude or Francatelli might cook as well or better, but they lacked Soyer's star quality. However, he now faced every star's dilemma. Where could he go from here? He was still only thirty-six—hardly the age for an energetic man to rest on his laurels. On the other hand, it was clear he had done as much as he could using the Reform Club as his sole platform. If he wanted to increase his audience, he would have to find a new stage.

His first book, *Délassements Culinaires,* which contained among other plums *La Fille de l'orage,* had been neither a literary nor a commercial success. But it had fulfilled one very important function, proving to its author that problems with writing need not prevent a person from producing a book. Now he proposed another. It would be quite different, and its sales, at least up to a point, assured. All the lords, ladies, and notabilities who wandered so freely around his kitchens wanted to know his recipes. Now he would tell them.

For his cookery book as for all other culinary tasks, Soyer called upon his faithful (if sometimes rebellious) supporting cast. His chief helper was "a very clever first kitchen-maid who had been some years under his tuition, and knew well the composition of all his soups, sauces, entrées, etc."[20]—in short, someone upon whom he might and did unquestioningly rely, in the comfortable certainty that she would never, however much she knew, present a threat, for the good and sufficient reason that she was a woman. Even though she might by now have learned to cook as well as Soyer (and could write into the bargain), she would never, as he had done, rise through the ranks to become a chef in her own right. She might become the pillar of some private kitchen, but that, with its aura of domestic servanthood, was very different from being a *chef,* in terms of both situation (subordinate rather than controlling) and salary (women generally commanded less than half the salary of men doing comparably responsible jobs). When M. Mirobolant, an undisputed *chef,* arrives at Clavering Park, his train of *aides* includes "a professed female cook . . . who had inferior females under her orders"—and who is clearly under *his* orders.

Soyer now requested of this competent female that, each time she made a dish, she should write down exactly what she used and how she proceeded; his chief apprentice was to do the same. The result was *The Gastronomic Regenerator,* published in 1846. He had, he claimed, been meditating this project for years, but previous attempts

[20]Volant and Warren, *Memoirs of Alexis Soyer,* p. 48.

had led to nothing. "Only within the last ten months that I in reality commenced afresh this work, in which lapse of time I had to finish twenty-five thousand dinners for the gentlemen of the Reform Club, and thirty-eight dinner parties of importance, comprising above seventy thousand dishes, and to provide daily for sixty servants of the establishment, independent of about fifteen thousand visitors which have seen the kitchen department in that lapse of time."

The *Regenerator* contained two thousand recipes, arranged, Soyer claimed, in an entirely new fashion. Most cookery books, he tells us, had hitherto been presented as a series of complete meals, while his presented dishes generically: soups, fish, roasts, salads, entremets, etc.

In fact, this claim of newness was not wholly justified. Beauvilliers's cookery book, which Soyer certainly knew (he gives many of the same recipes), was published in 1814, and arranged more clearly than Soyer's, his recipes grouped not (other than soups or desserts) by their place in their meal but by their main ingredient—as, beef, pork, fish, game, etc. That, admittedly, was in French. But Eliza Acton's *Modern Cookery for Private Families,* which uses Beauvilliers's method of classification, came out in 1845, the year before Soyer's work. Fortunately for our hero, however, these details did not detract from the new book's popularity.

The Gastronomic Regenerator was more than a mere recipe book. It carried large quantities of supplementary material—copies of articles on the Reform Club kitchens, puffs, dedications to a variety of Dukes, Duchesses, and Princes, and a biography of the late Madame Soyer almost identical to that later published in Volant's *Memoirs,* which was not surprising, since Volant was Soyer's secretary at this time and thus responsible for the transcription of the nonrecipe portion of the book. There were also advertisements for other Soyer products; for *The Gastronomic Regenerator* was not his only foray into commerce this year. If the English wanted a single sauce, who better to supply it to them than the renowned chef of the Reform Club?

Soyer's Diamond Sauce
FOR COLD OR HOT MEAT, POULTRY, GAME ETC ETC
BY A SOYER

Will shortly be ready for sale in Quart or pint bottles and may be obtained at all the principal Italian ware- houses in the United Kingdom.

The *Regenerator* found an immediate sale among Club members (many of whom were able to enjoy the added gratification of finding themselves mentioned in the book's copious acknowledgments); and of course Soyer could have hoped for no better advertisement than the Ibrahim Pasha dinner. "The bill of fare at the Reform Club was worthy of *the great Soyer,*" wrote Lord Panmure after this event. "Pray call at Ridgway's, and desire him to send me two copies of *'his'* book by Saturday next's Dundee steamer."[21] At the end of a year, two thousand copies had been sold at the considerable price of a guinea each; it reprinted twice in 1846 and again in 1847. By 1850 it was into its ninth edition, and carried on reprinting for years thereafter.

Not all the profits of *The Gastronomic Regenerator* went to Soyer—he had split the cost of publishing it with a friend, who nat-

[21]Volant and Warren, *Memoirs of Alexis Soyer,* p. 90.

urally took half the receipts. Nevertheless, the money poured in. Sala, who for a while knew him as well as anybody, reckoned that what with his salary and apprentices' fees, he was earning the impressive sum of £1,000 a year.[22] And *The Gastronomic Regenerator* was soon followed by *The Poor Man's Regenerator* and *The Modern Housewife, or Ménagère,* all of which sold in their hundreds of thousands; and then there were his gadgets and his patent sauces . . .

He announced his intention to spend some of this cash in fitting up his kitchen at home as the ideal bachelor's kitchen, with a view to opening it to those members of the public who might wish to see it. The visitors did not materialize—perhaps fortunately, since it seems clear that Soyer would have had trouble accommodating them; the kitchen, however, did, and like all his other kitchens was as admirable for what it was as what it produced.

It is in one of Congreve's comedies, I think, [wrote Sala] that one of the characters taunts a lady with having taken her "out of a shop no bigger than a birdcage"; and, as a matter of fact, Soyer's apartments were not of much more commanding dimensions than would belong to a series of moderate-sized aviaries; but the eminently assimilative and inventive nature of the man had enabled him to set up in two or three little exiguous dens on the top floor, a miniature kitchen and larder and scullery, as complete in their way as the wonderful kitchen and annexes which he had

[22]To compare: In 1839, the butler of the Reform Club earned £75 p.a.; in 1836, the House Steward's annual salary was £200. In 1907, Major Arthur Griffiths reports, in *Clubs and Clubmen,* that a chef "is not a cheap artist," commanding between £200 and £300 a year.

arranged for the Reform Club. He had his roasting-range, his oven, his screen and plate-warmer; his *bain-marie* pan heated by water from the adjacent boiler, his "hot-plate," his seasoning-box and fish sauce-box; his refrigerator, and his knife-cleaning machine; his dressers and tables, and plate rack. The larder was as completely furnished as the kitchen; and on the floor beneath was his dining-room. I remember that, after we had consumed an admirable supper, which he had cooked with his own hands, with the assistance of a very small but obedient and handy Irish servant-girl, with shoes hopelessly down at heel, he brought forth that which seemed to me to be a kind of conjuring apparatus. It was his "magic stove." A chop or a steak was placed on a metal tripod, of which the top was solid or barred, just as it was intended that the meat should be fried or broiled. At a little distance from this tripod, but quite independent of it, was a spirit lamp, and by means of some ingenious blowpipe arrangement, a prolonged tongue of flame, so to speak, was projected horizontally from the lamp into the tripod and under the frying-pan or the gridiron, as the case might be, where the flame assumed a circular shape, and cooked the meat to a nicety.[23]

Otherwise, he put his money safely into a bank deposit at 3 percent, where it sat quietly until another friend, a well-known conjurer called Philippe, got wind of it. The year 1846 saw a great bubble in railway shares, and Philippe, who had already made

[23]Sala, *Things I Have Seen and People I Have Known,* pp. 245–7.

large paper profits, persuaded Soyer to let him gamble in these shares on both their behalves. When in 1847 the bubble burst, the conjurer performed a vanishing act, leaving Soyer to settle the bills. However, although he found himself expensively out of pocket, the good-natured Alexis never let mere questions of money come between himself and his friends. Cash slipped through his fingers with the same inconsequential ease as it fell into his lap. If he lost it, why, he would earn some more. "London is full of people, advertise well, and Christmas will put us on our legs again," he wrote good-humoredly to the chastened Philippe.[24]

By now Soyer was as much one of the sights of London as the Reform Club kitchen. Just as in Paris, he had become the life and soul of the party—but this time, it was a much bigger party. "It was strange to see the great chef, after he had given the final turn of the sauce-pan to serve the last dish for Lord So-and-so," wrote Volant,

> throw off his red velvet cap, jacket and white apron and, while passing through a kind of spray of small jokes with various visitors, how soon he would dress himself up for the Opera or any other place of amusement. He was so delighted to leave the Club after his laborious duties, that he often forgot to take the refreshment prepared for him, and, when out, would enter any place where a piece of bread and a slice of *fromage de Brie* could be had to delight his palate, and he never enjoyed anything better.[25]

[24]Volant and Warren, *Memoirs of Alexis Soyer,* p. 59.
[25]Volant and Warren, *Memoirs of Alexis Soyer,* p. 167.

In Paris he had danced the night tipsily away with his little *soubrette;* now he frequented the opera, decked out in bespoke evening dress, with the day's leading ballerina on his arm. Then he had hung hopefully around the stage door of the Théâtre des Variétés; now, he had the entrée to all the theaters in London, and never need pay for a ticket. And when the show ended, he knew all the late-night dining clubs, and numbered among his friends the leading wits of the day. If you came upon a particularly animated group, as likely as not Soyer would be at its center, telling jokes.

This increasing personal success—or notoriety—was less and less easy to reconcile with his job at the Reform Club. As he had truly written to his conjurer friend Philippe, "My situation is all I possess." But what exactly was that situation? Was he a menial, to be ordered about, or an artist, to be respected as a talented quasi-equal? It seems clear that from the first, his status at the Reform had always, at least in his own eyes, been something more than that of simply "the cook"—a view reinforced by the solid core of Reform Club members who were his friends and champions, led by Lord Marcus Hill, for years the Club's chairman. There seems to have been a genuine intimacy between these two. Soyer records long conversations between himself and Lord M. H., in French, in *The Gastronomic Regenerator;* and it will be remembered that Soyer and Lord Marcus were both married in the same church (St. George's, Hanover Square) on the same day, April 12, 1837. This may of course have been a coincidence—but it seems unlikely. Like many Club members Soyer was a Freemason, most probably introduced to the Order during his days with Ailsa, who was the Grand-master of Scotland; and he also consorted with them in his persona as man-about-town. He could get theater tickets that were otherwise unobtainable, and when he did so would often join the party as a friend—"I got three tickets, for you, Madame and me," he informed one member for whom he had performed this service. Such a person might be a cook, but was surely in no sense "mere."

A number of members, however, found this presumption of equality highly inappropriate. Some, like Thackeray, simply laughed it off. When his M. Mirobolant challenges Pendennis to a duel, it is this question of status that forms the *casus belli*. "What has he said to you?" inquires a friend, to which Mirobolant hisses, "Il m'a appelé—*cuisinier!*" Others found it actively impertinent. Whatever view you took, it was an anomaly; and it led to occasional unpleasantnesses. Soyer's career at the Reform Club was punctuated with sessions at which he was required to account for himself in one way or another by the Committee. Mostly these supposed misdeeds turned out to have been misunderstandings, or were the result of other people trying to deflect blame—"his penetration was so accurate," Volant recalled, that "he could detect, at the very first question put to him, who was the delinquent."[26] Sometimes, though, they resulted from behavior that hovered on the borders of what was and what was not acceptable—acceptability, as always, depending on the viewpoint of the complainant: What is acceptable in a friend is not what you require from the cook.

On these occasions Soyer relied on his charm to carry him through. But although this strategy generally succeeded, the flamboyance and gaiety which many found so attractive, and which generally defused potentially awkward meetings so that they ended in

[26]Volant and Warren, *Memoirs of Alexis Soyer,* p. 165.

laughter and jokes, could also be seen as wholly inappropriate behavior in a Club servant. Thus, in August 1843 he was found guilty of insolence toward Captain W. G. Beare and "severely censured" by the Committee; he apologized, but the following March the Committee was again "consider[ing] the conduct of M. Soyer towards a certain member of the club." Then there were the *petits soupers recherchés* he liked to give in his room, after hours, to the many well-known personages whose company he kept. These were always paid for personally, the only Club property involved being the knives and forks. But they were viewed with suspicion, as was his ever-increasing group of "improvers," as the apprentices were called. For under Soyer, the Reform Club kitchens had become, in effect, a high-class cookery school, so well-known as a sure route to a good job that, far from demanding wages, people paid £10 a head to be admitted as an assistant. One of the few extant letters in Soyer's own hand was written in 1844 to his old employer Mrs. Lloyd, who had asked him to find her a new cook. Just the young man for her came in only the other evening, he replies: He will send him round to her residence directly.

Although his loyalty to the Club remained unbounded, even Soyer's energies were finite. He had simply amassed too many competing commitments and personae; and as the 1840s went on, it became clear that his days at the Reform Club were numbered. When, in 1850, the moment of his resignation finally arrived, varying stories circulated as to what the precipitating event had actually been. Sala says it was a decision to open the club coffee room (actually the main dining room) to strangers twice a week at lunchtime, thus making it in effect a restaurant. Soyer, says Sala, felt this an affront to his status, and resigned forthwith. The version given by Volant is that strangers were already admitted twice a week, and would now be able to come in daily. Not, says Volant, "that [Soyer] cared what they made of it," but he would need far more assistants in the kitchen, and was afraid that standards of cookery and service would lapse. However, the Annual General Meeting held on May 1, 1850, conveys a somewhat different view of events. It expressed its "dissatisfaction with the management of the coffee room and the attention of the cook to the comfort of the members"—a pointed reference to Soyer's lowly status, at least so far as the Reform Club was concerned. And three weeks after that the Committee instructed the house subcommittee to seek a new cook.

According to the Club's historian, Soyer resented the AGM's criticisms, and was worried not that he might have to take on new staff but that, on the contrary, the number of "improvers," or pupils, working in the kitchens was going to be limited.[27] This certainly rings true. Everyone knew that his present multifarious way of life relied upon a large and efficient supporting cast; there was also the question of the apprentices' fees, which went directly into his own pocket. Of course, he could always argue that these apprentices did not have to be paid. But they did have to be fed; and staff numbers, and the cost of feeding them all, was a never-ending bone of contention. Volant relates how Soyer "would calculate, with the clerk, the expenses, and often would delight at the prospect of announcing to the Committee, that the sixty or seventy servants of the establishment had been kept at the rate of 4s 6d. or 5s. per head per

[27]George Woodbridge, *The Reform Club 1836–1976*, London, 1978.

Punch depicts Soyer's departure from the Reform Club.

week!"[28] This was of course admirable, but surely betrayed a certain guilty conscience. After he left, cooks were allowed only very few such pupils, or none.

In May 1850, Soyer wrote his letter of resignation. It dwelled on his thirteen happy years in the Club's service, and pointed out that, although he was not yet forty, his hair was already turning white—such had been his assiduity in the Club's service.

There had been other such letters in the past; all had been rejected. This time, however, everyone knew the time had finally come to part. The committee regretfully accepted that their cook would leave as soon as a new one could be found. Sala records that

[28]Volant and Warren, *Memoirs of Alexis Soyer,* p, 167.

"there was not the slightest ill-feeling between [Soyer] and the committee when he left";[29] indeed, many members of the club remained his good friends, including Thackeray, Lord Marcus Hill, and Mr. Fox Maule, afterward Lord Panmure: a friendship, as it turned out, that would soon play an important part in his life.

Grapes

[29]Sala, *Things I Have Seen and People I Have Known,* p. 242.

5

Entrée Chaude: Famine Soup

The Ibrahim Pasha banquet marked the apogee of Soyer's career as a fashionable cook. By the time it took place, in 1846, he had been with the Reform Club nine years. Emma was dead, and Cerrito had left him for Saint-Léon. And he was still only thirty-six. Was the rest of his life simply to be more of the same? And if not, what? Although he would spend another four years at the Reform Club, it is clear that he felt restive. The world was a wider and more diverse place than Pall Mall liked to imagine, and he was beginning to feel constrained by its plushly padded horizons and insurmountable snobberies.

This change of gear is apparent in his list of publications.

Délassements culinaires, the volume commemorating his affair with Cerrito, had been published in 1845, and *The Gastronomic Regenerator* in 1846. And in 1847 these were joined by a booklet entitled *Soyer's Charitable Cookery: or, The Poor Man's Regenerator*, a book of cheap recipes for the "poor and labouring classes," from which the author donated a penny to charity for every copy sold.

This was hardly the new book one might have expected from London's most fashionable chef. As Soyer himself wrote, "Whilst semi-buried in my fashionable culinary sanctorum at the Reform Club, surrounded by the élite of society, who daily honoured me with their visits in that lounge of good cheer, I could not gain, through the stone walls of that massive edifice, the slightest knowledge of Cottage life." Indeed, why should he wish to do so? Few of Clubland's inhabitants, cocooned in the comfort that was its raison d'être, felt the slightest inclination in that direction. But Soyer, perhaps because of his own experience of poverty, could not so easily efface his awareness of the scummy tide washing around Pall Mall's islands of privilege. From 1847 until his death eleven years later, he took an increasingly active interest in the culinary welfare of those at the other end of society. *The Poor Man's Regenerator* drew upon these experiences, in Spitalfields with the London poor and in Dublin during the Irish potato famine.

Soyer put as much effort into his charitable recipes as into his grand extravaganzas, and did not hesitate to follow his usual Reform Club practice of treating his grand friends with samples in hopes of a puff. The recipe I picked was endorsed by no less a personage than the Duchess of Sutherland, who having tasted a sample sent to her residence by Soyer reported that "they could scarcely believe it was made from the materials used, it being so good." But even with this recommendation ringing in their ears, my pool of tasters did not greet this course with much enthusiasm. Indeed, they all groaned whenever I mentioned it. In the end, it was sampled only by my family, who had no means of escape.

Receipt for Soup No. 1

I first put one ounce of dripping into a sauce-pan (capable of holding two gallons of water), with a quarter of a pound of leg of beef without bones, cut into square pieces of about half an inch, and two middle-sized onions, peeled and sliced. I then set the saucepan over a coal fire, and stirred the contents round for a few minutes with a wooden (or iron) spoon until fried lightly brown. I had then ready washed the peeling of two turnips, fifteen green leaves or tops of celery, and the green part of two leeks (the whole of which, I must observe, are always thrown away). Having cut the above vegetables into small pieces, I threw them into the saucepan with the other ingredients, stirring them occasionally over the fire for another ten minutes; then added half a pound of common flour (any farinaceous substance would do), and half a pound of pearl barley, mixing all well together. I then added two gallons of water, seasoned with three ounces of salt, and a quarter of an ounce of brown sugar, stirred occasionally until boiling, and allowed it to simmer very gently for three hours, at the end of which time I found the barley perfectly tender. This soup will keep for several days when made as above described.

This soup, Soyer calculated, cost 3d. per gallon, including fuel—that is, just three farthings per quart serving; and since this calculation was based on London prices, and everything, as he observed, is cheaper in the country than in London, it would have cost even less elsewhere.

Seeing that only three of us were on hand for this course, and nobody seemed likely to ask for a second helping, not very much was required. However, so exiguous are the specified quantities of meat and vegetables that I saw no way of making less than a gallon of the soup. Halving Soyer's quantities meant that I used only two ounces of meat, the peelings of one turnip—I picked a big one—the whole of one onion, the top of one leek, and the top part of one celery (I couldn't bring myself to count the leaves). Then there was a little fat (sunflower oil, since no dripping was to hand), a quarter of a pound each of flour and barley, seasonings, and (mostly) water.

The preparation was straightforward—exactly the same, in fact, as for any of Soyer's other stocks or gravies, except for the minute quantities of meat and vegetables—and the result, somewhat to my surprise, smelled not unappetizing. When we sampled it, our hero's favorite word, "palatable," was the first that came to mind. "Palatable" implies acceptability without joy, which is exactly what Receipt No. 1 offers. You can eat it without any great hardship, but would probably choose not to if any alternative was to hand. In other words, it was institutional cooking. (My husband, who spent his formative years at an English public school, declared after the first mouthful that it reminded him of school meals.) It wasn't watery—the barley and flour thickened it out quite satisfyingly—nor, thanks to the plentiful salt, was it wholly without flavor; indeed, it teetered on the edge of being too salty, which may have been my fault rather than Soyer's.

The absence of herbs and spices seemed at first rather puzzling. Soyer, who liked strong flavors, habitually used them very freely. And herbs, if not spices, cost very little, and might disproportionately improve so plain a dish. But this turned out to be no accidental oversight. The introduction to *Charitable Cookery* explains that they were omitted on purpose, since their effect is to stimulate the appetite and "my object [was] not to create an appetite but to satisfy it."

Our appetites were certainly successfully unstimulated; nobody asked for more. Whether a quart of the mixture apiece would have satisfied them I am unable to say, since my tasters flatly refused to contemplate an entire meal composed of Receipt No. 1. I suspect it would keep you going, being hot and thick. The meat is cut up very small, a cunning trick that ensures a few morsels will be found in every portion; the same, of course, goes for the vegetables, which make a surprisingly large mound when chopped up.

The result, as I have said, wasn't bad. Rather, it was unmemorable; which, given the memorably horrendous mixtures habitually served out to those unfortunate enough to depend on public charity at this time, was probably an absolute commendation. One stew served out to the starving Irish during the great hunger consisted, per 30 gallons, of one oxhead, without the tongue, 28 lb. turnips, 3½ lb. onions, 7 lb. carrots, 21 lb. pea meal, 14 lb. Indian corn meal, and the rest water. Once was enough for the recipients of what the local schoolmaster described as a "vile compound": Even starvation was preferable. They declared it gave them "bowel complaints."[1] "The disclosures in the Andover Union have thrown quite a new light on the science of cookery, which not even the inspiration of a Soyer

[1]Woodham-Smith, *The Great Hunger*, p. 178.

could have hit upon," commented *Punch* under the heading "Work-house Cookery" in 1846. "Butter, according to the new poor law cookery, is made from the skimmings of greasepots, and parochial tea is made from boiling old leaves which have already had the strength drawn out of them." Of course, *Punch* may have been exaggerating in the name of satire. But the bite of its squibs lay largely in the fact that they rarely strayed far from reality. Compared to such products as this, Receipt No. 1 is gastronomy of another order.

Of course, any cook wants his products to be eatable—and a cook with Soyer's reputation must aim a good deal higher than that. But for Soyer, learning his trade in Paris, "palatability" had always been a question of nutritional as well as gastronomic importance. Health was a universal preoccupation, and just as all French ills legendarily originate in *la foie*, so the highest recommendation for any food was that it promoted *la santé*. Advertisements in the French press for chocolate, coffee, even mustard, all promoted their health-giving properties.

This concern for nutrition, which Soyer wholeheartedly shared and energetically propagated, strikes, for us, an unexpectedly modern note. For example, he advocated, on nutritional grounds, that where possible vegetables should be washed and used skins and all rather than peeled: a piece of advice we would certainly endorse today (though whether even that justified using, as in Receipt No. 1, *only* the peelings, is another question). And for the same reason it was important to fry meat and vegetables lightly in fat for some time before any liquid was added—a technique used in both his charity recipes and his high-class brown sauce, with the result that both, at least at first, gave off the same savory aroma (subsequently diluted in the famine soup, and intensified in the sauce). "Putting twelve onions into a gallon of water and boiling them for as many hours, no smell arises from it; but cut the half of one, and fry it, and the perfume will be diffused throughout the whole house; thus I extract the aroma of every ingredient which I employ."[2]

This was important for obvious reasons: Aroma gets the juices going, so that food eaten with relish is easier to digest than when it must be forced down. "As Hippocrates said, That which pleases the palate, nourishes."[3] But science had recently added even more weight to this ancient assumption, identifying the source of both palatability and nourishment in the brownish aromatic substance that results when meat is fried. This was known to Soyer's generation as *osmazome,* and considered highly nutritious, not only because it promoted appetite by smell and flavor, but because it was rich in nitrogen, which promoted bodybuilding. According to Brillat-Savarin, "It is in osmazome that the principal merit of a good soup resides; the brown of roast meat is due to the caramelization of osmazome; and it is osmazome that gives its rich flavour to venison and game." In Receipt No. 1 and its fellows, Soyer could boast the first charity cooking that preserved the osmazome of the ingredients. It was scant, as they were, but it was there.

The Sampayo and Ibrahim Pasha feasts took place in 1846. Who, reading those stupefying menus, could possibly imagine that 1846 was a famine year? Or that in any year, whether of famine or plenty,

---

[2]*Soyer's Charitable Cookery*, Introduction.
[3]*Soyer's Charitable Cookery*, Introduction.

hunger was the norm not five minutes' walk from the palaces of Pall Mall? Viewed across the proscenium of their thickly curtained windows, that other world must have seemed as unreal as a masque. Of course, one had inevitably to leave the club from time to time; and since they then shared the same streets, it was impossible for the rich wholly to avoid the poor. Wealthy ladies filled their days and assuaged their consciences by organizing fundraising committees, charitable balls, and bazaars for their benefit, while the peers and MPs they were married to shaped the lives poor people led. But poverty, for these fortunates, was strictly something that happened to others. Secure in their comfortable situations, protected by networks of relationships with the rich and powerful, they were unlikely, even should the worst of bad luck befall, ever to experience it themselves.

Living and conducting his business enterprises in various bohemian Soho rooms (at this particular time, he was living in Leicester Square and launching a bottled drink, Soyer's Nectar, from a factory in Rupert Street), Soyer traveled daily between these two worlds. Other people's misfortune was something he could not help but be aware of, and, democratic Frenchman that he was, he had no desire to shut himself off from it. On the contrary. "Like a joyful pilgrim of the olden time," he wrote in his *Charitable Cookery*, "I set forth on my journey, visiting on my route every kind of philanthropic and other useful institution, but more especially the domains of that industrial class, the backbone of every free country—the People."[4]

This empathy must partly have arisen from his own experiences.

[4]*Soyer's Charitable Cookery*, Introduction.

Unlike his parents, he was in the fortunate position of knowing he need never starve. Quite apart from the income that was now coming in from his book and his various inventions, he possessed a talent that was always in demand. On the other hand, though comfortable, he was most definitely not rich as members of the Reform Club were rich; and he had known, throughout his childhood, what it meant to be poor. He also knew, none better, how arbitrary were life's ups and downs. Because of a chance change of job at a crucial moment, the penniless son of a poverty-stricken laborer had transmogrified into a substantial personage with thousands in the bank, one of the most famous figures about town. Because of a fatally timed thunderstorm, the happiest young man in London had been transformed into a bereft widower. In every sense of the word, life was precarious.

The well-placed connections and lucky bequests that relentlessly dominate the plots of Victorian novels are there not only because they provide dramatic possibilities but because, in an urbanizing society with few safe careers open to any but the well-off, so many people's hopes of betterment relied upon them. But the ladders that led upward were in the nature of things scarce, while slippery snakes were many. Inheritances languished and diminished in Chancery. Run-of-the-mill occurrences—childbirth, a chill, an infected cut—might easily (as in Emma Soyer's case) prove fatal. An unexpected death, a business failure, the invention of a new machine—and the honest craftsman no longer had a living. Soyer's *The Modern Housewife, or Ménagère,* published in 1849, is framed up as a discussion between two middle-class ladies, Hortense and Eloise. Hortense has known better days and retired to live cheaply in the country with her husband, while Eloise and her extensive household inhabit the substantial Bifrons Villa in genteel St. John's Wood. Eloise, in reality a Mrs.

Baker, did indeed live at this address, where Soyer, a friend of her husband's, was a frequent visitor, and a great admirer of her efficient housekeeping. But Volant, writing in 1859—a mere ten years after *The Modern Housewife, or Ménagère* first celebrated the capable Eloise's bourgeois comforts—tells us that "through her husband's misfortunes poor Eloise . . . ultimately died in a hospital"[5]—i.e., destitute.

Soyer's Protestant birth probably also affected his attitude to the poor. This was partly political: French Protestants, even when well-off and at the center of affairs, were not natural members of the conservative establishment. On the contrary, they had traditionally been its victims; and the result was a generally radical mind-set. Guizot, Louis-Philippe's prime minister, the man who in 1830 replaced the hated Prince de Polignac, and who was thus part of the "revolutionary gang" detested by Mrs. Lloyd's friend the Duke of Buckingham, was a Protestant. But Protestantism also brought with it other traits, among them an ethic of work and application that had served Soyer well throughout his amazing, seemingly effortless, but in fact all-consuming journey upward. His restless energy constantly sought new outlets; every inefficiency, each gap in the market, cried out to him for a solution. Hence his unending stream of cookbooks and kitchen inventions, the "pagodatique" dishes, the tendon separators for clumsy carvers, the "magic" stove that stood on a tray and would let you fry, stew, or boil your dinner on any tabletop; hence his eager annexation of gas as a kitchen fuel.

This inventiveness was not matched by the persistence that might, had he cared, have made him a truly wealthy man. The only instance of his trying to take out a patent was in 1853, in respect of

[5]Volant and Warren, *Memoirs of Alexis Soyer*, p. 125.

an invention for "Improvements in Preparing and Preserving Soups" called "Soyer's Osmazome Food," some distillation of the magic essence presumably rather like Oxo (a condensed beef bouillon). Characteristically, however, the application was voided because he failed to proceed with it in time. Once the business of invention was over, he seemed to lose interest in its product. Like a child bored with yesterday's toy, he preferred, once the novelty was exhausted, to move on to something new. His commercial sauces and relishes were sold by his friends Mr. Crosse and Mr. Blackwell, not by Soyer; and it was Crosse and Blackwell, not Soyer, who made money out of them. Although he enjoyed money's pleasures, the fact of its possession was in itself of little importance to him, and he resolutely declined to undergo the tedium involved in the amassing of wealth. It came, it went; as Philippe the conjurer could testify, friendship was more important to him than cash.

It was in the winter of 1846–47 that Soyer took up the systematic concern with life's unfortunates that would characterize the rest of his life and that, alone of his inventions and preoccupations, was never cast aside for some newer and more compelling event. It was a bitter winter, and the plight of the poor had reached as-yet-untapped depths of misery. If they were not to starve as well as freeze, some way must be devised of feeding them; and this he determined to do. Of course, others had already made some efforts in this direction. Various charitable committees ran soup kitchens in deprived areas. But having now no domestic distractions, he was able to devote himself to this new interest with unusual single-mindedness.

The first recipients of his charitable attentions were London's Huguenot community, whose French Protestant ancestry perhaps echoed his own, and who so clearly fell into the category of deserving poor, starving meekly in their garrets rather than drowning their sorrows in gin. At the end of the seventeenth century, these skilled and hardworking emigrants had established themselves as silk weavers in Spitalfields, manufacturing a luxury product for which they were highly paid. Their early prosperity and success can be judged by the fine houses they built in the neighborhood of Fournier Street. But during the nineteenth century they, like all other handloom weavers, found themselves ruined. In 1801, Joseph-Marie Jacquard had invented a punch-card system by which machines could be programmed to produce even the most complex patterned fabrics. Cheap machine-made silks flooded the market, and the Spitalfields weavers starved.

Soyer was introduced to this now-destitute community by its pastor, the Rev. Joseph Brown, and on February 10, 1847, wrote a horrified letter to various papers, including *The Times*, recounting what he saw there.

We found, in many of the houses, five or six in a small room entirely deprived of the common necessaries of life—no food, no fire, and hardly any garment to cover their persons, and that during the late severe frost. In one of the attics we visited we enquired of a woman how they subsisted. Her husband, she said, had no employment during the last four months, and that they merely lived on what he could get by begging in the streets. She added, that she and her children had not touched a bit of food for twenty-four hours, the last of which consisted of apples partly decayed, and bits of bread given to her husband; which food we may consider, even if plentiful, to be pernicious to health. The only piece of furniture in that gloomy abode of misery was the weaving machine, now at rest, and which, in time of prosperity, was used to provide food, and made, if not a wealthy, at least a happy home for those now wretched and destitute families, and the scientific production of which has often, and even now, adorns the persons of thousands of the aristocracy and gentry of the country.

Soyer's first recourse, as always, was to practical invention. He produced a design for a new model soup kitchen, better, larger, and more efficient than anything that had been seen before. It would be paid for by subscription, and he would start the ball rolling himself, to the tune of £30.

> I immediately proposed that my subscription kitchen for the poor, which was being made at Messrs. Bramah and Prestige's factory, should be erected, without any loss of time, in the most populous district of Spitalfields . . . I am happy to inform you, sir, that my first experiment, made last Saturday, has been most successful, having been able to make a most excellent peas-panada and meat-soup in less than one hour and a half, and this at a very moderate expense—the quickness and saving of which are partly owing to the contrivance of my new steam-apparatus, and which food was distributed, in less than twenty minutes, to about *three hundred and fifty* children.[6]

[6]*The Times*, February 18, 1847.

On February 21, he wrote to the paper again.

> I am quite convinced . . . that the wearers of [silk] possess at all times the most charitable feelings towards their fellow-creatures in distress . . . I am aware that every nobleman, gentleman, and tradesman have to support their own poor, and therefore propose that not more than a guinea should be received from anyone as a subscription; but from sixpence to the above will be most thankfully received.[7]

It seemed, however, that his rich friends did not share his charitable impulses. The subscription list for *The Gastronomic Regenerator* on its publication the previous year had extended to two thousand, at a guinea a head, but there were only twenty responses to his soup-kitchen appeal. A grand total of £147 was raised, including Soyer's own contribution—by far the largest. Even an exhibition of the late Madame Soyer's pictures in the Prince of Wales's Bazaar, under the title "Soyer's Philanthropic Gallery," failed to raise any significant funds. "The fact is," wrote an indignant member of the Reform Club, who had visited the almost empty gallery and entirely missed the point, "that the upper ranks of this country have no real feeling for art."[8] Nevertheless, the construction of the kitchen went ahead.

In the meantime, Soyer had made an exhaustive study of the charity soup already available at the several soup kitchens already operating in London. Most he found so disgusting as to be uneatable—which made it useless even to the hungriest. This nastiness,

[7]*The Times*, February 21, 1847.
[8]Volant and Warren, *Memoirs of Alexis Soyer*, p. 134.

he thought, was due less to bad ingredients than to the soupmakers (probably charitable ladies who never otherwise cooked) being "entirely ignorant" of what to do with them. There was no seasoning. The rice, split peas, and barley that were used to bulk out the soup were usually underdone; and yet the end product often tasted burned. "In some parishes I find one hundred pounds of meat cut into pieces of a quarter of a pound each, put into one hundred gallons of water, at twelve o'clock of one day, to be boiled until twelve o'clock the next day; by such proceedings the osmazome of the meat is lost by evaporation from the boiler, and only the gelatine and fibrine are left . . . It contains no nutriment whatever . . . What would be said of a cook who would put a quarter of a pound of meat, or even a piece weighing 30 lb, to roast before a large fire for twenty-four hours?" This dismal state of affairs was not entirely surprising: "Twenty years' experience and practice in the culinary art has taught me that it requires more science to produce a good dish, at a trifling expense, than a superior one with unlimited means."[9]

It was evident that merely designing a model soup kitchen was not enough: Even the best equipment in the world would not be proof against such anti-cookery as this. Soyer would have personally to supervise the preparation of the soup. And since he could hardly be expected to oversee the feeding of every pauper in London, this meant he must give the world the benefit of his experience by publishing his recipes, as he had already done with such success for the wealthy, in *The Gastronomic Regenerator*, and was soon to do for the middle classes, in *The Modern Housewife, or Ménagère*. That way, he could at least be sure that ingredients were no longer wasted on

[9]Volant and Warren, *Memoirs of Alexis Soyer*, p. 134.

account of ignorance. The result was *Soyer's Charitable Cookery: or, the Poor Man's Regenerator*, published in April 1847.

This new culinary excursion of Soyer's did not go unnoticed. His letters to the press provided a detailed account of his charitable doings, and the editors—many of them his personal friends—needed little coaxing to print them, along with the stories and squibs they generated. Among the contents of these letters was the recipe with which this chapter began. And when Soyer's genuine beneficence is taken into account, not the least astonishing aspect of Receipt No. 1, from a twenty-first-century standpoint, is its almost perverse insistence on cheapness. It is undoubtedly true that leek tops are good in soup and are usually wasted. But *only* the tops of the leeks? *Only* the peel of the turnips? After I had peeled my turnip, its white inside stood reproachfully on my worktop. The same went (or would have gone, had I bought my meat in the quantities Soyer habitually did rather than a supermarket pack) for the bones to which that meat had once been attached. Not that Soyer advocated disposing of the bones; on the contrary, they were to be put aside for a separate batch of broth.

The contrast with his recipes for the better-off is particularly shocking. The amounts of meat that vanish into sauces, in the middle-class *Modern Housewife* as well as the unabashedly grand *Gastronomic Regenerator*, seem to twenty-first-century readers as amazing in their extravagance as Receipt No. 1 in its meanness. For the stock that formed the basis of our Soup course and the Reform Sauce—about three pints—I used, as directed, 4 lb. meat and bones, three onions, a turnip, a carrot, half a leek, and half a head of celery. And this was nothing out of the way. Brillat-Savarin, under the heading "Uses of Gastronomical Knowledge," tells the story of the Prince de

Soubise, who, discussing a dinner-party menu with his steward, found to his horror that the first item on the bill of fare was "fifty hams." Had the steward gone mad? the Prince inquired. Did he propose to feed the entire regiment?

> "No, Your Highness; only one ham will appear on the table; but I shall need all the rest for my brown sauce, my stock, my garnishings, my . . ."
>
> "Bertrand, you're a thief and I shan't pass that item."
>
> "But Your Highness," answered the artist, hardly able to contain his anger, "you don't know our resources! You have only to say the word, and I'll take all those fifty hams you object to and put them into a crystal phial no bigger than my thumb!"[10]

Tales such as this reflect the early beginnings of the restaurant as a house selling *restaurants*—tiny, restorative cups of the most concentrated possible *bouillon* for the regeneration of those worn out by fashionable exertion—a function echoed in the title of the *Gastronomic Regenerator*. The poor man, though doubtless even more in need of regeneration than the wealthy, could not—as Soyer's charity recipes make clear—expect the same level of refinement (in all senses of that word). Perhaps, too, given that the entire relief ethic in the mid–nineteenth century was directed toward making any proffered help so unpleasant that only the truly desperate would submit themselves to it, he felt he had no alternative but to take this

[10]Brillat-Savarin, *The Philosopher in the Kitchen*, p. 54.

grimly severe approach. If his recipes had seemed too lavish, then they would never have been taken up. "Nothing will be given away," he reassured potential subscribers to his new model soup kitchen, "except to those who are proved to be quite destitute; a quart of food or soup, and a quarter of a pound of bread, will be given for one penny."[11] Charity might be a virtue, but it must not, at all costs, be seen to wear a smiling face.

This policy, if indeed it was a policy, paid off handsomely. Soyer, the nation's most famous chef, with a recipe that promised one hundred gallons of palatable, life-sustaining soup for under £1? The designer of the most famous kitchens in the kingdom turning his hand to a new model soup kitchen, built (as all his kitchens were built) on the latest scientific lines, and capable of supplying twenty thousand meals a day? If it was true, it was a miracle. And as the British government was just then acutely concerned with the problem of cheap mass feeding, this particular miracle caught more than one hopeful official eye.

Relief efforts of this kind were a quite new preoccupation for the government. Generally speaking, destitution was not its business. The local poor rates provided outdoor relief for paupers, as well as supporting, if that is the word, the workhouses. But for the past two years the situation in Ireland had been so desperate as to be beyond any merely local remedy. In the summer of 1846, for the second year running, blight had wiped out the Irish potato crop. As a result, Ireland was starving, its inhabitants dying in their hundreds of thousands. It was not a situation that could be ignored, however hard one might try to do so; and the British government desperately needed

[11]Letter to *The Times*, February 21, 1847.

some new initiative that might enable it to regain control of an apparently hopeless calamity.

This blight, which had arrived from America, was not peculiar to Ireland. It had destroyed most of the crop throughout Europe. But although poor people everywhere, and especially in England, ate a lot of potatoes—a fallback food if you could afford nothing else—these did not constitute their sole nourishment. In Ireland, however, many people ate nothing else.

Because it had for centuries been run as an English colony—that is to say, for the benefit of the colonizers rather than the natives— Ireland at this time was less developed, more poverty-stricken, and more backward than any other country in northern Europe. "Commissariat officers serving in Irish relief declared that the English knew as little of Ireland as of West Africa; in fact, they knew less," says Cecil Woodham-Smith. "The distant parts of the Empire which Britain then ruled, in Africa, India, China, were more carefully studied than Ireland and their economic structure better understood."[12] Much of the land was owned by English landlords, often absentees, who drew rentals from it, grew cash crops for export, and took little interest in their tenants. Its fisheries were undeveloped, and its industries run down so as not to compete with those on the mainland. Production in the once-prosperous woolen industry had fallen about 50 percent in the past twenty years: Three-quarters of the woollen frieze cloth used by the Irish peasantry was now dumped by England. The Poor Enquiry of 1835 had found that three-quarters of the laborers in Ireland had no employment of any kind.[13]

[12]Woodham-Smith, *The Great Hunger*, p. 122. My account of the Irish famine is largely taken from this source.
[13]Woodham-Smith, *The Great Hunger*, p. 32.

This desperate situation was exacerbated, as the eighteenth century drew to a close, by a sudden population explosion. Until then, Ireland had been only thinly populated. But between 1779 and 1841 it increased by a minimum of 172 percent—perhaps even more. Girls married at sixteen, bore many children, and were soon grandmothers. And since these people had no money, it followed that if they were to keep alive, they must grow their own food. The resulting pressure on land was overwhelming, and rentals, despite the poverty, among the highest in Europe. Every available plot was divided and subdivided and divided again. And given these tiny holdings, the potato—usually the "lumper" or horse potato, a coarse variety that grew very large and prolifically—was the only possible crop. An acre and a half, laid to potatoes, would feed a family of five or six for a year; four to six times as much land, and some knowledge of agriculture, was needed to grow the equivalent amount of grain.[14]

Potatoes had other advantages. You grew them by strewing them on a six-foot-wide "lazy bed" and covering them with earth. The only tool needed was a spade, while corn required a plow; and spade tillage, unlike plowing, was as practical on a mountainside as in a valley. To cook them, a saucepan or the embers of a fire would do, with no need for milling, or yeast, or ovens. "Greens were unknown, bread was unknown, ovens were unknown," says Cecil Woodham-Smith. Where people did grow grain, it was not for eating but for selling. Grain paid the rent. That was the first priority. If the rent was not paid, the family would be evicted. And in that case, they would have nowhere to live and no land on which to grow next year's potatoes.

[14]Woodham-Smith, *The Great Hunger*, p. 35.

The potato was in many ways an ideal subsistence crop—nutritious, delicious, easy to cook, good for pigs, cattle, and fowls as well as people. But all monocultures are dangerous, and the potato was no exception. It did not keep; it could not be stored from one season to the next; it was prone to disease and vulnerable to the weather. The crop regularly failed, in whole or in part. There had been scarcities in 1728, 1739, 1740, 1770, 1807, 1821, 1822, throughout the 1830s, in 1841, and in 1844. On each of these occasions, there had been more or less widespread distress. But in 1845 and 1846, the failure was total, and the result: famine on a biblical scale unprecedented in Europe.

The British government's failure in the face of this famine was a litany of ignorance, dogmatism, party politics, and unbending bureaucracy. Why could not grain simply have been imported from abroad, duty-free, to make up the shortfall? Because that would have meant repealing the Corn Laws, which protected the price of British grain; and repeal of the Corn Laws was the most controversial and politically dangerous issue in British politics. It was opposed by the Tories, who were then in power; the real extent of Irish distress may be measured by the fact that the Prime Minister, Sir Robert Peel, who was also the Tory leader, was reluctantly forced to the conclusion that the only remedy for the desperate situation was "the total and absolute repeal for ever of all duties on all articles of subsistence."[15] The opponents of repeal at once turned on him, denying that the potato crop had failed "except to a very partial extent"; the Tory mayor of Liverpool refused to call a meeting for the relief of Irish distress; the Mansion House Committee in Dublin was accused

[15]Woodham-Smith, *The Great Hunger*, p. 50.

of "deluding the public with a false alarm." To profess belief in the blight, wrote Isaac Butt QC, "was as sure a method of being branded as a radical as to propose to destroy the church."[16] Why could not the export of food from Ireland have been prohibited? Because, in the words of Charles Trevelyan, the high-minded, public-spirited, and relentlessly inflexible civil servant charged with directing famine policy, "perfect Free Trade is the right course."[17] As it happens, the quantities in question would have been insufficient to supply the need; but the effect on starving people of seeing Irish food removed from the country under armed escort may be imagined. Why could not independent merchants use the money produced by the sale of grain to import low-priced foods to replace the potato, as Trevelyan urged? Because in the undeveloped state of Irish commerce, such independent merchants barely existed. By the time the British government agreed that some supplies must at all costs be bought, and that these should be of American maize, which did not compete with British farmers' produce, almost all maize stocks had already been bought up by other European countries. As a result, the amounts procured were wholly inadequate, and those in charge of the storehouses hesitated to open them for fear of riots when supplies ran out. Trevelyan was in any case opposed to opening the storehouses, as he felt relief distributed in this way risked "paralysing all private enterprise and having this country on you for an indefinite number of years."[18]

Trevelyan, when not occupied with famine relief, was the permanent head of the Treasury. His views were dictated not merely by the then usual deep-seated distaste for the notion of centrally funded

[16]Woodham-Smith, *The Great Hunger*, p. 50.
[17]Woodham-Smith, *The Great Hunger*, p. 123.
[18]Woodham-Smith, *The Great Hunger*, p. 89.

poor relief, but also by a horror of unnecessary taxation in general. He particularly disliked the idea that Irish relief should be paid for out of English taxes—something, he felt, that the English would never stand. Ideally, people should be enabled to buy their food with money they had earned; and to this end he set up a program of public works, to be financed from local rates. But most of these were of little real use. What Ireland needed was drainage, but ratepayers objected to paying for drainage schemes that would benefit someone else's land. The public works were therefore mostly roads from nowhere to nowhere else, benefiting no one. Or would have been— many remained hypothetical: Since all works had to be approved by Whitehall (Trevelyan actually moved into lodgings at this time so as to spend his entire time working, uninterrupted by family demands), the whole scheme became snarled up in a bottleneck of approvals and permissions. Meanwhile, people starved; and, to add to their miseries, the winter of 1846–47 was one of unprecedented severity, with snow and frost such as are rarely seen in Ireland. Irish peasant life during the winter was a primitive affair, but at least people could keep warm: Peat was plentiful, and every family had its supply to burn for heating. Now, if they were to eat, they had to brave the cold with no warm clothes and no reserves of strength.

There could be no end to this horrible situation until a new and hopefully healthy potato harvest could be gathered, in the autumn of 1847. In the meantime, even Trevelyan recognized that something more would have to be done. Until this moment, the government had been unwilling to supply cooked food: If you gave away ingredients and let people cook for themselves, then that at least maintained a certain independence. But there was nowhere near enough maize; and even when people managed, against the odds, to get hold of some, this, too, was not the end of their problems. Much of it had been bought unmilled, and the starving recipients had neither the implements nor the strength to reduce bullet-hard maize kernels to meal for porridge. So a new policy was introduced. The Destitute Poor (Ireland) Act of March 1847 brought the disastrous public works scheme to an end in favor of setting up soup kitchens throughout Ireland. "The soup system promises to be a great resource and I am endeavouring to turn the views of the Committees to it. It will have a double effect of feeding the people at a lower price and economising our meal," observed Sir Randolph Routh, the leader of the Irish Relief Commission. Routh was a product of the Commissariat department of the British Army, which, during the years of severe military economy following Waterloo, had developed parsimony into a high art—a policy that would have its own disastrous effects in the Crimea, when once again Soyer would try and help rescue the situation. But by this time even Routh had been driven to desperation by Trevelyan's perverse refusal to modify his ideas in the face of catastrophe.

February 1847, when Soyer published his letters regarding soup kitchens in *The Times*, happened also to be the moment when the Irish soup-kitchen legislation was being prepared. Volant's *Memoirs* of his old friend states that "In the beginning of February, 1847, M. Soyer turned his indefatigable thoughts to relieving the starving poor in Ireland." However, it seems far more likely that these thoughts were put into his head by others. As we have seen, he sent his famine soup recipes, as was his habit, to be sampled by various noble acquaintances; his letter to *The Times* mentions "nu-

Soyer's Irish soup kitchen.

merous noblemen, members of Parliament, and several ladies, who have lately visited my kitchen department and have found [the soup] very good and nourishing" (at least for others: Perhaps their opinion would have been different had they been expected to subsist on it). Many of these enthusiasts were either members of the government or their close friends or relatives; among them, as we have seen, was the Duchess of Sutherland, for whom Soyer had once worked and whom he had recently met again in her capacity as a member of the Poor Relief Committee. The Duchess now approached Lord Bessborough, the Lord Lieutenant of Ireland, who requested the Reform Club to allow their cook leave of absence in order to set up his soup kitchen in Dublin. The Club could hardly refuse; and by February 22 Routh was able to write triumphantly to Trevelyan that "Soyer is on his way."[19]

He was greeted by a desperate press—reflecting, no doubt, the fond wishes of everyone in Ireland and Whitehall—as a kind of wizard whose magic pot would somehow bring the famine to an end. "We learn that the Government have resolved forthwith to despatch M. Soyer, the chef de cuisine of the Reform Club, to Ireland, with ample instructions to provide his soups for the starving millions of Irish people," the *Cork Examiner* announced triumphantly on February 26, 1847.

> Pursuant to this wise and considerate resolve, artificers are at present busied day and night, constructing the necessary kitchens, apparatus, &c, with which M. Soyer starts for Dublin direct to the Lord Lieutenant. His plans have been examined both by the authorities at the Board of Works and the Admiralty, and have, after mature consideration, been deemed quite capable of answering the object sought.
>
> The soup has been served to several of the best judges of the noble art of gastronomy at the Reform Club, not as soup for the poor, but as a soup furnished for the day in the carte. The members who partook of it declared it excellent. Among these may be mentioned Lord Titchfield and Mr. O'Connell. M. Soyer can supply the whole poor of Ireland, at one meal for each person, once a day. He has informed the executive that a bellyfull of his soup, once a day, together

---

[19]Thanks to Frank Clement-Lorford, who was instrumental in helping to clarify this episode (as indeed many others).

with a biscuit, will be more than sufficient to sustain the strength of a strong and healthy man.

The food is to be "consumed on the premises." Those who are to partake enter at one avenue, and having been served they retire at another, so that there will be neither stoppage nor confusion. To the infant, the sick, the aged, as well as to distant districts, the food is to be conveyed in cars furnished with portable apparatus for keeping the soup perfectly hot. It would be premature to enter into further details. M. Soyer has satisfied the Government that he can furnish enough and to spare of most nourishing food for the poor of these realms, and it is confidently anticipated that there will soon be no more deaths from starvation in Ireland.

"M. Soyer," quipped Thackeray in *Punch*, "deserves to be called the Gastronomic Regenerator of Ireland. His receipt for cheap soup is the best practical suggestion which has been yet made for the relief of that unlucky island." Thackeray went on to propose a mass shooting of English game, to provide Soyer with extra meat for his soup, and with the added advantage that "if the Irish eat up the game the game will not eat up the farmer . . . Our scheme we know will sacrifice sport; but it is better to sacrifice that than human life."[20]

Whatever the merits or demerits of its product, Soyer's soup kitchen was undoubtedly a triumph of efficiency. He had clearly taken as much trouble and pleasure in its design as he had when fitting out the Reform Club kitchens eight years before, with the same attention to practical detail and optimum use of fuel and space. This

[20]*Punch*, March 1847.

paragon among soup kitchens was constructed in front of the Royal Barracks in Dublin and eventually opened on April 5. "The exterior and covering is of a temporary nature, being formed of boards and canvas, inclosing a space of forty-eight feet long, and forty feet wide," Soyer wrote in *The Poor Man's Regenerator*.

The interior consists of a steam-boiler, on wheels, thirteen feet long and four feet wide, with a glaze-pan over it, capable of containing three hundred gallons; and at the end an oven to bake one hundredweight of bread at a time; and all heated by the same fire. Under the boiler is an excavation to contain coals, and round it an elevated platform to give access to the glaze-pan. At the distance of eight feet round the boiler are eight iron *bain-marie* pans, with covers, six feet long and twenty-two inches wide, on wheels, and made double, to be boiled by steam, and contain, together, one thousand gallons. At each end, extending between the pans, are the cutting-tables—at one end the meat, and at the other the vegetables; and under which are placed wooden soaking tubs, on wheels, and chopping-blocks for the meat, drawers, and a sliding-shelf. Four feet beyond these are placed a row of tables, eighteen inches wide, in which a hole is cut, and therein is placed a quart iron, white-enamelled basin, with a metal spoon attached thereto by a neat chain: there are one hundred of these, and this table forms the outer boundary of the kitchen; leaving a space of two feet six inches between it and the wall. Inside of the tables are fastened tin water-cases, at the distance of ten feet apart, containing a sponge, etc., to clean out the soup-basins.

Round the two supports of the roof are circular tin boxes for the condiments. Seven feet from the ground, at each corner, is placed a safe, five feet square and seven feet high, with sides of wire, for ventilation, which contains respectively meat, vegetables, grain and condiments. At the same elevation as the safes are sixteen butts, containing 1792 gallons of water. At the entrance, in the centre, is the weighing machine. . . . Outside the tent is a zigzag passage capable of containing one hundred persons in a small space in the open air; at the entrance is a check-clerk, and an indicator or machine that numbers every person that passes; and on the other side is a bread and biscuit room, where those who have partaken of the soup, and are departing, receive on passing a quarter of a pound of bread or savoury biscuit; as I prefer giving it then instead of with the soup and food, it being sufficient for one meal without, and will not only save time, but when eaten afterwards will be more wholesome.

The *Illustrated London News* ran a picture of the soup kitchen's opening, showing the neat rows of pans, the white-clad cook on his platform, the grateful poor seated at their board, and, presiding over the whole, a full-length portrait of the Queen flanked by tasteful greenery. In the foreground stand the Duke of Cambridge, Soyer's old employer, Lord William Paulet, whom he would meet again in the Crimea, and their ladies, assembled on this occasion, or so we may assume, to admire rather than sample. Customers were allowed six minutes to consume a bowl of soup, permitting a through-put of one thousand per hour. This left three thousand uneaten quarts or more to be distributed at the kitchen door, in exchange for tickets or money. Containers "with fires attached" were also sent out, as promised in the *Cork Examiner*, on barrows or horse- or donkey-carts, "so that the food contained in them should be hot or cooking on its way to the place of distribution." The recipes were changed every day, with meager on Fridays.

The soup was hot; it was also, as I can testify, "palatable." And the response from Dubliners was almost overwhelming. The kitchen found itself supplying 8,750 rations daily, where five thousand had been considered the probable maximum.[21] However, Soyer's claim that a serving of his soup would sustain a grown man for a day was, to say the least of it, rash. "Medico," writing to *The Lancet* from the Athenaeum, denounced it as "soup-quackery" and "preposterous." Anyone "in the slightest degree acquainted with the elements of organic chymistry" would at once see that Receipt No. 1 was "utterly deficient in the due supply of those materials from which the human frame can elaborate bones, tendon, blood, muscle, nervous substance, etc." Furthermore, "The debilitating effects of a liquid diet are so well known to the medical officers of our hospitals, prisons and other public establishments that it is unnecessary to dwell on the subject." For skeptics such as this—and "Medico" was not alone in his doubts—the notion that the government seriously proposed a society chef as the knight in shining armor who would save a nation was so ludicrous as to be insulting.

In point of fact, this criticism, like Soyer's original claim, was probably exaggerated. There was some protein in the meat and dripping, as well as in the barley, which is also rich in iron, selenium, and niacin; and both barley and flour contain carbohydrate.

[21]Woodham-Smith, *The Great Hunger*, p. 179.

But such criticism could not be ignored. It was too near the knuckle; it undermined Soyer personally and the government politically. A report was therefore commissioned, to be undertaken by an independent nutritionist under the auspices of the Royal Dublin Society, Ireland's leading scientific body. They appointed a professor of chemistry, John Aldridge, who began with an exhaustive discussion of the metabolism of herbivores. He then transposed his findings to try and determine the nutrition needed by a four-stone child if it was to maintain its weight. On May 7 he personally sampled Soyer's charity soup recipes, announcing that the cheapest—the Fish Soup, Receipt No. 6—was also the most nutritious. In carefully chosen words he thanked Soyer "for what I believe to be his purely philanthropic intentions towards [the poor]. He has given to us two boons of no ordinary value, a model dispensing kitchen of great ingenuity, and a method of economic cooking far superior to any to which the poorer order of our countrymen have hitherto been accustomed."[22] Soyer took the opportunity to row back on his original claim. He announced in the Irish press that, although his soup was nourishing, it was not intended to replace a solid main meal. However, people could survive on it, if they had to, for several weeks.

The original plan had been for him to set up his kitchen, then return to his post at the Reform Club within a fortnight. But as always with complicated projects, things took longer than planned. He left for Ireland in February 1847; on March 11, Lord Bessborough wrote requesting that his leave be extended until April; and

[22]Quoted in Frank Clement-Lorford in his unpublished work, "The First Celebrity Chef."

on April 1, another letter was received from Soyer himself explaining that unexpected difficulties had delayed the opening of the Soup Kitchen and "begging further leave of absence until the end of next week in order to complete the undertaking he is engaged in." The Secretary was directed "to acquaint him that he might remain until Saturday the 10th inst."[23]

By the time he left Ireland on April 11, Soyer had been there almost seven weeks. As usual, it is difficult to know his true feelings; but some remarks in *Soyer's Charitable Cookery: or, The Poor Man's Regenerator* make it clear that (just as when he worked at Aston Hall) he found it hard to understand how such a country could have arrived at such a plight. "I do not mean to tax you with waste and extravagance," he wrote, "but merely to impress upon your minds that the country produces plenty of vegetable and animal substances, and the waters washing your magnificent shores teem with life . . . They only require to be properly employed to supply the wants of every one, with good, nourishing and palatable food." He was horrified to see fish being used, not for eating, but as fertilizer for potatoes, simply because "they know how to cook potatoes to perfection and are totally ignorant of the way to cook fish." In conversation with Lord Bessborough he suggested that public lecturers be appointed, "whose duty it should be to go round as often as the agricultural lecturer, and teach the people how to cook the food which that person now endeavours to make them cultivate."[24] Such a person could also show how to prepare the maize meal everyone so hated, making it "a blessing rather than a

[23]Reform Club archives.
[24]*Soyer's Shilling Cookery for the People*, p. 71.

curse." In a normal time and place, such a suggestion might have been worth considering. But Ireland in the 1840s was neither.

Later that year, Soyer reckoned up how many people his kitchen had fed, and what it had all cost:

From the opening of my model kitchen by me, on the 6th of April last, to the 24th, the number of rations of 2½lb. each was   40,000

From the 26th of April to the 22nd of May, by the South Union Relief Committee, the number of rations, averaging 12,500 per day, was   300,000

From the 24th of May to the 31st of July, also by the South Union Relief Committee, the number of rations per day, varying from 1,750 to 23,940, was   729,270

From the 2nd of August to the 14th, averaging 6,500 per day, was   78,000

Making 2,868,197lb. of food, and of rations,   £1,147,278

To supply that number of rations by the old plan of preparing food in different depots would have cost, at 3d. per ration (which is rather under the average), the sum of   £15,536

But according to my plan of preparing food with my model kitchen, as it was estimated in a report made to the Relief Committee, by its secretary, on the 23rd of April last, the cost of each ration, including coals, expenses of house, carriage, labour, etc., came to 1½d., making altogether, for 2,836,287lb. of solid food, a sum of   <u>£7,768</u>

Effecting a saving in favour of the South Union Committee of 50 per cent, or a sum of   £7,768[25]

Despite the abuse heaped on Soyer's head by such as "Medico," the citizens of Dublin undoubtedly appreciated his efforts on their behalf. A street ballad was written about him ("I must procure you a copy as a curiosity; but it is a vile production," wrote "W. J. K.," "a gentleman high in office"); others showed their gratitude in a more solid manner. Before he left Dublin a dinner was given in his honor at the Freemasons' Hall, on College Green, where about thirty gentlemen sat down to dinner and presented M. Soyer, after a suitably complimentary speech, with "a very elegant snuffbox, manufactured by Mr Bennett, of Grafton Street, as a memento of his visit to Ireland."[26] And on his return to London another dinner was given, this time a public one, at the London Tavern, "to commemorate his philanthropic and disinterested efforts for the relief of the starving Irish."

More than one hundred and fifty sat down to this dinner, which was, Volant assures us, "of the most *recherché* description, and the table service of gold and silver."[27] What can have been going on in their minds as they ate it? A banquet "of the most *recherché* description" off gold and silver to celebrate—a soup kitchen? Only twenty souls had seen fit to contribute when the very

[25]Volant and Warren, *Memoirs of Alexis Soyer*, pp. 109–10.
[26]Volant and Warren, *Memoirs of Alexis Soyer*, p. 111.
[27]Volant and Warren, *Memoirs of Alexis Soyer*, p. 111.

man they were now honoring had been trying to raise subscriptions to finance the kitchen in question. What, exactly, was being honored here?

The answer, surely, is neither Soyer's kitchen nor, really, Soyer himself. He was just the peg upon which this celebration was hung, and the relief celebrated was of conscience, not famine. Ireland might be a colony, but it was not on the other side of the world like India or Africa. Many English people are of Irish extraction; many of the banqueters would have visited Ireland, many must have had Irish friends or relatives. And there, in hedgerows and windowless hovels a boat ride away across the Irish Sea, the starving Irish were dying by their hundreds of thousands. It was a catastrophe so enormous that, for once, insulation was not possible. Surely they ought to do something about it? Surely the government ought to have done something about it? And now someone they all knew had actually gone over there and done that something, which was almost as good as if they had done it themselves. And their taxes would not be raised, and the potato harvest would turn out all right next time. (It did not.)

So that was all right.

Trevelyan was knighted for his devotion to duty during the Famine; in September 1848, a grant of money was awarded him for his good work overlooking Irish supplies of oatmeal and potatoes. *Punch* noted that Colonel Dunne, questioning this grant, wished to know why "M. SOYER, of the Reform Club," had not been rewarded for *his* commissariat services. "The hint has not been lost upon Ministers," it observed. "SOYER has been created a K.C.B.— Kettle Cook of the Broth."

Let Soyer himself have the last word.

Recipe of a distinguished Artiste for a favourite Soup, much in request of late at the Official Cabinet Dinners.

———————— Potage au Desir du Patronage ————————

Take for your stock anything capable of improvement—education, locomotion, sanitary administration, either will do very well; simmer very slowly, throw in occasionally a petition or two, flavoured with a spice of the marvellous and startling; now take it off, and stand by to cool down. Before putting on again, an inquiry or two as to any measure in contemplation will be proper. At this stage, a commission may be safely added, but be very careful to have your materials of the best, and such as you can depend upon; troublesome members, newspaper proprietors, reviewers, barristers on the look-out, and members of any powerful corporate bodies, are the best to select from. Do not choose such as are young or green, and your stock will run smooth and agreeable. Now skim the surface well, to remove facts as they arise; throw them on one side as worse than useless, and be very careful not to stir too deeply; reject or pare well down all conflicting and incongruous evidence—it would ruin your stock to have any contradictory flavours—thicken with a slice or two of gammon; and if it boil too clear, throw in plenty of statistical herbs—medical are the best—sage and honesty will not be proper, however. Now put by your first stock to stand, and you may garnish your tureen *après le livre-bleu*; it has a pretty artistic effect . . .

Note. To some English palates, it has been observed that this soup is attended with an unpleasant *après goût* of bitter herbs, in which *rue* is said to predominate; this objection is not valid, merely demonstrating that the English palate has not yet acquired a taste for the best French *cuisine*.[28]

[28]Volant and Warren, *Memoirs of Alexis Soyer*, pp. 148–9.

6

Roast: Quail
à la Symposium

Until he left the Reform Club in 1850, Soyer had always been an employee; and ever since his departure from France twenty years before, a servant. However autonomous he might appear, there was always a mark that could not be overstepped. If he went too far he would be disciplined; and discipline, however skillfully and charmingly defused, was a humiliation, emphasizing as it did the social gulf he so desired to annihilate. Now, though, all that would change. For the first time in his life he was his own master. He could choose for himself what he would do and when he would do it. And what he chose was to open a restaurant—a proper restaurant like the ones where he had learned his trade in Paris. Instead of the one or two regular dishes served in London's public eating houses, it would boast a full bill of fare from which to select the dinner of your desire. And instead of being restricted to a narrow group of privileged members, the only bar to the proffered pleasures would be inability to pay. Anyone who could afford to eat there would be welcome, whether he (or, importantly, she) be a lord, a lady, or a shoeshine man. And there would stand Alexis the genial host, welcoming his guests as a friend and equal.

In short, this chapter is about choice—which is appropriate, since at this stage in the meal the possibilities become almost overwhelming.

We are now, as it were, over the hump of our dinner. The compulsory and inevitable soup, fish, and meats have been offered and consumed. What remains is the pure pleasure of the second course—which in Soyer's day meant the array of dishes presented to tickle the palate before the desserts signaled the approach of the end. Some idea of this arrangement's infinite possibilities may be gained from his discussion, in *The Gastronomic Regenerator,* of "savory dishes for the second course":

> These dishes are divided into three classes, and in England all belong to the second course, but in France they are very frequently served in the first with a dinner of four or six entrées, that is, one or two of them, and are very commendable in the summer months; for breakfasts, luncheons or suppers, they are invaluable. The large pieces, such as pâtés of game, galantine of turkey, boars' heads etc., are in smaller dinners placed at the bottom of the table to face the roasts, but in a dinner of six or ten entrées they are served as flancs. All others, such as

small galantine of game à la volière, pâtés, chaud froids, salads, mayonnaise etc., by making them smaller may be served as savoury entremets in a corner dish.

This seems to mean that after a certain point (the fish) you can eat more or less anything you want in any order, and for more or less any meal.

At this point, then, I, too, had to choose; and since restaurants are the subject matter, I decided to make my selection as I would in a restaurant, on grounds of gastronomic balance. After fish and meat, it seemed time to try a bird; and after sauced fish and sauced chops, one would want something plain. The answer seemed to be a roast. For as Soyer observed in his inimitable franglais, "After the entrées have been well degusted nothing refreshes the palate or disposes it better for the second course than a fillet or cut from the fillet of a well-roasted capon, chicken, or some description of game."

Unfortunately, "some description of game" did not, I found, narrow things down very significantly.

These days we eat a relatively limited number of birds. There is the ubiquitous chicken; turkey, duck, and guinea fowl are also fairly universal. Then there is pigeon—though any inhabitant of central London must always be slightly worried by the possibility that it might be local. In season there is pheasant; also mallard and partridge, though for these you really need to live near a game dealer or a country market. At Christmas and Easter, but rarely otherwise, there are capons and geese, bred for traditional family gatherings. One may see the occasional grouse. And that's about it.

Soyer's list of possible birds speaks of a different age—a time when the countryside was a sort of Eden teeming with seemingly inexhaustible life and nothing was too small, or too precious, to eat. The list seems endless: turkey, capon, poularde (a specially fattened young hen), geese, ducklings, guinea fowls, pea fowls (excellent eating, Soyer assures us: He advises readers to save a particularly fine tail and buy a special silver holder for it, to decorate pea roasts), ptarmigans, black cocks and gray hens, partridge, dun birds, wild ducks, widgeons, teal, plovers, woodcock (the greatest luxuries, in his opinion, served on toast spread with their innards or "trail"), larks, snipes, quail, knot, knut or knout, ruffes and reeves, landrail, corncrake or dakerhen, water-rail, spotted gallinule or water-crake, fieldfare, redwing, curlew, gannet, terns, gulls (in his view, and I believe him, fit only for soup), coot, bittern, starlings, ox-bird, purre or stint, bustard, blackbirds . . .

I didn't want to cook chicken, since, however delicious, nothing could be more of a gastronomic cliché than roast chicken. And although nothing else is quite so hackneyed, none of the other more usual birds seemed particularly adventurous. On the other hand, who now eats purre or stint? Who even knows what it is? Soyer especially recommends corncrake, but corncrake is now an endangered species. The fact is that in the twenty-first century the fowl of the air are not, generally speaking, fair game. Even in Italy, where in the hunting season large men habitually crouch behind small bushes in the hope that passing sparrows will not notice them until too late, you no longer see those jars of little unnamed birds *sott'olio* that used to adorn the shelves of Tuscan *alimentari,* and that you crunched up whole, bones and all. They have all long since been blasted from the skies.

In the end, I decided upon quail. It's the kind of thing you'd eat in a restaurant—a little out of the ordinary: If you go to a restaurant you don't want to eat something you might cook at home. Indeed, roast quail was one of the dishes Soyer made for the grand press dinner with which he opened his restaurant. What is more, quail are now farmed, so you can eat them with a clear conscience. Those who know say, I am sure rightly, that the farmed birds don't compare in flavor with the wild. But wild quail, once so plentiful, have almost vanished, while farmed ones, though no doubt blander, are still delicious.

I got my quail in packets of six from the supermarket. Allowing two per head, they make a fine platter for a party. They look as though they would vanish in about two bites, but this is deceptive: There's plenty of meat in those plump little breasts.

—————————— Roast Quail ——————————

Eight quails are sufficient for a dish, they should be killed if possible forty-eight hours before dressing, draw and truss them by cutting off the wings at the first pinion, leaving the feet, and fixing the pinion of the wings and legs with a very small skewer; cover the breasts in vine-leaves, over which tie a thin square slice of fat bacon, then pass a long skewer through the pinions and thighs of each, tie them on a spit and roast them nearly twelve minutes at a convenient distance from a sharp fire of a nice gold colour, serve with a little gravy in the dish.

Soyer's gravy is essentially the same brown stock that had already formed the basis of the soup and the Reform sauce. In the end, I didn't bother with it, as the quail were juicy enough without.

Wrapping in vine leaves and bacon is the traditional French way with quail, whether roasted or grilled. I found the same recipe in Beauvilliers, whose book appeared in 1815, and in every other French cookbook I consulted up to and including *Memories of Gascony* by Pierre Koffmann, which appeared in 1990. On the other hand, Eliza Acton, the best and most comprehensive English cookery writer in Soyer's day, does not mention quail at all. They are a southern bird, and this, with its vine leaves, is a southern recipe. It was therefore a doubly appropriate choice, since Soyer, with his restaurant, was introducing (or trying to introduce) a very French concept into England.

It was summer when we cooked this dish, and extremely—indeed, excessively—hot; so there could be no question of building a fire in order to roast the quails before it. Instead we grilled them over charcoal, a process as like traditional spit-roasting as the twenty-first century gets. Indeed, some grills are equipped with battery-powered spits. As ours does not boast this feature, we simply laid the birds in rows on the gridiron, which was set in its highest position, as far from the coals as possible. Even so, this was not really Soyer's "convenient distance"—our quail kept being enveloped in flames as the bacon fat dripped into the charcoal. Of course this would not happen if your birds were in front of the fire, as Soyer recommends, rather than above it. But if you grill them, this is one dish where a revolving spit would really be an advantage.

Since we wanted to serve recognizable birds rather than cinders, we gave them a little less than the prescribed twelve minutes. But despite their rather blackened appearance on the dish, the quail, beneath what remained of their wrappings, were perfectly cooked—tender, aromatic, the breasts just pink. The vine leaves and bacon had transmitted their flavors while protecting the birds from the flames, which of course is exactly what they were intended to do.

Soyer's mention of white hairs in his resignation letter had the double advantage of both being quite true and sounding an appropriate note of melodramatic hyperbole. It also, however, accurately reflected his apprehensive state of mind at this juncture. His fortieth birthday, never an insignificant event, occurred in February 1850; and this, in addition to the inevitable reflections attendant on the gateway to middle age, posed for Soyer a momentous psychological barrier. Both his elder brothers had died before reaching this age; and the previous year he himself had almost joined them, falling through the ice while skating on the lake in St. James's Park. He was rescued in the nick of time by one of the Royal Humane Society's lifeguards, but the experience was doubly disturbing coming at this particular juncture. (It prompted not only a ten-guinea donation to the Society, which made him a life governor, but also, according to Volant, stimulated his ever-alert powers of invention: He at once devised "a novel way of saving life during the skating season.") In addition, during his last months at the Club he had felt himself weakening and fancied himself in decline. The doctor recommended a course of gymnastics, and he at once had the necessary apparatus set up in his apartment, with miraculously strengthening effect: Within three months he was returned to good health. His friends noted that, from this time, he even began to grow a little corpulent. Volant attributes this to the exercise, but weight gain is hardly its usual effect. A more likely cause is drink, always an occupational hazard for a cook. He was imbibing serious quantities, a glass of champagne always on hand while he worked—a weakness that the strains of the next few years were not calculated to alleviate.

It was in 1850, just after Soyer had taken his leave of the Reform Club, that George Augustus Sala, later one of Britain's best-known men of letters, then a coming young man, first glimpsed him. Sala and his brother were visiting Hungerford Market, London's fish market. They were just about to leave when Sala's eye was caught by an improbable figure bargaining for lobsters.

> The stranger was a stoutish, tallish gentleman, a little past middle age, with closely cropped grey hair and a stubbly grey moustache; and, but for his more than peculiar costume, he might have been mistaken for the riding-master of a foreign circus, who had been originally in the army. He wore a kind of paletot of light camlet cloth, with voluminous lappels and deep cuffs of lavender watered silk; very baggy trousers, with a lavender stripe down the seams; very shiny boots, and quite as glossy a hat; his attire being completed by tightly fitting gloves, of the hue known in Paris as *beurre frais*—that is to say, light yellow. All this you might think was odd enough; but an extraordinary oddity was added to his appearance by the circumstance that every article of his attire, save, I suppose, his gloves and boots, was cut on what dressmakers call a "bias," or as he himself, when I came to know him well, used to designate as *à la zoug-zoug*.[1]

[1]Sala, *Things I Have Seen and People I Have Known,* vol. 1, p. 240.

He must, Sala reflected, have been the terror of his tailor and hatter.

This idiosyncratic personage evidently knew what to look for in a fish. He "took the lobsters one by one, critically scanned them, poised them in one hand after another to ascertain their weight, examined their claws, rapped them on their back, poked their sides, and offered terms for them in a mildly authoritative tone"—terms which were eventually accepted with surprising good grace considering the evident hard bargain that had been struck: The fishmonger evidently wished to remain on terms with an excellent client. When Sala wondered who this might be, his brother exclaimed, "Why, of all people on earth, who could that be but Soyer?" and introduced them. Thus Sala met the man with whom he would spend the best part of the following year.

When Soyer took his leave of the Reform Club, he had told Lord Marcus Hill that he had some "very advantageous and important" offers and plans for the future, about which he hoped to consult Lord Marcus in his capacity as an old friend. This was no exaggeration. There were offers of well-paid employment, which he rejected; there were plans for gastronomic tours of Paris; he catered a number of vast banquets, one of them a literary event in London in honor of the visiting French playwrights Halévy and Scribe, another in Exeter at which oxen were roasted over a specially constructed gas apparatus while the rain poured down in torrents.

One of these feasts, however, was especially significant. It was given in York in October 1850, by the Lord Mayor of that city, and its guest of honor was Prince Albert, the Prince Consort. On this occasion, the Lord Mayor of York was returning hospitality. Six months earlier, he, along with nearly two hundred others—mayors of provincial cities, foreign ambassadors, generals, bishops, masters of the city guilds, prime ministers past, present, and future, and many others, all resplendent in official attire—had been invited to a banquet by the Lord Mayor of London, whose purpose was to set in motion Prince Albert's plan to organize a great exhibition of the world's art and industry the following year in Hyde Park. Albert had also been that evening's guest of honor, and everyone had hoped that the occasion would make the Exhibition unstoppable. From five-thirty in the afternoon, onlookers gathered to watch the guests arrive; at six-fifteen, Albert walked down the long corridor of the Mansion House; at seven, dinner was served. It included turtle soup, a choice of six kinds of fish, lobster, mutton, pigeon, and raised ornamental pies. In hiring Soyer to prepare the return match, the Mayor of York both gave notice that city sophistication was not confined to the capital and acknowledged our hero as its supreme gastronomic performer.

Soyer, for his part, made the most of this highly prestigious occasion. The centerpiece was one of his most impressive exercises in extravagance—a confection of turtles and ortolans reputed to have cost one hundred guineas, and known thereafter as the Hundred Guinea Dish. What it tasted like is not reported—it does not exactly sound like a marriage made in heaven; but in this case the flavor was perhaps less important than the effect.

This York dinner was crucially important to the Exhibition's prospects. Plans were still not finalized; the anti-free-trade lobby in particular was bitterly opposed, and still hoped to prevail. The purpose of the evening's festivities was to rally opinion outside London, and finally set Albert's great project on its way. Unfortunately, etiquette prevented the prince from actually producing Her Majesty his wife; nevertheless, his own presence departed from normal usage sufficiently to underline the royal couple's enthusiasm for the project—hers as well as his. Traditionally, the monarchy never went out in this way to meet the people, but waited for the people to come to them; on this occasion, however, as he explained in his speech, he had "come . . . to [York], not at second-hand from the mansion of some neighbouring landed lord, but direct from the presence of the sovereign herself, prepared to express as from her own royal mouth the interest she feels in the trade and industry of all her people." The speech included not only this direct endorsement from the Queen herself but also a eulogy for the recently deceased Sir Robert Peel, who had been one of the Exhibition's staunchest supporters, and whose sudden death had emboldened its enemies. Albert's speech, capitalizing on the nation's grief for an honored statesman, proved the crucial turning point, triumphantly rallying the room—and, through enthusiastic press reports, the nation—to his point of view.

Many of the Exhibition's committee members were also members of the Reform Club; as a result, Soyer had long been *au fait* with the plans for its staging. Indeed, he had already put forward his own ideas for it. In March 1850, while he was still working in Pall Mall, the Building Committee, which included his old friend Charles Barry, called for designs for the Exhibition building. There were 255 entries; all were considered, all rejected, and almost all are now, sadly, lost, including Soyer's, submitted from the Reform Club. But although he, like everyone else, was unsuccessful on this occasion (Paxton's Crystal Palace, the latest thing in prefabricated technology, was conceived and commissioned in a rushed two weeks some time after the competition had officially closed), the

Great Exhibition, one way or another, would nevertheless take up the next two years of his life.

This was by no means the first great international exhibition—Paris had staged one as recently as 1844. But it was the first to benefit from the railway age with all its revolutionary new travel possibilities. Until the big expansion of railway building that took place in the late 1840s, long journeys took days and cost hundreds of pounds. Now for the first time ordinary people might travel from Edinburgh to London in twelve hours and still be left with money in the bank. The result was a whole new way of seeing the world, not just physically but psychologically; and the Exhibition, which gave everyone a reason for traveling and to which almost everyone traveled, came to symbolize that change. Groups of people banded together to charter special trains; private tour operators such as Thomas Cook arranged deals by which parties, having traveled at discount rates, would be met and shepherded through the capital by Mr. Cook or his son, who guaranteed to return them to the appropriate station in time to catch the last train back; the railways offered their own deals, for, having cut their prices, they were anxious to make sure that not a seat was left unfilled. More than six million people—almost one in three of the British population—visited the Exhibition during its five and a half months' run.

Numbers like this were outside anyone's experience: No one in their wildest dreams could have anticipated such a thing. However, that the influx of visitors would be unprecedentedly large was clear from the outset. And once in London, these visitors would have to be catered for. They would need to be sustained bodily as well as amused: beds, food, lavatories must all be provided. The Exhibition's "monkey closets," designed by sanitary engineer George Jennings, where a penny bought relief in the comfort of privacy, were used by over 827,000 people—hence the phrase "to spend a penny."[2] Cheap dormitory accommodation was arranged for those who might need it, though most people preferred to lodge with private families, who happily cashed in on the fun by offering bed and breakfast. As for eating, the Exhibition's commissioners consulted Dr. John Lindley of the Horticultural Society, whose annual shows in Chiswick provided the only previous experience of mass catering on this scale. He had at first thought cold meat, cold chicken, and wine would be the most suitable provisions to offer. However, this had proved altogether too delicious, with the result that "many of our visitors thought more of eating and drinking than of the objects at the exhibition, and that the garden was converted into an eating-house, with just such consequences as might have been anticipated from the presence of wine, etc." Therefore, "We do not now suffer any meat or wine or spirituous liquors to pass our gates, and the consequence has been that the serious inconveniences formerly felt have disappeared . . . The articles usually to be found in a confectioner's shop—liqueurs, etc., excepted—are all that can be required."[3]

The commissioners took Lindley's point. They did not want their Exhibition upstaged by mere victuals, nor disgraced by unseemly behavior. Any refreshments, they decided, must be strictly teetotal. There would be three eating rooms: a tearoom, serving ices, pastries, sandwiches, fruit, tea, coffee, cocoa, lemonade, seltzer, and soda water, and two other rooms selling the same drinks plus

[2]Leapman, *The World for a Shilling,* pp. 94–5.
[3]Leapman, *The World for a Shilling,* p. 90.

ginger beer and spruce beer, along with bread, butter, and cheese. Free drinking water would also be supplied.

When tenders were invited for the catering contract, Soyer, with his matchless experience of mass catering at all levels, was foremost among those approached by the commissioners. However, to the astonishment of his friends, he declined to bid. The commissioners let him know that, if it would make a difference, they would be prepared to let him sell single glasses of wine with a meal: He was still not interested. In the event the contract was won, for a tender of £5,500, by a Swiss jeweler and soda-water manufacturer named Jacob Schweppe, whose subsequent career and still-resonant name go to show what a good thing Soyer turned down. Schweppe's eatables were not much admired—"dry" and "meager" were the adjectives most often used—but his beverages, including Schweppes soda water at sixpence a bottle, evidently passed muster. Doubtless they compared favorably with London water in those cloacally challenged days—in *Punch*'s words, "the Committee must have forgotten [when it specified free water for all] that whoever can produce in London a glass of water fit to drink, will contribute the rarest and most universally useful article in the whole Exhibition."

Soyer's lack of interest in the official catering contract did not mean he had no interest in feeding the Exhibition's visitors. On the contrary, this prospect interested him very much indeed—so much so that he was already immersed in a scheme of his own, very different from anything the commissioners had in mind. On Christmas Day 1850, the month before the refreshments concession came up for tender, he had signed the lease on a large house just opposite the site of the Crystal Palace, where he proposed to set up his own establishment in direct competition with whatever Mr. Schweppe might offer.

Gore House, the venue he had taken, was perhaps the best-known house in Kensington. It was a long, graceful building in white stucco set amid gardens full of fruit trees, roses, and shady walks. Until recently it had belonged to Lady Blessington, a famous hostess, beauty, authoress (she published, among other works, *The Conversation of Lord Byron*), journalist, and wit. Her parties were legendary. Everyone attended them, from Lord Melbourne to Thomas Moore and the future Napoleon III of France. However, her income was only £1,000 a year—a substantial sum, but not enough to sustain her lifestyle and that of her son-in-law and lover, the foppish Comte d'Orsay. In the end their debts were such that they were forced to flee the country. All their possessions were auctioned off, and the house let to Soyer, initially for six months, at £100 a year. In this idyllic setting he proposed to open a restaurant, "Soyer's Symposium of All Nations."

Soyer's plans for the Gore House venture were, to say the least, expansive. A Reform Club friend had advised him that simply serving the best food and wine in London would ensure commercial success, but this was altogether too boring for the newly independent Alexis. He had other notions, and they would require a very large initial investment. "Many thousands of pounds" were spent on Gore House, Sala recalled; and although Soyer had substantial savings, he could never have financed it alone. His backer was a Liverpool businessman named Joseph Feeny, who had been urging him to set up a high-class restaurant in the City of London—a proposition Soyer resisted because in his view all the potential clientele would already belong to one or another of the London clubs, which provided an exactly equivalent service. The Symposium was aimed at a much wider public, in whom Soyer hoped to instill the notion of good food as a recognized pleasure.

After signing the lease, he engaged three firms of builders and a firm of landscapers. Across the road, Paxton's Crystal Palace was rising at record speed from what had been the lawns of Hyde Park, and already attracting large numbers of tourists. Paxton's builders, Messrs. Fox and Henderson, were also one of the firms working on the Symposium; and Sala, to his delight, was thus able to wangle one of the coveted tickets that permitted entry to the Exhibition's building works. For Soyer and Sala had, in Sala's words, "struck up an alliance." Sala "officiated as Soyer's general adviser and keeper of his correspondence"—i.e., acted, among other things, as his secretary—"accepting no regular salary, as did his regular employés; but taking from time to time a moderate honorarium from an always open-handed but sometimes necessitous artist."[4]

Once the Symposium's makeover was under way (the builders, rather unrealistically, were sworn to the utmost secrecy), Soyer set off on a three-month tour to promote his stove. By the time he returned in March, the basic construction was done. He moved in, along with Feeny and Sala, and would stay there for the rest of the year. The 1851 census shows that on March 30, in the hamlet of Knightsbridge, Gore House contained "Alexis Soyer of Soyer's Universal Symposium, Joseph Feeny, Partner with Mr Soyer," two domestic servants, Charlotte Wildman and Emily Service, and "George Sala, visitor, artist."

Kensington, then only recently built up along the Park, and then

[4]Sala, *The Life and Adventures of George Augustus Sala,* p. 293.

as now the preserve of the well-heeled, was not at all pleased to find itself the focus of all this activity. Indeed, Kensington hated the very idea of the coming celebrations. Until now, one of its principal attractions had been the fact that there was nothing in the neighborhood to draw people from elsewhere in town. You would come there only if you lived there or had business with someone who did; and only the right sort of people lived in Kensington. The Exhibition would change all that, and Kensingtonians dreaded it. For them 1848, the year of European revolution, was still a painfully recent memory. It was true that the Chartists, who carried Revolution's banner in England, had come to nothing, their great meeting (against which the universal Lord Wellington had been recalled from retirement to protect London) washed out by heavy rain. Nevertheless, there had been a great many of them; and now, only three years later, a new influx of the working class threatened. Lord Brougham spoke for many when he voiced fears of being overrun by "socialists and men of the red colour." A petition of protest, signed by nearly every resident of Knightsbridge and Kensington Gore, was presented to Parliament in an attempt to divert the Exhibition away from Hyde Park. However, it failed; and when the Commissioners announced that after May 22 admission would cost only one shilling, Kensingtonians threw up their metaphorical hands. On July 1, the London Season ended and the aristocracy traditionally left for the country: They had hoped the price of entry might be kept at five shillings until then. Now they would have to sit out May and June in a London overrun with undesirables. *The Times,* which had begun by supporting the Exhibition and had enthusiastically reported Albert's speech at York, now predicted that "Hyde Park and . . . the whole of Kensington Gardens will be turned into the bivouac of all the vagabonds of London as long as the Exhibition shall continue. The annoyance inflicted on the neighbourhood would be indescribable."[5]

Kensington's forebodings can only have been exacerbated by the goings-on at Gore House. For if the Exhibition's official refreshments prudently eschewed wine in the interests of decency and composure, Soyer's establishment promised no such restraint. So grandiose were his plans that they overspilled even Gore House's generous grounds: He had to rent additional land from a neighbor, George Rummey, at £35 a year. And that was just the beginning. When neighbors and passersby peeked through gaps in the "close-boarded seven-foot fence" that his lease required Soyer to erect around the property, what did they see? Where once only the very best people had wandered, vulgarity incarnate! Gore House's lessor, a lawyer named John Aldridge, wary of Soyer's overconvivial propensities, inserted a clause in the lease forbidding "the said Alexis Soyer his executors his assigns his administrators" from "hav[ing] or hold[ing] or permit[ting] or suffer[ing] to be had . . . in at or upon the premises hereby demised or any part thereof any Balls or Concerts or any Fetes Fireworks or Exhibitions of any nature or kind whatsoever and shall not carry on or permit or suffer to be carried on in or upon the said messuage and premises hereby demised or any part thereof any trade or business whatsoever other than and except that of an Hotel or Restaurant or both but shall and will conduct the same in an orderly and proper manner." That seemed watertight enough. Soyer signed it, along with the rest of the lease. It seems impossible, however, that he for one minute imagined adhering to it.

[5]Leapman, *The World for a Shilling,* pp. 47–9.

Soyer's Universal Symposium perhaps gives us an idea of what his lost scheme for the Exhibition itself might have comprised. For although it was first and foremost a restaurant, or rather many restaurants, it was also what would today be called a theme park. From the outside, it was comparatively tasteful. The garden wall on Kensington Gore remained much as before, save for a legend declaring its new identity: SOYER'S UNIVERSAL SYMPOSIUM. Once inside, however, you were in another world. You entered through the Vestibule de la Fille de l'Orage, where you experienced "what you are probably prepared for, but not in such a form—a "thundering reception" from M. Soyer." Immediately above your head, "looming in the glittering indistinctness of blue and silver," was a monstrous hand, clutching "the arrows of Jove— sinuous wreaths of bright forked, snaky lightning," and above the inner door, the words *Soyer's Symposium* depicted in flashes of

Soyer's Symposium—the discreet street frontage.

lightning. (The lightning flashes were, or so he claimed, contrived by a magic lantern specialist called Lillywhite, who was probably also responsible for the Symposium's other lighting effects.)[6] This set the tone for the rest of the building's marvels, which were so numerous that they required a whole book to explain them—*The Book of the Symposium, or, Soyer at Gore House,* written by Sala: a "catalogue raisonné, artistic, historic, topographic and picturesque." They included the Hall of Architectural Wonders, the Blessington Temple of the Muses, the Temple of Danae, or, the Shower of Gems, La Forêt Péruvienne, or, the Night of Stars, the Gallic Pavilion, or, Avenue des Amours, the Temple of Phoebus, the Bower of Ariadne . . . Perhaps the most spectacular was the Grotte des Neiges Eternelles, or Rocaille des Lueurs Boréales. "From all the fiery splendour of the Temple of Phoebus we find ourselves instantaneously transported to the North Pole," burbled Sala's guide. "Craggy masses of stalactite-like ice are hanging over us, threatening a momentary decadence, and glistening with the crystallised brilliancy of icicles. In a small cavery couches [*sic*] an arctic fox, making his bed on the ice, and burrowing, as it were, in the snow. Large mirrors—their edges artistically concealed by pendant icicles—enhance the effect." This was real ice, refreshed every morning—an effect not easy to maintain, especially in the heat of the summer.

Sala's own masterpiece was the Grand Staircase, which he had adorned with a panorama of figures mounted on exotic beasts. These were caricatures of celebrities, living and dead, from Pitt the

---

[6]For this information and much else relating to the Symposium, I am indebted to Frank Clement-Lorford.

Younger and Napoleon to Charles Dickens and Douglas Jerrold, editor of *Punch*. Soyer insisted that it be called "a Demisemitragimimicomigrotesquepanofunnisymposiorama," or "Such a getting up stairs to the Great Exhibition of 1851, painted in Fresco by Mr George Augustus Sala." "I groaned as I interpolated this hideous rubbish in my manuscript," Sala recollected, "but it was a case of Ancient Pistol and the leek. I wrote, and eke I swore."[7]

The more expensive meals were taken inside the house; more economical diners were seated in the Gigantic Encampment of All Nations, "a covered gallery 130 yards long," marveled *The Times,* "in which is a table reaching from one end to the other, and a tablecloth of commensurate dimensions." This tablecloth, 207 feet long, was, Soyer emphasized, of British manufacture. Elsewhere patrons could enjoy demonstrations of Magic Cookery, on Soyer's magic stove, marble statues and fountains, bacchanalian vases, emerald pyramids of morning dew . . . And from twelve until two they might view the Symposium Kitchen, "in which no less than 600 Joints can be cooked with ease in the course of a day."

From ten a.m. until two p.m these and other wonders were open to the public whether or not they intended to eat at the Symposium. Entry was one shilling; a season ticket cost one guinea, a double ticket a guinea and a half, a family ticket, admitting five, three guineas. These tickets would "admit to all parts of this monstre and unique Establishment, which is capable of providing Dinners and Refreshments of every description for five or six thousand persons daily, the charges for which will not preclude persons of

[7]Sala, *The Life and Adventures of George Augustus Sala,* p. 291.

every station from partaking of the hospitality of the *Maison Soyer*." After two the establishment closed to nondiners and the entry fee was taken as part payment for any meal eaten.

The Wonders of the Symposium.

*La Forêt Péruvienne;
or, the Night of Stars.*

*La Salle des Noces
de Danaë; or,
The Shower of Gems.*

La Chambre Ardante
d'Apollon; or,
The Temple of Phoebus.

The Grotte des Neiges
Eternelles; or,
The Rocaille des
Lueurs Boréales
(Aurora Borealis).

The Bower of Ariadne;
or, The Vintage Palazzo.

Soyer's progress afforded particular pleasure to his old friend Thackeray, who had been observing it in the Reform Club for many years, and now documented it gleefully in the pages of *Punch.* They were contemporaries, both at this time just forty, Thackeray's hair, like Soyer's, rapidly turning white. He had just become famous as the author of *Vanity Fair,* and was then engaged upon *Pendennis,* in which, of course, Soyer would figure as the comic French cook Alcide Mirobolant. Thackeray had for Soyer (records Sala) "the friendliest of feelings and genuine admiration to boot; since the mercurial Frenchman was something more than an excellent cook—that is to say, Alexis was a man of sound common sense, a practical organiser, a racy humorist and a constant sayer of good things." As for Soyer, he "almost worshipped" Thackeray.[8] "It is rumoured," *Punch* reported, with that mix of affection, humor, and patronage that characterized all Thackeray's portraits of Soyer,

> that active arrangements are in progress for the opening, on a grand scale, of a grand Baked Potato Can of all Nations, or Eel Pie and Kidney Pudding Symposium, under the immediate direction of BINKS, the renowned *chef* of cosmopolitan cookshopery. The Can has been fitted up, regardless of expense, from an original design furnished by the famous Rusti Khan, and dug up on the banks of the Thames, by one of the Coolies, or Coalies, of the neighbourhood. Each department of this elegant moveable Symposium will be got up in a style appropriate to its particular object. The salt will occupy a space arranged as a salt mine; and the potatoes will

[8]Sala, *Things I Have Seen and People I Have Known,* vol. 2, pp. 14–15.

appear in the celebrated jackets supplied by the masterly hand of nature.

On April 27, the press was invited to look around. "Gore House and the grounds attached to it, now in the possession of M. Soyer, of gastronomic celebrity, have undergone a perfect metamorphosis," reported *The Times*. It was particularly struck by the tremendously long tablecloth, and remarked that "preparations seem to have been made to furnish refreshments to all the nations of the earth." But although the Crystal Palace itself was miraculously ready to open, with all its exhibits, by the agreed date of May 1—"Dearest Albert's name is for ever immortalised," Queen Victoria contentedly wrote in her diary that evening—it was clear that the Symposium would take a little longer. During the first half of May, although it could be viewed by appointment, it did not yet provide meals. Sala, as Master of Ceremonies, happily displayed its marvels to visiting

Punch *meditates the logistics of laundering the Great Table-Cloth.*

celebrities; the acquaintances he struck up then were to stand him in excellent stead in the future. Indeed, he concluded that "my connection with the Symposium was, in the long run, productive of much more benefit to me than it was to its founder."[9]

The Symposium's gastronomic christening took place on May 9, when dinner was served to the Metropolitan Sanitary Association. This body, despite its unpromising title, included most of London's prominent citizens, including both Thackeray and his then friend Charles Dickens, who was to be one of the day's speakers. This was not as surprising as it might seem, for in the 1850s, sanitation—or the lack of it—was a problem no inhabitant of London, whether rich or poor, could possibly ignore. In 1876, *Building News* recalled how, years before, it had been suggested that the Thames Embankment should be converted into a boulevard, lined with "cafés, restaurants, little paradises, and pavilions," but that this proposal had been "denounced, as if there had been suggested another burning of St Paul's."[10] *Building News* contrasted this London stuffiness unfavorably with the gaiety of Paris; what it chose to forget was that such a suggestion, whatever its social pros and cons, would have been seriously impracticable. Cafés and little paradises are strictly summer entertainments, and the stench of untreated sewage made London's summer riverside anything but a resort of pleasure. The situation reached crisis point in 1858, when during an unusually warm summer what became known as the Great Stink made it necessary to hang sacking soaked in deodorizing chemicals in the windows of the House of Commons. Meanwhile,

---

[9]Sala, *Things I Have Seen and People I Have Known,* vol. 1, p. 293.
[10]Quoted in Olsen, *The Growth of Victorian London,* p. 107.

the Sanitary Association pondered what should be done—and ate dinners.

As the main house was still not quite ready, the dinner took place in the Baronial Hall, a pavilion roofed with what looked like spare parts from the Crystal Palace across the way—as was indeed the case, the builders being Paxton's own Messrs. Fox and Henderson (who constructed the Oxford Railway Station, which they were then also building, in the same way). It was adorned with "the late Madame Soyer's celebrated Pictures, and the complete Gallery of Eminent Characters by the Count d'Orsay, munificently presented to M. Soyer by J. Mitchell, Esq., of Bond Street." Thackeray, on first visiting it one Sunday morning in the company of *Punch*'s cartoonist Richard Doyle, remarked that it was not so much a baronial hall as a *Marquee:* A small joke, but everybody laughed. Its sides, like much

Inauguration of the Baronial Hall: the Grand Sanitary Dinner.
Notice the cast-iron and glass construction, echoing that of the
Crystal Palace across the way.

else in the Symposium, were hung with calico. "What, think you, are the decorations of the Palace?—Of calico!" marveled Thackeray in his *Punch* persona as the French tourist M. Gobemouche.

> Calico in the emblematic halls, Calico in the Pompadour boudoirs, Calico in the chamber of the Sun—Calico everywhere. Indeed, whither have not the English pushed their cottons—their commerce? Calico has been the baleful cause of their wealth, of their present triumphant condition, perhaps of their future downfall!
>
> "That is the Baronial Hall of All Nations," says a gentleman to me—a gentleman in a flowing robe and a singular cap, whom I had mistaken for a Chinese or an enchanter. "The hall is not open yet, but it will be inaugurated by the grand Sanitary dinner. There will be half-crown dinners for the commonalty, five shilling dinners for those of mediocre fortune, ten shilling dinners for gentlemen of fashion like Monsieur. Monsieur, I have the honour to salute you."— And he passes on to greet another group.
>
> I muse, I pause, I meditate. Where have I seen that face? Where noted that mien, that cap? Ah, I have it!—in the books devoted to gastronomic regeneration, on the flasks of sauce called Relish. This is not the Crystal Palace that I see— this is the rival wonder—yes, this is the Symposium of All Nations, and yonder man is Alexis Soyer!

The establishment was finally ready for the public the following week. On May 16, advertisements in every newspaper announced that

This Vatican of Gastronomy will be opened to the public TO-MORROW, the 17th instant, when dinners and refreshments of every description may be obtained at the following reasonable scale of prices:—Collation Anglo Française in the Encampment of all Nations, 2s 6d; dinners in the Baronial Hall, built by Messers. Fox & Henderson 5s; dinner à la Française in the Blessington Temple of the Muses; Danaë's abode; la Forêt Péruvienne, or the Night of Stars; the Temple of Phoebus; the Bower of Ariadne; the Grotto of Eternal Snow; the Hall of the Golden Lilies; 7s 6d.

On May 15, the day before the opening, there was a press lunch. It began with asparagus, progressed through red mullet and lamb with green peas, revived jaded palates with roast quails and ortolans, and culminated in "Miroton d'homard, Gelée à l'ambrosie, Asperges en branche, Pain d'orange, Croustade d'abricot, and Pâté de foie de volaille." Karl Marx attended as the representative of the *Neue Rheinische Zeitung;* his friend Engels noted, with some surprise, his name on the guest list, and hoped he had enjoyed the homards *à la Washington* and the *champagne frappé,* though he could not imagine how Soyer had found Marx's address. What Marx thought, neither he nor the *Neue Rheinische Zeitung* recorded. The *Morning Chronicle,* however, was bowled over. After the roast beef was placed upon the table "description became hopeless! Imagination might do something; but experience alone could convey an idea adequate to the occasion." Afterward, Soyer made a speech. *Punch* recorded his best line. "Why," asked M. Soyer, "why is this dinner the reverse of an omelette soufflée?" Everybody gave it up.

"Because," said the cook, "an omelette soufflée is puffed to be eaten; now the dinner is eaten to be puffed!"

For the first few weeks, Soyer was in heaven. The Symposium was all he had ever hoped it might be. It offered a choice of dishes such as the London public had never before known; there was wine for anyone that cared to order it; there was even soda water to compete with anything Mr. Schweppe over the way might provide. Everyone who was anyone, from Disraeli to Cerrito, came to see the fun—the guest book, Sala remarked, must have constituted an autograph hunter's paradise. Every day an ox was cooked in one of the roasting pits near the Encampment of All Nations; every night (despite the restrictions in the lease) there were fireworks; occasionally, there were even balloon rides (one of which, when the balloon burst, nearly did in George Sala). Jugglers, clowns, and troubadours mingled with the guests; more than a hundred pages in costumes of the proprietor's own unmistakable design waited upon the diners.

The Symposium's fame, along with that of its proprietor, spread even as far as Paris. Jean Lamain, the natural son Alexis had abandoned as a baby, chose the month of August 1851 to write to his father and renew acquaintance—surely no coincidence, nor attributable to a chance upwelling of filial feeling. After a lifetime of poverty—Jean was a locksmith and general mechanic—he must have hoped, not unreasonably, to share in his father's good fortune. Soyer, after an initial moment of hesitation and utter astonishment, invited his son to London, recognized him, and took the necessary legal steps to assure his rights of inheritance: In 1853, Jean adopted the name Soyer. Whether they met again, however, we do not know.

Finally, Soyer was his own man; finally, he was making his

mark upon his adopted city. London, post-Soyer, would be transformed into a second Paris, full of the *gaieté* that had hitherto been
so exclusively *parisienne*. He hoped, too, as time went on, to revive
the system that had served him so well at the Reform Club, establishing the Symposium as a college of domestic science where apprentices would pay for the privilege of helping in his kitchen.

But, however delightful, being his own master also held dan-
gers that he had not previously had to face. Until now, when things
went wrong, the Reform Club had always been there to pick up the
pieces. Its kitchens had been built to his design, but he had not had
to pay for them. When Emma died and he was incapacitated by
grief, his salary had continued. When the Irish soup kitchen had
taken longer than expected to set up, his position had been held
open. If a meal went wrong, if he offended someone, there was always tomorrow, and his friends on the committee to defend him.
His cookbooks, his gadgets, his bottled sauces, his apprentices' fees,
had been mere icing on this cake. Obviously, he wanted these enterprises to succeed, but if they failed it didn't really matter.

In these forgiving circumstances his impatience with tedious
detail, his desire always to move on and try something new rather
than follow up the project in hand, had not brought him down, or
even held him back. But now business realities could not be so easily escaped. For Soyer's dream was not working out as it should;
and this time there was no safety net between himself and reality. It
was his mess, and he would have to sort it out.

The first and main problem was a wildly overoptimistic business plan. The Symposium's finances, which included not just the
building works and decoration but hire of "butlery"—tables, chairs,
linens, silverware, china, and glass, as well as the cooking and wait-

ing staff—had been based on a projection of five thousand visitors a day. Unfortunately, the real figure was nearer one thousand. Soyer had assumed, quite reasonably, that people spending a day at the Exhibition, given a choice between Mr. Schweppe's miserable provisions and those of the famous Soyer, would take the opportunity to slip across the road for something to eat rather than risk their digestions in-house. Unfortunately, however, although the Exhibition was far too large to be covered in a single morning or afternoon, the rules governing admittance and readmittance discouraged any such popping out. The entrance fee did not buy you a day ticket. If you left, there was no going back unless you paid all over again. This naturally meant that far fewer people than Soyer had hoped crossed Kensington Gore to sample the Symposium's delights. They preferred to sit by the fountain with a picnic, or buy a sausage roll, however dried up, from Mr. Schweppe. And at one thousand customers a day, it was not possible for the Symposium to make a profit.

This was a fundamental miscalculation. But it was not the only problem. Another was Soyer himself. Just as the Symposium reflected his talents, so many of its difficulties were exacerbated by his weaknesses—his dazzlement with wealth and title, his slapdash habits, his inability to persevere with boring detail. If all had been going to plan in the numbers department, these deficiencies might not have mattered, or not so much. But all was not going to plan, and as a result, they became disproportionately significant.

If people were to be attracted in sufficient numbers, word of mouth was all-important; and since the rich were a small minority, the satisfaction of the not-so-rich was imperative. The trouble was that Soyer, though genuinely desiring to welcome all classes, took little personal interest in any but the best people. All his life he had deeply desired to be his employers' friend rather than their servant, and was now in a flutter of excitement at personally entertaining his erstwhile masters at his very own establishment. The result was a two-tier service. Everyone—or everyone who was anyone—could be sure of an excellent meal at the Symposium. You told Soyer when you would arrive and how many would be in your party, and you put yourself in his hands. He would oversee your dinner himself, and you would eat the best food in London. But such dinners were not cheap; and there was only one of Soyer. If he was occupied with the quality, he could not attend to the shilling diners in the Grand Encampment of All Nations. Responsibility for the cheaper meals therefore fell to others, and this lack of interest on the part of the establishment's moving spirit soon began to show. Service was unsatisfactory in the shilling dinner department; orders got muddled, the food took a long time to arrive, and was often cold when it came. Naturally, people began to grumble. Soyer's food was not, after all, as good as all that. The Symposium was not all it was cracked up to be. *The Art of Dining,* a British attempt at the *Almanach des Gourmands* published in 1852, expressed the general view: "Soyer . . . is a very clever man, of inventive genius and inexhaustible resource, but his execution is hardly on a par with his conception."[11]

Our hero, happily occupied with his aristocratic friends, tried to ignore the mounting difficulties. These trivia would sort themselves out. If worse came to worst, someone else could look after them—for instance, Volant, for Soyer's old ally and secretary was now the Sym-

[11]Hayward, *The Art of Dining.*

posium's manager. However, by the middle of June it was clear that things could not go on as they were. Feeny was discontented with the return on his investment; George Warriner, another old ally, now in charge of the Encampment of All Nations, complained about the staff, over whom he had no control, as they were hired in along with the rest of the butlery. Volant suggested a system in which each partner should concentrate on what he did best: Feeny would manage the finances, Soyer the cooking, and Volant the day-to-day running. However, Feeny decided he wanted no more of the Symposium. He had had enough, and withdrew.

At this point, things looked very black. Soyer had neither the financial resources nor the expertise to manage such an enormous enterprise single-handed. In despair he turned to an old friend, Alexander Symons. Symons had already helped him publish *The Gastronomic Regenerator* and *The Modern Housewife, or Ménagère,* and was also his partner in the Magic Stove. All these had produced an excellent return on the initial investment: Perhaps he hoped the Symposium might yet do likewise. He agreed to come in as manager, on condition Volant was relieved of his responsibilities.

For the next three months the Symposium kept going—just. There was another crisis in July. The butlery contract had been set up on a percentage basis: Soyer paid his supplier £1 for every hundred 2s. 6d. diners, £1 10s. for every hundred at 5s., £2 10s. for every hundred at 7s. 6d., and £3 for every hundred at 10s. 6d. But because of the shortfall in customers this percentage amounted to much less than had been expected, and the supplier threatened to remove his stock from the premises unless he was paid £100 a week for it. Symons agreed to this arrangement—"It couldn't do any harm," he said, "at least for a few weeks." And so things went on until September, when the supplier sent in a bill for £680. Soyer and Symons remarked that this was a very large sum, and murmured that a check would be forthcoming. Meanwhile, in October the Great Exhibition would close, and the crowds that now thronged Kensington would melt away.

Some new cat must evidently be pulled from the bag, and another of Soyer's friends, Louis Jullien, produced it. Jullien, a fellow member of London's French community, was then a well-known musician and composer; he is now remembered as the inventor of "promenade" concerts. He suggested that the Encampment of All Nations be replaced by a music hall, overseen by himself, in which, after dining, people would be able to enjoy the music and dance, as they did in Paris's *bals musettes*. Soyer, much taken by this idea, which doubtless recalled the jollities of his Parisian youth, at once applied to the Middlesex magistrates for an extension of his music license.

But with the end of the Exhibition things had changed—or rather, reverted to normality. The inhabitants of Kensington, having endured the invasion of hoi polloi, wanted their park back, along with their well-bred peace and quiet. They had put up with Soyer's festivities for five months; enough was enough. And Mr. Thomas Pownall, the chairman of the magistrates and (as it transpired) a confirmed temperance man, was, for his own reasons, wholly with them on this. During the summer of 1851, London had been pervaded by an uncharacteristic spirit of uncensorious pleasure. Mr. Pownall disliked this, but had been unable to do anything about it. Now, however, he decided to pay a surprise visit to the Symposium to see what sort of place it might be. Soyer's plans sounded unwholesome, and he wished to make quite sure things would not get out of hand.

What Mr. Pownall found, on the evening he visited, was more people than usual having rather a lot of fun. On that particular day a party of two hundred, up from the country to visit the Exhibition and led by their parson, had booked themselves in to the Symposium for the evening. While Soyer, as was his habit, entertained the quality indoors, the country party ate and drank their fill at the Encampment of All Nations. When the magistrate arrived they were enjoying themselves, as Volant described it, "over the entire premises—some drinking at the various bars, others skipping about to the bands of music; in fact taking as much pleasure as they could for the few hours they had to remain."[12] These, in addition to the four or five hundred other diners and strollers, made the place even noisier than usual, though in the Baronial Hall gastronomy continued undisturbed. Mr. Pownall, expecting the worst, found it, and was agreeably horrified. The parson's presence counted for nothing with him: Parson or no parson, such unconstrained conviviality—and in the presence of ladies!—confirmed all his views regarding the effect of the demon drink upon morality. Appalled, he reported that a near-riot had occurred, and that the Symposium was a "receptacle of the commonest description." On no account, given the orgies he had witnessed, should the Symposium's music license be extended.

Soyer, through his lawyers, at once signaled his intention to sue Pownall for defamation; and faced with a battery of the chef's influential friends, all affirming their experience of the Symposium to have been pleasant and orderly, Pownall eventually withdrew his charges. But the damage was done. There was no chance of a music

---

[12]Volant and Warren, *Memoirs of Alexis Soyer,* p. 233.

license now, and without it, the business could not continue. On October 11, the Great Exhibition opened to the public for the last time. Three days later, a notice was posted on the gate of Gore House announcing that all creditors should apply to Soyer's business office at 5 Charing Cross Road, where they would receive half what they were owed—the outstanding moneys to be paid once accounts were finalized.

It transpired that the Symposium had been a financial disaster. Although it had made £21,000, its outgoings had been even greater—to be precise, £28,000, leaving a deficit of £7,000: a huge sum. Soyer personally saw to it that everyone was paid off; he signed over all his royalties to Symons in an attempt to pay back what had been lost, and his company, A. Soyer and Co., which owned the Magic Stove, was taken over by a businessman named David Hart, who paid off the remaining creditors. Even so, the next year was darkened by a flurry of lawsuits, including a particularly black moment when his old friend Volant took him to court for an alleged £54 18s. owed. This suit was almost certainly directed at Symons, not Soyer—an attempt at revenge for Volant's summary demotion. Volant later apologized to Soyer, but it was too late: He had behaved unforgivably, and was never forgiven.

"Since the last time I had the pleasure of seeing you at the Symposium, I have had to endure the most dreadful and unpleasant experiences, all because of the unjust remarks of the magistrate Pownall," Soyer wrote to Lord Marcus Hill, "My Dear Protector," on December 29, 1851. "Finally, with perseverance and a great deal of philosophy, my affairs are almost paid up and in order. I now intend to make M. the Magistrate give us proof of what he said about my establishment; your friend Lady Vernon and other close friends often came to see me there in the evening; I am certain they never saw any thing *immoral* . . . p.s. Please accept this sample of my new Pâté à la Symposium and a bottle of my Courvoisier. Don't forget to slice the pâté."

The Symposium's crash left Soyer with just £100 to his name. In retrospect, it could never have succeeded. It was overblown, chaotically ill-organized, and (for anyone thinking beyond the end of the Exhibition) in the wrong place. When, twenty years later, London did finally acquire some proper restaurants, they were located where the crowds gathered, in the West End and at the big railway terminals. Nevertheless, although he naturally preferred to blame an unjust outside agency rather than be forced to admit his dream had quite simply failed, there can be no doubt that Soyer was right in thinking Pownall deeply biased in his judgment. The Symposium, with its public jollity and universal welcome, embodied everything the magistrate detested, both as a temperance man and as a representative of the upper classes. He wanted to shut it down, was looking for a pretext, and would probably have found one whatever the circumstances. The country party simply made his job easier.

So died England's first restaurant. Like quails in vine leaves, it was too southern a notion for these foggy shores. The Exhibition had been a one-off: London was not yet ready for a permanent institution that so promiscuously mixed all classes and both sexes while at the same time claiming to be respectable. A few years later, *Building News* reported the opening of a new and admirable establishment where the "well-appointed costume of the tables [is] almost appetite-provoking . . . Now that the example has been set it will, perhaps, be followed by similar establishments . . . where the stranger in London could get a dinner, without having no other alternative of choice than between the cook-shop eating-house, the mere chop and steak tavern, or such places as the Old and New Hummums in Covent Garden." However, this disturbingly democratic notion should not be pushed too far. "It occurs to us to ask if it would not in some instances very well answer to ingraft the club-house system upon a public dining establishment; one floor being appropriated exclusively to subscribers, who would have their own coffee-room, reading-room, &c., to which strangers would not be admitted."[13]

Financially speaking, the Great Exhibition did rather better than the Symposium. When all its debts were discharged, the Commissioners found themselves £186,000 in profit. And it had already been decided what would be done with the money. For £336,000— the extra £150,000 contributed by the government—they bought Gore House, its grounds, and the adjoining plant nursery, upon which would be built the complex of institutions that now line Exhibition Road. They include the Victoria and Albert Museum, the Science Museum, the Natural History Museum, Imperial College, and the Royal Geographical Society. And on the site of the Symposium itself, in place of Soyer's grottoes and boudoirs and projected dance hall, we now enjoy promenade concerts *à la Jullien* in the Albert Hall.

[13]Olsen, *The Growth of Victorian London,* pp. 103–4.

7

Entremets: Turkish Delights

In 1851, when the Symposium crashed, Soyer was forty-two. For more than a decade he had been one of London's best-known figures. But his name would mean little today were it not for what turned out to be virtually the final act of his dramatic life: his sortie to the Crimean War.

For Britons, safe in their sea-secured island, war (other than the civil variety) generally happened elsewhere. When, in the spring of 1854, fighting began in a place called the Crimea, few had heard of it and fewer still knew where it was. Enlightenment, however, was about to set in. Just a decade earlier, on May 24, 1844, Samuel Morse had transmitted the first telegraphic message, and the result was a shrunk world. When William Howard Russell used the new technology to transmit dispatches direct from the battlefront to *The Times,* his readers discovered, for the first time, war's true horrors. And enemy bullets were by no means the worst of them. Men were frozen in their tents, Russell reported as winter set in that November. Disease was rampant, and there were regimental hospitals at the front "where the sick men in wet marquees had only one blanket to lie upon." So many had died since the start of the campaign that there remained scarcely a face Russell recognized from the army he had set out with six months before.

The main British army hospital, at Scutari on the other side of the Black Sea, was little better than the field hospitals. Despite all Florence Nightingale's tireless efforts, it was disgustingly unhygienic and terribly overcrowded, and the food barely edible. "We have not seen a drop of milk," reported the *Illustrated London News*'s correspondent in January 1855, "and the bread is extremely sour, the butter most filthy. It is Irish butter in a state of decomposition; and the meat is more like moist leather than food. Potatoes we are waiting for till they arrive from France."

Most people, reading this, could feel only helpless misery and anger. Soyer, however, at once realized that he was uniquely qualified to help. He offered his services forthwith, leaving England for Constantinople the following month, and not returning until 1857. This course, our entremets or dessert, is taken from the invalid diet recipes he devised for Scutari.

Turkey is of course famous for its delicious sweetmeats, and Soyer, who developed a great admiration for Turkish food, doubtless did them full justice. However, the honey-based Turkish confections—baklava, lokoum, and the rest—are too dense and rich for invalid stomachs. The sweet dishes he cooked for Miss Nightingale's patients are quite another matter. They are light and delicate, though not without their touches of luxury: port, sherry, and marsala are frequent ingredients. The Victorians were great believers in the invigorating properties of fortified wine, which formed part of the official medical supplies both at Scutari and at the front. Indeed, Soyer's account of his Crimean excursion positively swims in alcohol. Not a day seems to have passed in total sobriety; and this is hardly a surprise. How could the men possibly have got through those dreadful months without the blurring effects of the champagne that accompanied officers' dinners or the generous rations of issue rum, or the rough wine and brandy served out to the French army by its valiant *vivandières?*

Looking through Soyer's list of Scutari recipes, my eye was particularly caught by the wine-flavored jellies. They sounded delicious, reviving fond memories of a port wine jelly that used to be served at Miller's Restaurant on King's Parade in Cambridge. I therefore selected one for our dessert, to the delight of my sampling panel, whose passion for jelly I rarely gratify.

Soyer's jellies did not, needless to say, come red- or green-flavored in packets. They were made from either sago or calf's-feet, neither especially inviting to the twenty-first-century imagination. The horrid frogspawn texture of school sago puddings remains a particularly clear and loathsome memory. I knew I'd never manage to swallow a single spoonful of that. So I chose the feet.

Jelly Stock

Made from calf's feet, requires to be made the day previous to being used, requiring to be very hard to extract the fat. Take two calf's-feet, cut them up and boil in three quarts of water; as soon as it boils remove it to the corner of the fire, and simmer for five hours, keeping it skimmed, pass through a hair sieve into a basin, and let it remain until quite hard, then remove the oil and fat, and wipe the top dry.

What could be more nourishing than calf's-foot jelly? And what, nowadays, more utterly unheard-of? Even I can hardly believe that there was a time when I used quite frequently to prepare this culinary fossil—it felt, even then, as though I was probably the last living person to do so. My jelly (a recipe handed down from a Russian grandmother) was savory not sweet, highly seasoned, and made with carrots and onions and parsley. You blanched the feet, threw away the water and scum, then simmered them in clean water with the vegetables and seasonings until the meat fell away from the bones, which you took out, leaving the rest to set in a bowl. The result was a very firm jelly, eaten spread with mustard. Delicious; though it was almost better hot, when it made an ever-so-slightly gelatinous, strong-tasting soup.

Even then it wasn't easy to find the necessary feet, and nowadays, as supermarkets replace high-street butchers, it would doubtless be even harder. I used to get mine at Randall and Aubin in Brewer Street, Soho, but they years ago abandoned their French butchery and replaced it with an oyster bar. Doubtless the wonderful Mr. Portwine, at whose Seven Dials establishment I found those excellent mutton chops, could have got me some, but tragically his shop closed while I was writing this book—to be precise, between the mutton cutlets and the famine soup. I was bracing myself for a visit to Smithfield when I noticed Soyer's saving sentence:

> *Note.*—I find that the preparation now manufactured by Messrs. Crosse and Blackwell, of Soho Square, London, is preferable to any other, being also cheaper than boiling calf's feet on purpose, which takes a very long time, and is more difficult to make.

Clever old C&B! The Victorian housewife, toiling in her gadget-less home, needed convenience foods even more than we do—and Mr. Crosse and Mr. Blackwell provided them, making a fortune in the process. Of course, Soyer was here up to his old trick of using his books to puff a business partner: It was Crosse and Blackwell who marketed Soyer's Patent Relishes. He had, by contract, to supply new recipes regularly and keep them provided with up-to-date portraits to adorn the bottles; they would do the rest (and make the money). Unfortunately, since Crosse and Blackwell's was long ago swallowed by Nestlé, I could no longer buy their gelatine. Still, gelatine is gelatine; the crucial thing is that even then it came ready-prepared, making all that boiling and straining and wiping, even for Soyer's generation, a thing of the past.

> Put in a proper-sized stewpan 2¼oz. of calf's-foot gelatine, 4oz. of white sugar, 4 whites of eggs and shells, the peel of a

lemon, the juice of three middle-sized lemons, half a pint of Marsala wine; beat all well together with the egg beater for a few minutes, then add 4½ pints of cold water; set it on a slow fire, and keep whipping till boiling. Set it on the corner of the stove, partly covered with the lid, upon which you place a few pieces of burning charcoal; let it simmer gently for ten minutes, and strain it through a jelly-bag. It is then ready to put in the ice or some cool place. Sherry will do if Marsala is not at hand.

I didn't bother with the egg whites and shells, as these are purely a clarifying agent, and no longer necessary with today's high-tech gelatine. Otherwise I simply followed the recipe, with the important difference that powdered gelatine, which was what I used, is not added first but is sprinkled onto the hot liquid, which must not subsequently boil.

I did rather wonder, when pouring in the water, whether Soyer's pen (or his secretary's) might not have slipped. Four and a half pints for a quarter-pound of sugar and a half-pint of Marsala? The mixture did indeed taste distressingly weak: With memories of that port wine jelly in mind, it was all I could do not to tip the Marsala bottle and add a bit more sugar. But no: When I checked other similar recipes, this appeared to be the standard dilution. And of course this dish was not intended for normal dinner tables. This is invalid food: It speaks of an age before antibiotics, when illnesses ran their course and survival was as often as not a matter of chance. In the absence of effective drugs, recovery was a slow business; convalescent patients, in their weakened state, needed bland, nourishing food that could be digested by the most delicate stomachs.

Soyer even gives instructions for that Dickensian concoction toast-and-water, which is exactly what you might imagine—a large piece of toast steeped in boiling water and strained; the water is then drunk neat or may be flavored in a variety of ways—with a piece of baked apple, with figs, raisins or plums, or even a little ginger. This valetudinarian cuisine is the context in which our jelly, light but nourishing, should be judged; and bearing this in mind, it is clear that instant gelatine, though better for the housewife, was far less good for the invalid. Messrs. Crosse and Blackwell were interested in the end result, not the protein, and their proprietary product, however convenient, must have been far less nutritious than the original feet jelly.

After a couple of hours in the fridge (Soyer would have used an insulated wooden icebox), I had a clear brown jelly. It was not particularly sweet; we could taste the lemon quite distinctly, but the Marsala was so dilute that nobody could detect any trace of it other than the brown color, though it must of course have contributed to the overall effect. The flavor that did emerge, everyone agreed, was tea: It was like eating jellied iced tea. And, like iced tea, it was genuinely refreshing. In the heat of a Turkish summer this dish would be wonderfully cooling, far more so than if it had been strongly flavored and too sweet.

The value of these delicate dishes transcended the merely nutritive. Amid the stench and overcrowding of that ghastly war, refined morsels like a weak wine jelly not only relieved distressed stomachs but came as a welcome reminder that civilization still existed, even in hellholes like Scutari and Balaklava. Many witnesses noted the disproportionate comfort the mere sound of a woman's voice afforded sick and wounded men, marooned far from home and yearning for their wives and mothers. Soyer's Marsala jelly was the culinary equivalent of this soothing sound.

Soyer's departure for the Crimea was the logical continuation of a career that, ever since 1847, had taken an unusually radical direction. Most upper servants, like Ude, or Charles Pierce, his old friend from Aston Hall days—now *maître d'hôtel* at the Russian Embassy in London—drew a kind of reflected prestige from the exalted households in which they worked, and were in many respects even more snobbish than their masters. But Soyer had always found service demeaning, however much he might enjoy the culinary and social opportunities it afforded. Paradoxically, given that his attitude to the rich and powerful was little short of fawning, his social views—expressed, as always, through his cooking—were singularly democratic. He felt (as we have seen) that even soup kitchens should dispense reasonable food in decent surroundings, while the Symposium had been, among other things, an attempt to put into practice the egalitarian principle that good food should not be the sole preserve of the moneyed classes.

When it collapsed, he seems, perhaps unsurprisingly, to have suffered from something as near depression as was possible in so buoyant a character. It is certainly hard, otherwise, to account for the one truly dishonest act of his life—the publication in 1853, under his own name, of a history of cooking in the classical world, *The Pantropheon*. This was in fact the work of a M. Duhart-Fauvet: Soyer had merely translated it. But although Duhart-Fauvet's pride undoubtedly suffered, little if any money was misappropriated: The public, it seemed, had little interest in gastronomic history, and the book did not sell.

The two may have met during one of Soyer's frequent visits to France, where he now spent a considerable amount of time, conducting gastronomic tours, taking the opportunity to renew his friendship with Fanny Cerrito, and stocking up on luxuries such as foie gras which he sold on to private clients in London. He also had a line in devising and preparing grand dinner parties for the rich; but word got around that his services, these days, cost even more than appeared on the bill. He was drinking heavily, and employers were required not only to pay his fee but also to provide large quantities of champagne to lubricate the cooking.

Still, they could afford it; and so, too, thought Soyer. He renewed his interest in soup kitchens, concerning himself in particular with one at Ham Yard, off the Haymarket. To this he brought his Dublin-acquired expertise, to such effect that the nearby Leicester Square soup kitchen also requested his services.

Soyer's soup kitchens were far from being the usual gloomy affairs. He saw no reason why charity should *ipso facto* be miserable; the poor might be unfortunate, but that did not make them inferior, and they were as entitled to enjoyment as the next person. He persuaded his musician friend Jullien to attend from time to time with his band, and entertain the customers with the waltzes and polkas for which he was famous. And at Christmas 1852, he organized and participated in a grand fund-raising ball at Willis's Rooms, from whose proceeds he organized a sumptuous banquet for the poor at Ham Yard. It included:

9000lb. of roast and baked meat

178 beef pies, 50 hare pies, 60 rabbit pies, 50 pork and mutton pies, each weighing from 10 to 30lb., and one, the "monster pie" weighing 60lb.

Twenty roast geese

3300lb. of potatoes

5000 pints of porter

5000lb. of plum pudding

50 cakes

6000 half-quartern loaves

One cask of biscuits

18 bushels of Spanish nuts

18 bushels of chestnuts

6 boxes of oranges

3000 two-ounce packets of tea

3000 three-ounce packets of coffee

5000 half-pounds of sugar

and

One whole ox, roasted by gas—supplied by the Western Gas Company, under the gratuitous superintendence of Mr Inspector Davies of that establishment.

It is safe to say that such a feast was unique in the experience of Ham Yard's habitués.

This concern to ensure that the poor ate, if not as well as the rich, at least as well as possible, he now extended to cookbooks. *The Gastronomic Regenerator* was only one of many recipe collections written by grand chefs and aimed at the rich; *The Modern Housewife, or Ménagère,* though concerned with economy, was strictly middle-class in tone. And this, hitherto, had been the full extent of the cookbook market. The poor, even if they could read, were assumed to have neither the money nor the equipment to cook properly, and their hard lives would anyway leave them with neither the time nor the energy to do so.

But Soyer came from another tradition, where everyone, even the poor, not only cooked but took an interest in food; and just as he had tried to subvert the middle-class appropriation of eating out with the Symposium, so now he turned his attention to home cooking. His new compendium of recipes for the poor, *Soyer's Shilling Cookery for the People,* assumed a small and simple kitchen, and relatively few utensils: a gridiron, a frying pan, an iron pot, and a new invention, Soyer's "baking-stewing pan," with a tight-fitting lid that would retain all the aroma of whatever was cooking, ingeniously fitted with a lock and key "to prevent any person raising the lid while cooking, as by so doing the best part of the flavour would immediately escape."[1] The book contained recipes divided generically in the usual manner—soups, then fish, etc.—and, within those categories, by the cooking utensil used: Thus the fish section is divided into "fish on gridiron" (beginning not with "the king of the ocean" but with the plain red herring), "fish boiled in pot, pan or stewpan," "fish in tin pan in the oven" and "fish in frying pan."

The book was published in 1854, and was an instant and over-

---

[1] *Soyer's Shilling Cookery for the People,* p. 69.

whelming success. On the day of publication, the entire 10,000 print run sold out; within four months it had sold 185,000, and by the time it had been out a year, a quarter of a million. This time Soyer had underwritten publication himself, without a partner; so once again, he found himself in the money.

He still led as convivial a life as ever, and it was while waiting for friends over a late post-theater supper at the Albion Hotel, Russell Street, one January evening in 1855, that he read the fateful dispatch from the Crimea.

The Crimean War had begun the previous March. The combatants were on the one side Russia, and on the other Britain, France, and Turkey. All had their own reasons for war. Britain feared that if Russia gained a foothold on the Black Sea coast she might use it to dominate Constantinople and the entry to the Mediterranean; France wanted to break down the continental alliance that had paralyzed her for half a century; Turkey feared Russian encroachment onto the borders of her empire. The actual fighting began with a quarrel between Russian Orthodox monks and French Catholics over precedence at the holy places in Jerusalem and Nazareth. Tempers frayed, violence resulted, and lives were lost. Tsar Nicholas I of Russia demanded the right to protect the Christian shrines in the Holy Land, and to back up his claims moved troops into Wallachia and Moldavia, now part of Romania, then belonging to the Ottoman Turkish empire. His fleet went on to destroy a Turkish flotilla off Sinope in the Black Sea. British newspapers reported that the Russians had fired at Turkish wounded in the water, and the march to war began.

To start with, there was great public support for this war: It was "popular beyond belief," Queen Victoria reported to her uncle the

King of the Belgians. Not, however, for long. The Crimean campaign was a nightmare from the moment the troops embarked on their old-fashioned sailing ships, which so unnecessarily prolonged the voyage out, and in which so many cavalry horses died as the journey dragged on.

Tactically, the war was disastrous. The British army had seen no action since 1815; the only officers under sixty who had any actual military experience had acquired it serving in India, an unfashionable posting that effectively debarred them from the highest command. And the inadequacy of this command was soon only too plain. Its strategy was lamentable, both actively, as in the disastrous charge of the Light Brigade under the Russian guns at Balaklava, and passively, as when the army failed to capitalize upon its extraordinary victory at the Battle of the Alma to take Sebastopol, thus condemning the troops to an extra eighteen months' unnecessary suffering.

The conditions in which all this took place could hardly have been worse. From the moment the army landed it was decimated by epidemic disease and undermined by extreme weather. Dysentery and cholera were rife; great heat was followed by torrential rain; an unprecedented hurricane in November 1854 sank supply ships in Balaklava harbor, destroyed the encampments, and carried away everyone's clothes and possessions. Such men as remained on their feet were exhausted before a blow had been struck. "If we were beginning with healthy men, I think we could get on capitally," wrote George Frederick Dallas, a young lieutenant of infantry, during a welcome spell of fine weather. "As it is the numbers in hospital don't decrease, and the poor fellows have not stamina to get well . . . We have actually buried, since we came into the country, 432! Conceive that there are about as many more in Hospital, here and at Scutari, many of whom will probably never get home. I am always afraid to ask after any soldier, whom I perhaps have not seen for a day or two."[2]

By the time the winter of 1854–55 set in, with its alternate horrors of freezing snow and deep mud, things were looking desperate.

"At the commencement of 1855," W. H. Russell reported,

> We had no means of getting up the huts—all our army could do was to feed itself. Captain Keane, R. E., was in charge of 4000 tons of wood for hutting, but he could not get anyone to take charge of it, or unload it out of the ships. Each hut weighed more than two tons. As to the "warm clothing," the very words immediately suggest to us all some extraordinary fatality. Some went down with the ill-fated and ill-treated "Prince" [lost in the hurricane with all hands], some of it was lost, and we heard that a ship with clothing for the officers had been burnt off Constantinople; that some of it had been saturated with water; and I had an opportunity of seeing several lighters full of warm greatcoats, &c., for the men, lying a whole day in the harbour of Balaklava beneath a determined fall of rain and snow . . . At the close of the year there were 3500 sick in the British camp before Sebastopol, and it was not too much to say that their illness had, for the most part, been caused by hard work in bad weather, and by exposure to wet without any adequate protection. Think of a tent

[2]Mawson, *Eyewitness in the Crimea: The Crimean War Letters (1854–1856) of Lt. Cl. George Frederick Dallas,* p. 98 (March 11, 1855).

pitched, as it were, at the bottom of a marsh, into which some twelve or fourteen miserable creatures, drenched to the skin, had to creep for shelter after twelve hours of vigil in a trench like a canal, and then reflect what state these poor fellows must have been in at the end of a night and a day spent in such *shelter,* huddled together without any change of clothing, and lying packed up as close as they could be stowed in saturated blankets. But why were they in tents? Where were the huts which had been sent out to them? They were on board ships in the harbour of Balaklava . . .

The situation at the main British army hospital, situated in a barracks at Scutari, a district of Constantinople on the Asiatic side of the Bosphorus, was no better. The men, Mary Seacole remarked, "had a very serious objection to going into hospital for any but urgent reasons"[3]—and rightly so: They were almost always better off in their own tents, however miserable. In contrast to the French hospital at Pera, where every patient had a proper bed, clean sheets and towels, and warm clothes, the British in Scutari lay close-packed on mattresses on the floor, often naked under a greatcoat. The place stank; the main water supply was for weeks contaminated by a dead horse; the barracks washhouse had been turned into a store, so that it was almost impossible to keep up a supply of clean linen. "I am really cook, housekeeper, scavenger, (I go about making the orderlies empty tubs) washerwoman, general dealer, store keeper—the Purveyor is supposed to do all this, but it is physically impossible," wrote Florence Nightingale in a private letter to

[3]Seacole, *Wonderful Adventures of Mrs Seacole in Many Lands,* p. 166.

her friend the Secretary for War, Sidney Herbert. "And the filth, and the disorder, and the neglect let those describe who saw it when we first came." Scutari's mortality rate at the beginning of 1855, despite the best exertions of Miss Nightingale and her corps of nurses, was 47.5 percent of cases treated.

"Medical stores . . . have been sent out in profusion, . . . by the ton weight," Mr. Herbert assured Miss Nightingale in October 1854. "15,000 pair of sheets; medicines, wine, arrowroot, in the same proportion . . ."[4] But they had not arrived. And even had they done so, there was no guarantee that Miss Nightingale would have been able to extract them from the purveyor, "an old man," as *The Times* described him, "upward of sixty years of age, who had probably been an excellent officer in his youth . . . with two inexperienced lads as assistants."[5] Russell in Balaklava complained of "a system of 'requisitions,' 'orders,' and 'memos,' which was enough to depress an army of scriveners." And Scutari was impeded by the same ineffective bureaucracy. To take an example from what would soon become Soyer's department, "The practice of drawing *raw* rations, as here seen, seems invented on purpose to waste the time of as many Orderlies as possible," wrote Miss Nightingale to Mr. Herbert in January 1855,

> *who stand at the Purveyor's office from 4 to 9 a.m. drawing the patients' breakfasts, from 10 to 12 drawing their dinners, and to make the Patients' meals as late as possible—because it is impossible to get the diets thus drawn, cooked before 3 or*

[4]Sidney Herbert to Florence Nightingale, October 15, 1854, Wellcome Library.
[5]*The Times,* January 4, 1855.

4 o'clock . . . I saw meat, drawn too late to be cooked, standing all night in the wards.

She herself ran an efficient special diet kitchen, where dainty invalid dishes were prepared from stores she herself procured. Between December 15, 1854, and January 15, 1855, it supplied, daily, 25 gallons of beef tea, 15 gallons of chicken broth, 40 gallons of arrowroot, 12 gallons of sago, 120 quarts of barley water, 10 quarts of rice water, 8 quarts of lemonade and 20 quarts of milk, 40 chickens, 4 dozen eggs, 15 lbs of jelly, 250 portions of rice pudding, 5 bottles of port wine, and 3 bottles of Marsala. But as *The Times* put it, "Even if these arrangements secured regular meals, well and cleanly cooked—which I am afraid cannot be stated unreservedly—there would still remain a vast number of special cases to prepare for."

Such was the situation drawn to Soyer's attention that January night at the Albion Hotel. On February 2, *The Times* printed a letter under the heading THE HOSPITAL KITCHENS AT SCUTARI:

Sir,—

After carefully perusing the letter of your correspondent, dated Scutari, in your impression of Wednesday last, I perceive that, although the kitchen under the superintendence of Miss Nightingale affords so much relief, the system of management at the large one in the Barrack Hospital is far from being perfect. I propose offering my services gratuitously, and proceeding direct to Scutari, at my own personal expense, to regulate that important department, if the Government will honour me with their confidence, and grant me the full power of acting according to my knowledge and experience in such matters. I have the honour to remain, Sir, your obedient servant, A. Soyer.

Soyer at once set about getting the necessary permissions for his trip. Fortunately for him—and the potential recipients of his good offices—he was well-placed to do so. For by no means all such offers of help were welcomed. Miss Nightingale herself, though a personal friend of Sidney Herbert, the Secretary for War, was deeply resented by the Army medical establishment, who, with a few exceptions, did all in their power to obstruct her. The Jamaican Mary Seacole, a nurse with long experience of comparable conditions, waited in vain for an interview with Mr. or Mrs. Herbert even though she had many friends in the army and had traveled to England all the way from Panama, at considerable expense, simply in order to offer her services. But neither could find time to see "the yellow woman whom no excuses could get rid of, nor impertinence dismay"; and after many hours spent fruitlessly hanging about in anterooms, a conversation with one of Miss Nightingale's friends convinced her that even "had there been a vacancy, I should not have been chosen to fill it." So she bought the necessary stores and took herself to the war anyway, putting up a "hotel" behind the lines and (since she had after all to live) selling, rather than giving, the comforts so badly wanted by the troops. "When a poor fellow lay sickening in his cheerless hut and sent down to me," she wrote, "he knew very well that I should not ride up in answer to his message empty-handed. And although I did not hesitate to charge him with the value of the necessaries I took him, still he was thankful enough to be able to *purchase* them."[6]

Soyer was in a rather different position. Being a man, he did not arouse the endemic military distaste for female hangers-on—or, what was even worse, bossy women who tried to tell chaps what to do. Moreover, he had already demonstrated his capacity for practical action in an emergency. Although his Dublin soup kitchen may not have lived up to its somewhat rash nutritional billing, in many ways it had been a triumph, producing decent, cheap food for vast numbers at speed and in an orderly manner. He had ridden to the government's rescue then; if he offered his services now, who were they to turn him down? Several of the gentlemen who had associated themselves with the Dublin soup kitchen, such as Lord William Paulet and the Duke of Cambridge, were now senior officers in the Crimea. And, most important of all (as Miss Nightingale herself could testify), he knew the Secretary for War. By the time Soyer wrote his letter, this was no longer Sidney Herbert: The Earl of Aberdeen's administration, in which he served, had been brought down by Russell's dispatches from the front. Lord Palmerston was now Prime Minister, and his Secretary for War none other than Soyer's old friend Lord Panmure, whom we last met in his capacity as head of the Royal Humane Society after our hero's near-death experience on the ice.

Soyer spent the next two weeks doing what he most enjoyed—making practical arrangements and showing them off to the *gratin*. He shuttled between the War Office and the drawing room of another patron, the Duchess of Sutherland, regaling the assembled

---

[6]Seacole, *Wonderful Adventures of Mrs Seacole in Many Lands,* p. 166.

SOYER, THE GOOD SAMARITAN.

Soyer rides to the rescue on his turtle.

ducal household with "a few samples of diets and aliments I had prepared from the soldiers' rations" and treating Lord Panmure to a selection of model hospital diets, which were pronounced, with wonderful inevitability, "very palatable."[7] He also designed a field stove that he thought would be a great improvement on anything the Army currently possessed: a combination of the steam boiler he had used in his soup kitchens and the all-purpose "baking-stewing pan" from the *Shilling Cookery*. In appearance it was very like the Tortoise stove that heated so many Parisian garrets: cylindrical, with a lidded cauldron suspended over an internal firebox, and an elbowed chimney to vent the smoke and increase the draft. Since

[7]*Soyer's Culinary Campaign*, p. 20.

both the fire and the food were enclosed it would work indoors or out, and in all weathers, and as no giveaway flames or smoke would be seen, could be used even in the trenches. To cap its many virtues, it needed very little fuel: 300 lb. of wood per thousand men as against the then current army allowance of more than ten times that. "Salt beef, Irish stew, stewed beef, tea, coffee, cocoa, etc." could be prepared in the cauldron, which might also be fitted with a grid for baking, roasting, and steaming.

After viewing a model of this stove, Panmure sent Soyer to visit the famous engineer I. K. Brunel, then designing prefabricated huts for a field hospital to be built at Erenkeni on the Dardanelles. Brunel was extremely enthusiastic, declaring it just what he needed for his hospital kitchens; and the first consignment was forthwith ordered from Messrs. Smith and Phillips of Snow Hill, old friends who had already manufactured several gas cooking appliances to Soyer's design. Unfortunately, neither stoves nor huts would arrive in the Crimea until the war was almost over, when they provided a tantalizing glimpse of how much better things might have been had the proper preparations been made. Some of Brunel's huts served for many years to house the sculpture department at the Royal College of Art in Kensington; as for Soyer's stoves, they were so efficient, economical, and practical that the Army went on using his design, or a variant of it—still called the Soyer stove—as late as the first Gulf War.

The result of all this was a commission to leave at once for Constantinople, the War Office paying Soyer's expenses and those of his staff—the inevitable secretary plus "a few [cooks] from Paris."

These would not be the first French cooks in the English army of the Crimea. Many officers—the Commander-in-Chief

Lord Raglan, Lord Cardigan, and the Duke of Cambridge, to name but three—had taken their personal chefs (as it happened, all friends of Soyer) with them to the front. Now the rank and file would receive the same service. Of course, Soyer's team would not be large enough to cook food for an army. What they could do, however, was teach the soldiers how to cook decently for themselves. They would assess the situation, work out good recipes, and provide clear instructions. After that there should be no problems: Were not soldiers trained to follow instructions from the moment they joined the army? "Being under discipline, [they] might prove as useful as any cooks," Soyer declared.

The cooks were comparatively easily found, their leader being the son of Soyer's old friend Louis Jullien. The secretary, though, presented more of a problem. Volant had once fulfilled that function, but Volant was no longer a friend. Sala was offered "very handsome terms" if he would take the job on, "but somehow . . . shrank from accepting the offer."[8] Soyer eventually engaged a friend referred to only by his initials, T.G.; an incidental reference describes him as "a gentleman of colour." "My dear fellow," Soyer represents himself as saying, "I can tell you what, there is a chance for you—it is only for two or three months—you will be well paid, and all expenses defrayed."[9] T.G. agreed; whereupon Soyer entrusted Emma's precious paintings to Messrs. Crosse and Blackwell (though he took one with him for company), and set off for Constantinople.

That journey, overland to Marseille and thereafter by sea, is a delightful one if the sea is not too rough; and, like many other

[8]Sala, *Things I Have Seen and People I Have Known,* vol. 2, p. 101.
[9]*Soyer's Culinary Campaign,* p. 29.

travelers undertaking this very particular version of the Grand Tour, Soyer made the most of it. In Boulogne he hobnobbed with an old friend, now valet-de-chambre to Louis-Napoléon, and learned that the Emperor had personally expressed his pleasure and relief on hearing of Soyer's Scutari expedition. In Paris, Brunel, who happened also to be there, procured permissions to visit the city's military hospitals. In Marseille he was treated to the local bouillabaisse, whose recipe he thoughtfully recorded for the benefit of his readers. In Corsica, where his ship waited out a gale, he visited the Buonaparte family house, sending a detailed description of its kitchen to the editor of *The Times*—unfortunately never printed because it was inadvertently posted without a stamp. In Athens he cooked a *petit déjeuner à la fourchette* with his patent Magic Stove "on a fallen capital of the stupendous ruins." And at last, on a foggy morning toward the end of April, they entered the Dardanelles and approached Constantinople across the Sea of Marmara. The Topkapi Palace, St. Sophia, and the Blue Mosque with its six minarets clothed the hill of Stamboul to the left; Pera, where the best hotel and the French hospital were situated, lay straight ahead on the spit of land berween the Golden Horn and the Bosphorus; and to the right, on the Asian shore, lay Üsküdar, or Scutari, dominated by a giant cemetery, with jumbled graves tight-packed between trees, and the monstrous rectangular barracks, with a tower at each corner, that was the British hospital, scene of Florence Nightingale's labors.

When Soyer first saw the barracks hospital, he tells us, "my mind was quite overpowered." And this is hardly surprising. This huge building—three hundred yards long, two hundred wide—was, as everyone knew from *The Times*'s graphic reports, full to capacity with the sick and dying, the wards overflowing into the corridors.

Each patient, Soyer calculated, "would require three to four articles of diet daily, making a total of several thousand per diem." And the Scutari hospital would not be the only one needing his attention. A little to the right, in a large red-brick building, was the General Hospital, housing another five or six hundred patients; there was yet another hospital nearby at Kululee, and an officers' hospital, to say nothing of the field hospitals behind the lines in the Crimea itself.

The scale of what he had undertaken suddenly appeared so stupendous that for a while panic took over and his mind went blank. Then he recollected that before setting out from London he had decided upon a plan of action. The trick was not to attempt an instant, wholesale conversion but to take it gradually, beginning on a small scale, with a hundred patients, and extending his operations from there. "In a few minutes my puzzled brain was as clear as a bell, and I felt confident of success. 'If I succeed with a hundred,' said I, 'in a very short time I can manage a thousand, providing I meet with proper support.'"[10] In this confident frame of mind (though plagued now with diarrhea, which afflicted him, on and off, for the next several weeks), he prepared to commence operations.

Having found some temporary lodgings and presented himself to Miss Nightingale, Soyer toured the hospital's main kitchen and the various special diet kitchens, to try and get an idea of what he would need to do. His professional eye noticed, first of all, the very bad quality of the charcoal, which "smoked terribly, and was nothing but dust." No deficiency could have been more basic. Charcoal was the main fuel; unless its quality could be assured, cooking became almost impossible. Inferior charcoal filled the kitchens with

[10]*Soyer's Culinary Campaign,* p. 45.

The Barrack Hospital kitchen at Scutari, after Soyer had set it in order.

smoke, and needed far too much wood in order to catch. And then, when this was finally achieved, the food cooked too fast—which left a choice between raw or burned.

Some of the special diet kitchens, located wherever space could be found in towers and hallways, were smoky and unpleasant; but the main kitchen came as a pleasant surprise. It was huge and magnificent, built by the Turks, who were past masters at vast kitchens (that in the Sultan's new Dolmabahce Palace accommodated between three and four hundred cooks and boasted twenty large chimneys) and fitted with twenty huge boilers—more than enough for the hospital's needs, and of excellent quality.

Unfortunately, however, the boilers were made of copper—in Soyer's words, "the worst metal which could possibly be employed for hospital uses." Copper, although traditionally prized in cookware for its heat-conducting qualities, immediately rang alarm bells for any Frenchman. The French medical press was full of articles explaining how this was one of the most dangerous possible cooking materials: toxic verdigris "combined" (in the words of one lawyer) "with all the most delightful dishes and stews most likely to please our taste and senses,"[11] and was the more perilous for being undetectable. At the very least, it must be carefully tinned on the inside, to prevent direct contact with food—and retinned when, as in this case, the original tinning had been worn away; which would not be easy, as each boiler was screwed to its marble base. Nevertheless, "I am far from despairing," Soyer assured Miss Nightingale. "Indeed, I feel confident that I shall succeed." With which he bade her adieu and prepared to return at seven the following morning, to watch the system in action.

What he found was chaos. Each mess had an orderly who cooked its meat in a batch, tightly tied to a rough piece of wood or "skewer" and plunged into the boiler; and each batch was marked in a different way—some by a piece of cloth cut from an old jacket, others by buttons, knives, forks, or scissors; one ingenious fellow used a pair of old candle-snuffers. Wasn't this a little unhygienic? Soyer wondered. No, came the reply; the snuffers had been boiled so many times, they must be clean by now.

By any standards, whether hygienic or gastronomic, it was hard to imagine a more dreadful method of cooking. The meat swelled as it boiled, and being so tightly tied the inside remained virtually uncooked even when the outside portions were overdone. All was completely tasteless; and since it was cooked unboned, some patients' portions consisted almost wholly of bone and were

[11]Quoted in Spang, *The Invention of the Restaurant,* pp. 29–30.

thus doubly uneatable. This question of boning the meat was one of the points at issue between Miss Nightingale and her enemies in the medical establishment. "It would seem unnecessary to trouble you with the kitchen details," she fulminated to Sidney Herbert. "But Cumming [one of the doctors] etc tell me it requires a new 'regulation of service' to 'bone the meat' etc!!!"

In the wards, Soyer noticed that patients ate their meat first, and only afterward their soup; and as the meat took a long time to carve, the soup, which was anyway tasteless and watery, was quite cold by the time anyone got around to it. On inquiring why they ate their meals in this order, he was told it was because each patient had only one plate—a round, deep, tin dish—and they wanted their meat first, to make sure no one else ate their portion before they got to it. His first recommendation, then, was that soup and meat be served together, the meat cut into small pieces and the soup poured over it; in this way, soup, meat, and potatoes would all be warm, and more easily eaten and digested.

After this he returned to the kitchen and requested six rations of everything allowed for making soup. He received four pounds of meat, a quarter of a pound of barley, and some vegetables, to which he added eight pints of water and some salt and pepper, producing, after an hour, a soup pronounced by all who tasted it "nourishing and palatable." The purveyor, Mr. Milton, arriving at this point, was treated to two sample basins, one containing Soyer's soup, the other made in the hospital, with no seasoning and of "a blackish appearance." The former was excellent, the latter he could barely swallow; he could hardly believe it when Soyer assured him that the good soup had been made from the regular rations at no extra expense. "All the soup," Soyer assured him, "will in future be like the sample

I have made, and I can greatly improve it by the addition of a few pounds of brown sugar and a little flour extra."[12] Following which demonstration the hard work began.

Soyer's task fell into two distinct categories. The first, and most straightforward, concerned what we might term hardware: finding younger chickens, fresher vegetables, and better charcoal, cleaning the kitchens, retinning the coppers, rebuilding collapsed and smoking chimneys, recommending slight changes in existing practices, such as tying the meat more loosely before putting it to be boiled. Such tasks were concrete and clearly defined. It was obvious to everyone why they needed doing, and they were soon done. An excellent interpreter was found, a Mr. Black, fluent in English, French, Turkish, Greek, and Armenian (and incidentally, to Soyer's delight, married to the Maid of Athens once celebrated by Lord Byron); with his help, the requisite supplies were assured and the necessary help engaged. Within a few days the coppers were tinned, a new charcoal stove built, an oven, a storeroom, and a larder partitioned off from the main kitchen, and a kitchen dresser and chopping block made. He turned his attention to tea—hitherto made by boiling water in the copper just used for soup, tying the leaves up tightly in a cloth, and throwing it in the water. The cloth shrank so much as it got wet, however, that water barely penetrated the compressed mass within, and the tea failed to diffuse. Soyer put a coffee filter into a two-gallon kettle, placed twenty men's tea rations in the filter, poured in the boiling water, and "to my astonishment made about one-fourth more tea, perfectly clear and without the least sediment."[13] Four of these

[12]*Soyer's Culinary Campaign,* p. 72.
[13]*Soyer's Culinary Campaign,* p. 77.

The Scutari teapot.

kettles made enough tea for the whole hospital, and their success prompted Soyer to design a "Scutari teapot," its filter elegantly topped with a model of the Galata tower, surmounted by a crescent moon and a star. Miss Nightingale ordered one for her own personal use; the design, slightly modified, is still in use today and may be bought at any kitchenware shop.

But there was a second category of problem, which we might define as software, altogether more amorphous, and harder to deal with. It concerned attitudes—the attitudes, in fact, which had led to many of the hardware deficiencies. And it boiled down to this: that no group of Frenchmen, in any circumstances, would ever have treated food, of whatever quality, as the British soldiers treated—or mistreated—theirs.

Of course, the fact that the French army ate better than the British—which it did—was not wholly a question of culture. Organization also played its part. British army budgets had been cut after 1815, resulting in the culture of parsimony that had already borne such lethal fruit during the Irish famine. "Of the four thousand now in hospital, three quarters at least are suffering from causes which . . . a greater attention to the material wants of an army placed in such circumstances must have vastly mitigated," reported the *Times* correspondent from Scutari that January. The French army, by contrast, was still run on Napoleon's efficient lines. As a result, it was incomparably better set up, in almost every department, than the English: better housed, better supplied, better led. And this was as true in the hospital service as in the field. The French military hospital at Pera, unlike Scutari, was clean, warm, and well fitted out. The patients not only had good beds and plenty of warm clothing, they also had convenient shelves for storing that clothing and any other personal possessions, such as their ample crockery and cutlery and their government-issue pipes and tobacco. Where the washhouse at Scutari had been turned into a storeroom, that at Pera still fulfilled its original function, permitting a supply of clean linen; and although the French had fewer doctors per head than the English, they were helped by fifty Sisters of Charity. The French hospital also benefited from the services of students from the Constantinople medical schools, who acted as dressers.[14]

But as Soyer's life in England over the past twenty years had so vividly demonstrated, even had the British army been as well-provided as the French, it would still not have eaten so well; and it was this antigastronomical culture that he now had to try and

[14]Report in *The Times*.

change. At Aston Hall and in Ireland, it had shown itself in the (to him) inexplicable inability of agricultural laborers to produce decent food from the land on which they lived, as French peasants did. At the Reform Club, he had been grieved and puzzled at the lowly place English society afforded cooks, even the best and most celebrated cooks, compared with the French celebration of culinary artistry. He had tried to change the culture with the Symposium, but without success: It had foundered partly on business miscalculation, but partly, too, on the British assumption that gastronomy was a pleasure strictly for the moneyed, and that no establishment providing such delights publicly to all classes and both sexes could possibly be truly respectable. But although its failure had been infuriating and expensive, it was just that: a business failure. Now, in Scutari, this project of gastronomic reform took on a new and urgent dimension. The terrible mortality in the hospitals had many causes, but decent, clean, and palatable food was essential if it was seriously to be alleviated. And such food could not be produced unless Soyer could succeed in radically reeducating the cooks—products of the system he had spent his entire professional life failing to change.

The ignorance of the soldier-cooks was like nothing he had ever seen before, save possibly in Ireland during the famine (perhaps not so surprising, since, by a terrible irony, many of the English army's soldiers were Irishmen). Not only did they not know how to cook, they constantly threw valuable food away. The gizzards, heads, and feet of chickens were discarded, instead of being used to make broth; so, too, was the water in which meat had been boiled. The patients got the *bouilli,* but what happened to the *bouillon,* that fundamental article of cuisine?

When all the dinners had been served out, I perceived a large copper half full of rich broth with about three inches of fat upon it. I inquired what they did with this?

"Throw it away, sir."

"Throw it away?" we all exclaimed.

"Yes, sir; it's the water in which the fresh beef has been cooked."

"Do you call that water? I call it strong broth. Why don't you make soup of it?"

"We orderlies don't like soup, sir."

"Then you really throw it away?"

"Yes, sir; it is good for nothing."

I took a ladle and removed a large basinful of beautiful fat, which, when cold, was better for cooking purposes than the rank butter procured from Constantinople at from ten to fifteen piastres per pound. The next day I showed the men how to make a most delicious soup with what they had before so foolishly thrown away. This method they were henceforward very glad to adopt. Not less than seventy pounds of beef had been daily boiled in this manner, and without salt. It would hardly be credited, but for its truth I can appeal to Miss Nightingale.[15]

Given this absolute ignorance, Soyer's insistence on bringing a team of Frenchmen with him made sense on the most practical level. If the British army was to feed itself in anything approaching an acceptable manner, it would have to be taught not only how to cook,

---

[15]*Soyer's Culinary Campaign,* pp. 74–5.

but if possible how to think about food in an entirely new way—that is to say, with interest and attention. And since no Britons—certainly no working-class Britons—*did* think about food in this way, they would have to be taught by Frenchmen.

The first necessity was to write out the new recipes he had devised in the utmost detail, since the cooks using them would rely entirely on instruction and not at all on instinct. Every slightest step must be described, leaving no possibility for error. Thus, the first recipe in Soyer's hospital diets, "Semi-stewed mutton and barley soup for 100 men," is an object lesson in basic principles:

> Put in a convenient-sized caldron 130 pints of cold water, 70lbs. of meat, or about that quantity, 12lbs. of plain mixed vegetables (the best that can be obtained), 9lbs. of barley, 1lb. 7oz. of salt, 1lb. 4oz. of flour; 1lb. 4oz. of sugar, 1oz. of pepper. Put all the ingredients into the pan at once, except the flour; set it on the fire, and when beginning to boil, diminish the heat, and simmer gently for two hours and a half; take the joints of meat out, and keep them warm in the orderly's pan; add to the soup your flour, which you have mixed with enough water to form a light batter; stir well together with a large spoon; boil another half-hour, skim off the fat, and serve the soup and meat separate. The meat may be put back into the soup for a few minutes to warm again prior to serving. The soup should be stirred now and then while making, to prevent burning or sticking to the bottom of the caldron.
>
> The joints are cooked whole, and afterwards cut up in different messes; being cooked this way in a rather thick stock, the meat becomes more nutritious.

Note.—The word "about" is applied to the half and full diet, which varies the weight of the meat; but ½lb. of mutton will always make a pint of good soup; 3lbs. of mixed preserved vegetables must be used when fresh are not to be obtained, and put in one hour and a half prior to serving, instead of at first; they will then show better in the soup, and still be well done.

Following this to the letter, no one could fail to construct a perfectly passable meal; and by cooking *en masse* in this way, the original chaos was quickly reduced to something approaching order. The dirty and inefficient extra-diet kitchens were closed and their soldier-cooks discharged, and soon all the food was being prepared in the large central kitchen under Soyer's own supervision. Two of his civilian cooks were put in charge of the special diets, each assisted by six soldiers, whom they instructed and who would eventually be able to instruct others. Before long, indeed, it would have been possible to feed many more patients than the hospital could possibly accommodate, "the receipts being regulated by weight and measure, from an ounce for certain articles to seven or eight cwt. for others."[16]

But, however clear the recipe, there is, in cookery, no substitute for practice. Soyer needed to create an army culture in which cookery, instead of being a chore performed by a ragtag of ignorant and uninterested orderlies, became a recognized and necessary skill,

[16]*Soyer's Culinary Campaign,* p. 82.

with at least one competent cook to each unit. And so he pointed out, in a letter to Lord William Paulet written that May:

> *Important regulations to insure for the future a good, clean, wholesome and nutritious class of food, and delicate beverages, to be daily produced for the comfort of the sick and wounded in all the hospitals of the East, as well as for the standing army, which will prove economical both in a saving of time, and also in a pecuniary sense. . . .*
>
> *First requisite.—That for every important hospital, a professed man-cook shall be engaged, with a civilian assistant, instead of military, as is now the case, and the principal to be under military rules and regulations.*
>
> *Second.—That all military men now engaged cooking in the hospitals and barrack kitchens shall be immediately instructed in the art of camp cooking. As they are already acquainted with the plain mode of cooking, it will only require a few lessons from Monsieur Soyer, under his new and simple style, to become throughly conversant with this branch of culinary operations . . . Monsieur Soyer feels assured that if present in the camp for a few weeks he will be enabled to carry out this important object, at the same time introducing wholesome and nutritious food made out of the usual allowances of provisions supplied to the army.*

In short, he proposed to set up an apprentice system, as he had at the Reform Club and had proposed to do at the Symposium—with this difference: that where his former apprentices had been destined to provide dainty cuisine for the well-heeled (and incidentally, a handsome income for their teacher), these would be taught, gratis, good basic cooking for the British army.

The convivial mode that, even in these circumstances, came most naturally to Soyer was now revived in the unlikely setting of Scutari for a "grand opening" of the new kitchen. All the heads of the medical department in the various hospitals would be invited, as would "some of the most eminent among the French and Turkish medical staff." Lord William Paulet was to invite the officers, and the head medical officer did the same for the doctors. All that remained was for Soyer to produce the spread. He would present samples of his own recipes—for beef-tea, chicken-broth, mutton-broth, beef-soup, rice-water, barley-water, arrowroot-water with and without wine, sago with port, calf's-foot jelly—alongside ostensibly similar dishes prepared by the soldiers. The company would taste the samples, and vote on which they preferred. "This, I was aware, was a bold experiment," Soyer observed, "for had I failed—and many unforeseen events might have caused such a result—my reputation would have suffered."

This catastrophe was only just avoided. The Grand Opening was to take place on a Monday. And on the Friday it looked as though Soyer would indeed fail; for he was suddenly taken ill with what seems to have been a sort of mini–nervous breakdown. "I seemed to have forgotten everything, and experienced at the same time a sensation of brain fever. There were, however, none of its symptoms. Although I was quite conscious of what I had to do, I was entirely incapable of doing it, or of ordering anything or directing

The Grand Opening of Soyer's Crimean field kitchen.

anyone."[17] The doctor—Macgrigor, one of Miss Nightingale's few allies among the medical establishment—put this disorder down to constant worry together with the unnerving and ubiquitous presence of the sick, the wounded, and the dead. He prescribed quiet and provided a soothing medicine; by Sunday afternoon, the patient had recovered.

The Grand Opening was a triumph. Although bad weather kept some of the invitees from crossing the Bosphorus, then only possible in rowing boats called *caiques,* the kitchen was crowded with officials from the various hospitals, while fifty Sisters of Mercy added the feminine touch without which no social occasion was, in Alexis's view, complete.

By the beginning of May, the necessary reforms had been set in

[17]*Soyer's Culinary Campaign,* p. 79.

place in all the hospital kitchens. "The hospitals are now in perfect order," Lady Stratford de Redcliffe, the British Ambassador's wife, reported on April 23—a slight exaggeration perhaps, but everything is comparative. Miss Nightingale and her friend and ally Mr. Bracebridge were preparing to visit the Crimea; Soyer and his team were invited to accompany them. He left the Scutari kitchen in care of a handpicked corporal, and advised the doctors to send from time to time for samples of different dishes. If standards deteriorated after his departure, they were to complain and make sure the cooks brought everything back up to scratch, according to the detailed recipes that had been printed out.

After which, on May 2, 1855, the party set sail for the Black Sea and Balaklava.

The Crimean War was a social as well as a military event. The camp was awash with nonparticipants. There were the journalists and photographers, whose use of new technologies such as the telegraph and the camera was creating a new type of journalism that brought the realities of war to their readers almost in real time. There were traders, like Mary Seacole, supplying various military and nonmilitary wants. There were nonfighting men, dubbed by Russell "T.G.s," or Travelling Gents, who viewed the spectacle from a safe distance. There were even ladies. A few officers brought their wives, while for some as yet unmarried girls the theater of war represented an extension of the social whirl, offering an unrivaled selection of suitable young men with little female competition for their attention.

For each of these the Crimea was a different place. For W. H.

Russell, sharing and describing the hardships of camp life during the bitter winter of 1854–55, and witnessing, day, after day, the tragic consequences of utter disorganization, it was a shameful waste of brave men's lives that must never be allowed to happen again. For Mary Seacole, guarding the precious stores that constituted the stock of her British Hotel, it was home to the most accomplished thieves in Europe. For Mrs. Frances Duberly, accompanying her husband, an officer in the 7th Hussars, it was quite simply hell. "If ever anybody should wish to erect a model Balaklava in England, I will tell him the ingredients necessary," she wrote.

> *Take a village of ruined houses and hovels in the extremest stage of all imaginable dirt, allow rain to pour into and outside them until the whole place is a swamp of filth ankle-deep; catch about, on an average, 1,000 sick Turks with the plague and cram them into the houses indiscriminately; kill also about 100 a day and bury them so as to be scarcely covered with earth, leaving them to rot at leisure—taking care to keep up the supply. On one part of the beach drive all the exhausted . . . ponies, dying bullocks, and worn out camels and leave them to die of starvation . . . Collect together from the water of the harbour all the offal of all the animals slaughtered for the use of the occupants of above 100 ships, to say nothing of the inhabitants of the town—which, together with an occasional human body, whole or in parts, and the driftwood of the wrecks, pretty well covers the water—and stew them all up together in a narrow harbour, and you will have a tolerable imitation of the real essence of Balaklava.*[18]

[18]Mrs. Henry Duberly, *Journal Kept during the Russian War,* London, 1885.

Soyer visits Mary Seacole's British Hotel.

Yet for Miss Ellen Palmer, visiting her brother in the 11th Hussars, this same Balaklava, where Miss Palmer's ship anchored on December 26, 1854, was "a wonderful little harbour." Lord Raglan lent her his horse; she flirted with various desirable fellows, including Captain William Peel, son of Sir Robert, and his cousin Archy, whom she eventually married; she went riding out into the hills; and four weeks later, at the end of January—a month that saw 8,000 sick and wounded men sent down from their camps to Balaklava, thence—eventually—to embark for Scutari—she exclaimed: "Our last day at Balaklava! The Peels, Lord Burghersh, Capt. Colville, Coln. Seymour, M. Dorel came in to 'say good-bye.' Walked for the last time to the Genoese castle, another favorite haunt of ours. A very sad evening; we walked anticipating our departure with sorrow."[19]

The view as described by Soyer, an oddly revealing mix of the professional, the social, and the culinary, contains aspects of all of these. Neither soldier nor sightseer, with a foolhardy fascination for the scene of battle and a tourist's determination to miss nothing of interest, he combined genuine dedication with party spirit in a unique mix that ensured more or less universal affection. Sartorially he was as gorgeous as ever, sporting a white burnous, a blue and silver stripe down his trousers, a gold-braided waistcoast, and a red and white cap. His secretary, T.G., wore white, and his fiery Zouave servant, Bornet, hired from the French camp, an indescribable variant on the anyway gaudy Zouave uniform, with its sky-blue baggy trousers tucked into riding boots. The self-styled Captain Cook and his brigade became, Soyer remarks, as familiar a sight around the camps as *le chien du régiment.* Thackeray, reviewing *A Culinary Campaign,* dubbed this "radiant apparition" Alexis the Succulent, while Russell's John Bull assumed it must at the very least be General Pelissier. "Who's that?" he is made to inquire, to which comes the reply, "That! Why, that's Monsieur Soyer, *chef de nos batteries de cuisine;* and if you go and ask him, you'll find he'll talk to you for several hours about the way your meat is wasted."

There were two hospitals in Balaklava, as well as sailors' hospitals, a field hospital in the camp, and a hutted sanatorium on the Genoese heights that Miss Palmer had found so picturesque. All required fundamental reorganization in both the medical and the

[19]Askwith, *Crimean Courtship,* pp. 63, 90.

kitchen departments—not easy to achieve in the shambles of the Crimea, where supplies were so ill-organized, the weather (and hence the possibilities of transport) so unpredictable, the soldiers so exhausted, the stream of invalids unending, and the Turkish workmen entirely unreliable. Miss Nightingale was faced, besides, with the unremitting hostility of the Chief Medical Officer, Dr. John Hall, who was stationed at Balaklava. Despite all this, improvements were eventually effected: nurses organized, new huts built, kitchens set in order.

Soyer's remit in the Crimea, however, covered the healthy as well as the sick. He was particularly concerned to show the troops how to make better use of their rations—no easy task, since neither the food nor the means for cooking it were at all satisfactory. As the new stoves had not yet arrived the old tin camp-kettles were still in use, and the daily necessity of cooking a hot meal remained a heavy chore. Mary Seacole remarked on the "clumsy, ignorant soldier-cook[s], who would almost prefer eating [their] meat raw to having the trouble of cooking it."[20] But who, in the circumstances, could blame them? Unlike the French, who prepared their food in messes of twelve, taking it in turns to act as cook for the day, the British assumed each man would carry and cook his own ration. The soldiers had first to construct a windbreak, then a fireplace of loose stones held together with iron hoops. Inside this structure they made their fire, and the small tin issue canteen Soyer thought so detestable was set on top. This was hard work, requiring a lot of fuel; and when it rained, cooking became almost impossible. As for the rations, fresh meat was by now rarely available, and the salt pork and beef rations

[20]Seacole, *Wonderful Adventures of Mrs Seacole in Many Lands,* p. 167.

were very hard and very salty. Vegetables were scarce: Fresh vegetables were not conveniently portable, and those that did arrive, sent weekly from Constantinople, were often rotten. Lime juice, though provided, remained unissued for many weeks because "neither the medical nor the Commissariat officer would make up their mind to ask the commander of the army if it were to be regarded as a medical comfort or an article of Commissariat issue."[21] As a result, many of the men suffered from scurvy, which weakened the teeth and gums, making it almost impossible to eat the hard salt meat and stale bread.

Soyer at once set about remedying these problems. He recommended that the meat ration be issued the night before it was to be eaten, allowing time for it to be well soaked before cooking, both to soften the meat and to get rid of excess salt. He invented weekly "menus" using the soldiers' rations to the best and most varied effect—for camp soup using pork or beef, pea soup, stewed beef and rice, suet dumplings and puddings—and had his recipes printed and distributed to the men. He recommended that the unreliable fresh vegetables be replaced by dried ones, which were not only dependable but portable. These were prepared in cakes by the firm of Cholet et Prevet, who also supplied the French army. (Cholet's factory, set up in 1848, was at Meaux, so it seems possible that Soyer may have had some long-standing connection with the firm.) These cakes, weighing one hundredweight each and designed for one hundred men, were marked into slices of ten rations, so that not too much would be used at a time. They contained cabbages, leeks, carrots, potatoes, parsnips, turnips, and onions, cut up into a coarse *julienne,* then dried, and mixed (this being a French firm) with one

[21]G. A. Furse, *Commissioning of Armies in the Field,* London, 1899.

pound of aromatic seasoning—thyme, bay leaves, winter savory, pepper, and cloves.

As at Scutari, fresh bread was the one reliably excellent foodstuff, especially after a floating bakery was fitted up, producing both white and brown loaves. The officers universally preferred the white, but Soyer, as so often echoing modern views where nutrition is concerned, recommended the brown—"there is less show and more nutriment in it." However, even the best bread soon loses its freshness, so he invented a sort of bread-biscuit, which neither went stale, as bread did, nor became teeth-breakingly hard, as biscuit did, and which was particularly excellent when soaked in soup.

All this was hard work, in appalling surroundings. Yet Soyer remained extraordinarily cheerful. He experienced, as everyone did, the hardships and difficulties of war—the squalor, the misery, the constant presence of death; his very presence proved, were proof needed, that he was not a heartless man. Yet his tone, when writing about it all, remained oddly urbane. His book *Soyer's Culinary Campaign* constantly reports conversations with old Reform Club friends that might as easily have taken place in Pall Mall; the familiar and uplifting memory of Madame Soyer, in the shape of one of her pictures, "The Young Bavarian," transformed the meanest berth into a memory of home. Even the most ghoulish exploits, as recounted by Soyer, take on an almost courtly air. For example, this account of an investigation into tainted air on the occasion of the celebration of the Queen's birthday aboard ship in Balaklava harbor:

> We went to breathe the fresh air, and to watch the frolics of the joyous but rather tumultuous crew . . . Captain Heath, the harbour-master, who was then living on board, also gave

a dinner-party that day; and as his numerous guests appeared upon deck, there was quite an array of naval and military men.

I seldom smoke, and I remarked that the air we were so anxious to breathe was anything but wholesome or agreeable. Thereupon the commander of the *Diamond* observed that an unpleasant odour arose from the sea.

"It does not come from the water," I replied, "but from the shore."

"What can it be, Monsieur Soyer?" said he.

"Don't you know, captain—you who daily visit your naval hospital on the heights, that on the bank are the bodies of the poor unfortunate fellows lost in the *Prince,* and the sea has washed away the earth which covered them? Some of them are actually on a level with the ground."

. . . Some of those who overheard our conversation begged Captain Shepherd to let us have a boat, with which request the captain complied. It was a fine moonlight night when we started, and we soon reached the spot. The smell had disappeared, so he said I was mistaken.

"Not at all, captain," said I. "Pray thrust your oar through the soil we are standing upon."

It was covered with lime, and he did as I requested, and found that what I had stated was correct.[22]

This curiously detached tone is doubtless partly the result of the account being dictated to a secretary in a foreign language. Partly, too,

[22]*Soyer's Culinary Campaign,* p. 155.

it may have been that horror was so general as to become almost normal. As Mary Seacole put it, "a day was a long time to give sorrow in the Crimea"[23]—though this did not dim the power of W. H. Russell's prose. But Soyer's tone is actively cheery. His letters to John Delane, editor of *The Times,* positively bubble with enthusiasm.

> Sir—
>
> *I shall do myself the pleasure of forwarding you by the next post a* résumé *of my culinary progress in the Crimea, adding to it the promised receipts, as well as some of those which I have already very successfully introduced into the camps, made out of the rations issued to the troops. I am also happy to inform you, that although so close to Sebastopol, I have not yet met with a single enemy; and were it not for the continual roaring of the cannon, the bursting of the shells, and the heat of the sun, I could fancy myself in England's happy land . . .*
>
> Camp before Sebastopol, June 3

Like all truly passionate artists, he talked and thought of little but his calling. "Mr Soyer is . . . is exceedingly egotistical, but has all the marks of a great man in his own line," observed one officer who met him at this time. "His conversation is all about his work, he soars beyond mere sauces and ragouts, but goes into the expense of different markets and different sorts of food, and examines whether fresh vegetables from Constantinople are not better than compressed ones from France. He has given me a recipe for making ship's beef and pork delicious, and says if he could have had his way it would (five

---

[23]Seacole, *Wonderful Adventures of Mrs Seacole in Many Lands,* p. 193.

or six years ago) have been preserved with far less salt than at present, and would not have cost a bit more or been more liable to decay."[24]

This singular combination of ghastly circumstances and tunnel vision struck more than one observer. It seemed to carry with it, they noted, an assumption that vital work erases social boundaries. Just before Soyer's Grand Opening at Scutari, Lady Stratford de Redcliffe observed, in a letter to the Queen, that M. Soyer, although "quite perfect in his way" was "a most ridiculous man." And in the Crimea W. H. Russell remarked, rather testily, on his inappropriate manner and overfamiliarity with Miss Nightingale. "Soyer is here eating whatever he can get and obstinately deaf to all hints that he ought to come in time to cook the dinner. Miss Nightingale is very ill, poor soul. Soyer dragged her into a battery—the mortar battery out of fire—and put her on the stern of a gun with the elegant expression meant to be neat and well-turned—'Voila! The Child of Peace had her breech on the breech of the Son of War!'"[25]

Miss Nightingale was indeed ill—about to come down with the "Crimea fever" that nearly killed her; so the expedition was incontestably ill-judged. But it is clear that this was not what really irked Russell. What he minded was Soyer's manner. The man simply did not know his place—wherever that might be: in Russell's view, clearly, at the stove. Where it certainly was not was as an equal engaged in dubious banter with Miss Nightingale. Indeed, such behavior was not merely an impertinence—as from a jumped-up servant to a lady—but almost sacrilegious. For as soon as she set

[24]Sir Leopold George Heath, May 26, 1855. *Letters from the Black Sea, during the Crimean War,* 1854–1856, London, 1897.
[25]May 1855.

foot in Scutari, Florence Nightingale had ceased being an ordinary young woman and become a saint. She wafted through hell, a vision of pure, English, angelic goodness, bringing comfort and cleanliness wherever she alighted: as Lytton Strachey put it, "a legend in her lifetime." And you don't flirt with legends or saints.

Yet not only did Miss Nightingale not seem to mind Soyer's absurd behavior, she appeared positively to enjoy it. Despite feeling, as we may imagine, distinctly unwell, she "very gracefully and kindly"[26] allowed him to take her hand, to help her climb the rampart to the gun carriage, and finally—as Russell describes—to seat her upon the gun itself. It was the affectionate act of a friend.

Ordinarily, this would not be anything very remarkable. But of course Miss Nightingale was not ordinary. On the contrary, she was highly singular, not least in the uniqueness of her position and experience; and the corollary (as with most saints) was extreme personal isolation. For friendship implies shared experience, and who in the world had lived a life comparable to hers, that indescribable combination of upper-class confidence, fierce politics, hard practical labor, and gentle empathy? A few old allies from her earlier life—the Herberts, the Bracebridges—had accompanied her on her journey, the Herberts politically and psychologically, the Bracebridges in person. Otherwise, her interest extended only to those in a position to help her further her professional aims. Soyer was such a one; but during these few months he was perhaps, too, almost a friend—the person whose experience and interests approached, more nearly than anyone's, her own.

And one aspect of this shared experience, it might be argued,

[26]*Soyer's Culinary Campaign,* p. 107.

was that despite its horrors, the Crimea was for these two a positive, even exhilarating, experience. They were not there because it was their job to fight, or (as with the army doctors) go where the fighting was. They did not, as the equally intrepid and benign Mary Seacole did, have to worry about money. They simply devoted themselves wholly and unreservedly to bettering the lot of a brave and unfortunate body of men, as best they were able; and unlike their subordinates—Miss Nightingale's nurses or Soyer's cooks—they were able to influence policy rather than merely implementing it. In that sense, whatever the disparities of personality or social status, they met on an equal footing. This, of course, was something Russell could not understand.

For Soyer, this heady sense of acceptance was something he had yearned for ever since arriving in his adopted country. The visible excitement that, alongside the constant professional preoccupation, pervades both his Crimea letters and his book, reflects the delightful awareness that here, at last, he is operating on a man-to-man basis with the best people. He is invited aboard the Admiral's flagship by the Admiral himself, with the words, "Monsieur Soyer, I assure you I am delighted to make your acquaintance. You are doing much for our brave soldiers, but you must not forget our worthy sailors." General Barnard, meeting him en route to a gathering that will consider the possibility of supplying a daily pint of hot soup to the men in the trenches during winter, says "Hallo, General Soyer! I'm not so much behind as I thought; for you are only just going to the general meeting, or the meeting of generals." At last, he has broken through the barrier. He is no longer a servant; he is *one of them*.

Of course, the fact that his presence ensured, if nothing else, a good dinner, still played a large part in Soyer's popularity. This was no problem for him: He enjoyed nothing more than showing off his skills. He reprints a story from the *Illustrated London News* in which, at the end of a long day, the writer, an officer, is visited in his tent by an unknown gentleman who has mistaken it for the tent of a friend. The visitor, who speaks "tolerable English but with a strong French accent"—not particularly surprising, since there were French troops quartered all around—is "a tall, stout, rather handsome-looking man, aged about fifty years."

The officer's Maltese servant has said that dinner will not be ready for an hour, and distraction is welcome. So the visitor sits and chats, and finally dinner appears. It is woefully undercooked. The visitor takes matters into his own hands, and rather to his host's annoyance—for "I can cook with any fellow in the Crimea except perhaps Soyer," who is reputed rather a humbug, but whose Shilling Cookery Book he has often used—

> my potatoes were in slices, a large onion was dissected piece-meal, my beef was submitted to the knife, a pinch or two of ration salt and pepper completed the preparations, and my little canteen-pan was on the fire . . . After a few minutes the stranger gave the pan a graceful wave or two over the fire, and then replaced it on the table. There was a dinner fit for Sardanapalus . . .
>
> "How do you like it?" said the stranger.
>
> "Don't talk at present," I answered; "I consider dinner one of the most serious duties of life."
>
> "Ah! Ah! Then you would not call Soyer a humbug to make this?" . . .

. . . At last the dinner was over. "One more glass of sherry," said the stranger, "and then I go. I am very glad to have made your acquaintance, and I hope you will come and see me when you come down to Balaklava . . ."

"With very great pleasure. And your name?"

(But this detail we have all, of course, known from the start.)

But although his popularity in the camp undoubtedly included an element of cupboard love, his gaiety, charm, and invincible good spirits ensured him a welcome wherever he appeared. "Alexis Soyer is living up with our Division, and is great fun," reported young Lt.-Col. Fred Dallas in a letter home. "He is a most pleasant amusing man, and great friends with my Chief, with the power of whose stomach he is much struck. He has known and met such a variety of people, and tells his anecdotes so well, that he is capital company."

Miss Nightingale's illness preoccupied the entire army, from the men, who worshiped her and hoped for her swift recovery, to the doctors, who did not, and hoped for her swift removal. "Sir John McNeil has just been here who was with F at Balaclava and exceedingly horrid to her, Mr Bracebridge says," reported her sister Parthenope that summer. But "Soyer was most attentive to F's comfort . . . and never failed to go up twice a day to . . . prepare a little something for her with his own hands"—doubtless calf's-foot jelly with Marsala, or something very similar.

At the beginning of June 1855, as soon as Miss Nightingale had regained enough strength to be moved, she and Soyer returned together to Constantinople, where the various hospital kitchens were now functioning more or less satisfactorily, with two tolerably good cooks replacing Jullien, who had inexplicably vanished, along with a good deal of money. But Soyer did not stay there long, for during July the long-delayed field stoves arrived. Since these were not needed at Scutari, he resolved to take them forthwith to Balaklava, where they could be of real service.

Arriving in the Crimea once more, he selected a suitable spot for the first demonstration of his stoves, then returned to his billet. To his astonishment and delight, when he came back next day, they were already in use. The Highland Brigade had found them, had at once realized what they were and how they should be used, and were cooking their dinners with notable gusto and success. No more eloquent testimony to the success of Soyer's design could be imagined—for, as he put it, "a soldier . . . is not a cooking animal."

The grand opening of the field stoves was held in a large marquee on August 26. Several hundred distinguished visitors were invited to a feast of plain boiled salt beef, with or without dumplings; plain boiled salt pork, with or without peas-pudding; stewed salt pork and beef with rice; French *pot-au-feu;* stewed fresh beef with potatoes; stewed mutton with haricot beans; ox-cheek and ox-feet soups; Scotch mutton-broth; and curry, made with fresh and salt beef. A happy Soyer divided his time between serving his guests and explaining, in detail, the inner workings and multiple advantages of his stoves. He was particularly delighted to welcome "a charming group of the fair sex, ten in number, escorted by their cavaliers. After taking some refreshment in the monster tent, they came to add their charms to the martial banquet, and taste with gusto the

A CULINARY CAMPAIGN

BY A. SOYER

ILLUSTRATED BY H. G. HINE

Soyer with a field stove in full operation.

rough food of the brave."[27] More and yet more guests arrived, the band struck up *Partant pour la Syrie*—and then, to cap this day of days, General Pelissier, the C.-in-C. of the French forces, arrived fresh from being invested with the Order of the Bath by Lord Stratford de Redcliffe. He tasted the *pot-au-feu,* which had been made using ox-heads (which were usually thrown away, few being able to face the task of cleaning them) and remarked to witty General Barnard that "he felt as interested in this unexpected exhibition as in the ceremony of the morning." To which General Barnard replied: "Your Excellency must agree with me that this day has been remarkably well spent: We devoted the morning to the *cordon rouge,* and the afternoon to the *cordon bleu."* "Nothing could have succeeded better than this opening," a delighted Soyer declared.

Even he, however, had to admit that it was put in the shade by the next great event—no less than the fall of Sebastopol itself, which took place the following week, on September 8, 1855.

At five that morning, the Guards began their silent march toward the city so long under siege, followed by the Scots Fusiliers. Soyer's combative Zouave wanted to go along, too, but was detained by the collar. Instead, he and his master set off on horseback, and finally managed to persuade a sentry to let them watch the drama from a nearby hillside.

The weather, which had been fine, turned stormy just before the attack, hiding Sebastopol behind a sheet of hail. Then the earth was shaken by gunfire, and the rattle of musketry was heard. When, after a while, a gale blew away the smoke, the telescope revealed a French flag flying over the Malakhoff. An hour later, aides-de-camp

---

[27]*Soyer's Culinary Campaign,* p. 217.

brought the news that the French had indeed taken the Malakhoff, and the English the Redan. It was all over.

On hearing this, Soyer and his Zouave left their viewpoint in order to make their way to the hospitals, where they would certainly be needed. Things were still quiet, however, so they went to their tent, returning to the hospital at four in the morning, where Soyer took over from the cooks who had been up all night. After a while he returned to camp, prepared "a quantity of lemonade, arrowroot, beef-tea, arrowroot-water, barley-water, rice-water, and pudding, boiled rice, etc.," and had it sent up to the hospital before going back there himself. He spent the rest of the day at his post, doing what he could to help amid the terror and the amputations, then returned to camp, "where an invitation awaited me to dine at the Carlton Club."

Thence, at eight, he repaired; there were eight or nine guests, who ate every morsel of a large and excellent dinner (not, this time, prepared by him). Everyone had something to tell—not least Soyer, whose "description of the hospitals was" (he assures us) "the great feature of the evening."

They had just toasted the Queen of England, the Emperor of France, and the Sultan of Turkey when news came that Sebastopol was burning. Soyer at once proposed that they should order their horses and go to see the show. To his surprise, however, no one seemed inclined to move. "'Surely,' said I, 'gentlemen! you don't expect the Russians will set a Sebastopol on fire every day at a few hours' notice to please you?'" But they had had enough of Sebastopol, and were tired out.

He returned to his hut, but even his majordomo at first refused to get up, though being an old campaigner he had gone to bed fully clothed so as to be ready for any emergency. This, however, was no emergency. "Not tonight," he said. "Oh, hang the place, let it burn." Soyer, however, desperate not to miss the spectacle, and equally desperate not to venture out alone, persisted; and they eventually set out together.

The night was very dark, so they made their way on foot. "The camp was silent, and apparently deserted. Although only eleven o'clock, we did not meet a soul, with the exception of sentries, on our way." They eventually found the vantage point of Cathcart's Hill, whence fourteen different conflagrations could be made out, the heat of which could be felt from where they stood. Not another soul was to be seen: Everyone else was simply too worn out to watch.

Early the following morning, Soyer went to the hospital, and then, having made sure there was nothing for him to do, set out for Sebastopol, whose condition he records in unique culinary detail:

> My Zouave knew the road, as he had been there the day before. Our first visit was to the Redan, where we were refused admission. My intrepid Zouave, not contented with this rebuff, took me round another way, and, leaving our horses outside, we scaled the works and got in . . . Nothing but the effects of a devastating earthquake can give anyone an idea of the *débris* of the interior, or of the destruction caused by the fire of the Allies, and the explosions that had ensued . . . The town was still burning. On reaching the large barracks, we visited the kitchens and bakeries. In the former, some of the boilers contained cabbage-soup; others, a kind of porridge made with black flour. In the bakeries, loaves of bread were still in the ovens, and dough in the troughs. We re-

moved a loaf from the oven and tasted it. As we had brought no provision with us, and there was none to be obtained in the burning city, we ate about half a pound of bread each, and finished our frugal repast with a good draught of water . . . "Come," said I, "let's go and taste the soupe-aux-choux." To this invitation [Bornet] most definitely objected . . . In my culinary ardour I tasted it, and found it extremely bad and entirely deprived of nutritious qualities, but no doubt in it was to be added some black bread which would improve it.[28]

Even Soyer's souvenirs reflected his interests. Where others looted guns, swords, church relics—anything that might be turned into money—our indefatigable hero took a long iron fork, a ladle, some of the dough from the troughs, some biscuits, and a large piece of black bread taken from the oven which he intended to try out when he and his Zouave got back to camp.

No one could keep up this pace for long, and a few days later Soyer finally succumbed. Diagnosed with Crimea fever, he waited out his illness in Constantinople, his condition not helped by constant assurances that he was unlikely to live. He abandoned his gloomy and comfortless house near the Scutari cemetery for the Grand Hotel d'Angleterre at Pera, and for three months lay there in a sort of semicoma. A German doctor recommended rigorous starvation, but since he was already skeletally thin this unnatural treatment did little good. He therefore transferred his allegiance to a young English doctor named Ambler, and after a few days was concocting "nice things for myself"—iced drinks, a little solid food,

[28]*Soyer's Culinary Campaign,* pp. 234–5.

raw eggs beaten with port wine—following which he began to feel strong enough to think once more about work.

He was finally, and highly appropriately, cured by Lady Stratford de Redcliffe's grand fancy-dress ball, held on January 31, 1856. Soyer was of course overjoyed to be invited to this event, one of the social highlights of Constantinople fashionable life. The Sultan himself was to attend—no small coup for Lady Stratford, since no Turkish monarch had ever before attended an infidel celebration. Soyer reveled in the gorgeous costumes and jewels, the brilliant *mise en scène,* the *tableaux vivants.* By the time the Sultan arrived at nine the ballroom was full, and at five the next morning the ball was only just ending.

As Soyer and his friends were leaving, the weather, which had been mild, suddenly produced a snowstorm, and they floundered back to the hotel in their flimsy costumes through streets already, in some places, six inches deep in snow. As they knocked fruitlessly on the hotel door an endless defile of donkeys passed, carrying coffins to the French hospital nearby. Soyer resigned himself to an early death, comforting himself with the wonderfully characteristic thought that, "after all, I should very much regret not having been, no matter what may be the consequences. To be present at an entertainment which the Padischah for the first time had honoured with his presence, is far from being a common thing."

When, at six-thirty, they finally effected an entry—the hotel offered the excuse that it had not expected them back so early—he gave orders that he was not to be disturbed, except by the doctor. But scarcely had he fallen asleep than he was roused again. Following the triumph of his field stoves the previous July, he had ordered a new consignment of four hundred, of a smaller size suitable for the front.

These had at last arrived and were on their way to Balaklava, and his presence was urgently required there to receive them.

There was nothing for it but to get up and get going. But to his astonishment, instead of feeling—as he expected—on the point of collapse, "I felt as strong again as the day before the ball, and to this event alone I attribute my cure. This proves that a sudden change may often be beneficial in cases of violent disease."[29]

The stoves had only just arrived in time, for the war was now almost over. In Constantinople, only the Barrack and General hospitals remained open. In the year since Soyer's arrival his innovations had become the rule. A Medical Staff Corps of cooks had been thoroughly and satisfactorily trained, and he proposed to leave Scutari in their hands as he would now need his civilian cooks in the Crimea. In the future, he recommended, such a corps should be introduced at all military hospitals. Soldier cooks were too often moved on just when they had mastered the necessary skills, while civilian cooks, not being subject to military discipline, were less reliably efficient.

For Soyer, the Crimea during these summer months of 1856 constituted the nearest he ever approached to heaven—a sort of combination soup kitchen and banqueting hall, in which he was everyone's best friend, constantly in demand. "All [the officers] appeared to have caught a giving-parties mania," he reports, listing invitations from a string of generals, colonels, and lords, and adds, revealingly, "I cannot but feel grateful—not alone for their liberal welcome, but also for the honour of having been admitted to their friendship." And between-times, the troops must be introduced to the wonders of his beloved stoves, a task in which he was ably

[29]*Soyer's Culinary Campaign*, p. 244.

helped by young Mr. Phillips of the manufacturers Smith and Phillips, who had been sent out with the consignment. "Short, fair, fat, and full of London jokes," he soon became such a firm friend that his first son, born that November, was named Alexis Soyer Phillips. Mr. Phillips was lent an old French cavalry pony, which was apt to fly off, as soon as mounted, in unpredictable directions; but it didn't matter, since wherever he found himself, he would be sure to find a stove in need of explication.

In the pages describing Soyer's life at this time, paragraphs setting out the daily savings of wood afforded by his stoves (450 lb. per company per diem, thus in a regiment of eight companies a daily saving of 3,600 lb. of wood, and in an army of forty thousand men 180,000 lb., that is, 90 tons, or 32,850 tons per annum) are followed by *recherché* menus for officers' dinner parties. And of course he gave his own dinners in return—*petites fêtes Anacréontiques,* beginning with delicate dishes and fine wines and ending in song. A drawing of his Crimean *villarette* shows a neat and festive hutment, its front path edged with stones and carefully spaced plants, its doorway decorated with bunting, and the camp cat—much in demand for its rat-catching abilities—brooding benignly from a nearby roof.

The culmination of all this festivity occurred when General Lüders, the Russian C.-in-C., was invited to visit the British camp in order to celebrate the peace with a grand lunch followed by a review of the troops. Now that the fighting was over, the opposing factions were on the most amiable terms, constantly exchanging visits—indeed, the Russians seem to have been touchingly anxious to show their erstwhile enemy the beauties of their country.

Soyer, who of course had been charged with the preparations for the lunch, felt it incumbent upon him to produce a dish worthy of the occasion. Time was short; and after a little consideration, he decided it would be best to concentrate upon one truly spectacular dish rather than dissipate his energies on several small and insignificant ones. The result, the *Macédoine Lüdersienne à l'Alexander II,* bears witness both to the canning and bottling skills of the Victorians and their awe-inspiring digestive powers. If we imagine a scale of richness and digestibility having calf's-foot jelly at one end, the *Macédoine Lüdersienne* shoots off the other, uncontested. It consisted of: 12 boxes of preserved lobsters, 2 cases of preserved lampreys, 2 cases of preserved sardines, 2 bottles of preserved anchovies, 1 case of preserved caviar, 1 case of preserved sturgeon, 1 case of preserved thunny *(sic),* 2 cases of preserved oysters, 1 lb. fresh prawns, 4 lb. of turbot, 12 Russian pickled cucumbers, 4 bottles pickled olives, 1 bottle mixed pickles, 1 bottle Indian pickles, 1 bottle pickled beans, 2 bottles pickled mushrooms, 1 bottle pickled mangoes, 2 bottles of pickled French truffles, 2 cases of preserved peas, 2 cases of preserved mixed vegetables, 4 dozen cabbage lettuces, 100 eggs, and 2 dozen of preserved cockscombs. And for the sauce, 6 bottles salad oil, one of Tarragon vinegar, half a bottle of Chilli vinegar, two boxes of preserved cream (whipped), four ounces of sugar, six eschalots, salt, cayenne pepper, mustard, and "a quarter of an ounce of Oriental herbs which are quite unknown in England." This tour de force, which I could not conceivably replicate (*pickled truffles? preserved lampreys?*), and from which I would not expect to recover for some days if at all, marked the high spot, both gastronomic and emotional, of Soyer's Crimean campaign.

After that, all was anticlimax. The camp began to empty; farewell party followed farewell party. Soyer gave a notable one in his *villarette,* for which he prepared a lawn of fresh-dug turf. The sun was particularly fierce that day; watching in despair as the new grass turned inexorably brown, he was inspired to commandeer some paint from the camp theater and get some soldiers to paint it green.

> Twilight was conquered by ration-fat, lampion-shells were profusely and artistically placed on the then green grass, tables sumptuously laid out, the chandelier and wax lights ignited, the globe lamps in front of the villarette blazing in volcanic splendour, the band of the Rifles playing, and the noble company as nobly arriving. . . . I, like you, immortal Vatel, had all the horrors of an unexpected failure before my eyes. The idea of suicide did not come into my mind, noble defunct and incomparable *chef!* probably because I had not the honour of wearing the sword of the courtier . . . On the contrary, though inclined to despair, I lost no time, but opened a bottle of champagne for a friend who had just popped in. At the second glass—*mirabile dictu!*—the thick curtain which shaded my brow vanished; the unsightly brown grass turned green, and everything appeared *couleur de rose.*[30]

The regiments began to leave now, and the semideserted camp presented an increasingly glum prospect. Soon, hardly anyone remained; even the debris disappeared, commandeered by the Crim Tartars who, in the absence of armies, inhabited the peninsula. But Soyer, unlike his soldier friends, had no particular desire to return home. On the contrary: The Crimean campaign had been the great-

---

[30]*Soyer's Culinary Campaign,* p. 280.

Painting the grass green.

est and most satisfying adventure of his life, and he wished only to draw it out as long as he possibly could. He justified his continued presence with the explanation that the soldiers needed to learn the use of his stoves, but as the regiments vanished even this excuse faded. The job was done: He had (to borrow Thackeray's phrase) fed his regiments to victory. Such an opportunity does not occur twice in a lifetime.

A final jollification offered in the shape of an impromptu yacht trip to Odessa. General Lüders, the city's governor, smoothed the way, obtaining a suspension of quarantine; the weather was fine; and the participants (who included W. H. Russell), released from the gloom of the abandoned camp, were in the highest of spirits from first to last.

Odessa contains many sights worth seeing, but as usual Soyer had his own priorities. He had told General Lüders that he wished to visit institutions, military hospitals, and public buildings—or rather, their kitchens. This the general had kindly arranged; with the result that for him, Odessa consisted of a succession of new and interesting variants on institutional cooking, which he described in detail for the readers of *The Times*. The kitchens, he was pleased to see, were clean and well-constructed, their boilers made of wrought iron "which I at first sight feared was copper, but the lids only were made of that showy but dangerous metal." He tasted the food being served to some orphans, and pronounced it good; he tasted their drink, *shchi,* "made with rye, mead, and a small portion of hops, requiring only a few hours to prepare it," and declared it "to the uninitiated palate anything but a pleasant drink, but, no doubt, very refreshing and agreeable when used to it." It had, he admitted, quenched his thirst for several hours on a hot day (or perhaps even thirst was preferable to another dose of *shchi*).

Duty thus performed, he was glad to add "a few words for epicures"—words which, a hundred and fifty years later, when Black Sea sturgeon face extinction and caviar sells for $56 an ounce, read particularly poignantly:

> The sturgeon, which is here abundant, and in England despised and valueless, forms a principal and an exquisite article of food, which is partly owing to the method they have of dressing it. On my return I intend to try and reinstate this queenly fish to its pristine fame.
>
> Fresh caviar, which is made from the roe of the fish, is daily eaten by the Russian population as an introduction to the dinner. Crawfish of an extraordinary size are caught in the small rivulets close to the town; they are cheap and very plentiful. The tail and claws are generally the only parts

eaten, and tons weight of the part which makes the exquisite bisque d'écrevisses are monthly thrown away.

The receipt of this excellent soup I have promised to send to the worthy host of the Europa Restaurant, he having promised to give it a trial, and thereby enrich his already luxuriant bill of fare.

Back at Balaklava, all was in the final stages of dismantling. Soyer spent one last day riding around the late scene of so much activity—the camp theater, now deserted and melancholy, the huts and tents where his friends had lived, now inhabited only by rats and a few returned Tartars, the thirty-seven cemeteries. Then, gathering up his mementos, including Miss Nightingale's carriage, which he rescued from the hands of some Tartar traders and sent back to London, he took ship for Constantinople, and left the Crimea never to return.

The danger, after so much excitement, was unendurable flatness and depression. Perhaps sensing this, Soyer did not at once return to London. He had become very fond of Constantinople, and in particular wished to collect more material for his next project—an international cookbook to be entitled "The Culinary Wonders of All Nations."

This was in many ways an astonishingly modern concept. *The Gastronomic Regenerator* had been written for the world of grand houses and gentlemen's clubs, where cookery was an art form presided over by chefs; *The Modern Housewife, or Ménagère,* though more modest, still assumed a full complement of servants. The *Shilling Cookery,* though innovative in its assumption that even the most modest households were entitled to good food, saw cooking as a daily necessity rather than a pleasure. But "The Culinary Wonders of All Nations" would, had it appeared, have been something quite different. Here is cookery seen through Soyer's own eyes, as an absorbing hobby, a pleasure in itself—a guise it would not acquire in the real world until the following century, when a combination of increased leisure, mass communications, and electrical appliances would develop the cookbook culture. Its range was to extend as far as China, whose cooking he found "resembl[es] much to the Turkish" (not in content but from their habit of serving many small dishes rather than one or two substantial ones) and whose Bird's Nest Soup he extolled: "The nests are small in the form of a half hollow . . . Their composition, which has a slight taste of salt, in colour is of a yellowish white, and semitransparent, but if old is black; it softens in warm water without disforming, and increases in volume . . . Nothing is more fortifying than a potage made with these nests and some good meat stock"—and he planned to close it with "the roast-beef and plum-pudding of Old England, which they are at present totally incapable of cooking properly in Paris, but which I intend compelling them to do."

In pursuit of recipes, he now spent a happy few weeks eating his way around the eastern Mediterranean. The Hachji Bachji, the official in charge of the Sultan's kitchens, who had under his command about six hundred male cooks, hearing of Soyer's project, invited him to a dinner replicating the repasts served daily to the Sultan, at which more than seventy different dishes were served. Of course, no one was expected to eat the whole of such a spread,

Soyer explained: The Turkish style was rather to sample mouthfuls of whatever caught the diner's fancy, each meal revealing a different gamut of possibilities. Turkey also offered opportunities for tasting Armenian food, which he found very similar to Turkish; and Greek, which he thought "sloppy and greasy." He also intended to include dishes from Russia, Malta, Italy, and France, especially French provincial cooking.

The book was never published, but some of its recipes found their way into a miscellaneous collection of dishes "for London suppers" at the back of *Soyer's Culinary Campaign*—for instance, "Pork Chops *à la Tartare*," in which the chops are marinaded in vinegar about an hour before being fried or broiled, and served with thin slices of raw onions and "a kind of cucumber peculiar to Russia and most delicious when properly pickled," also sliced thin. The chops are placed on a bed of half the onions and gherkins and covered with the remainder "until it forms a vegetable sandwich." (This dish, Soyer admitted, was "seldom to be obtained, even in Crim Tartary, and when it is, the animal is in no very nice condition.")

He lingered awhile in France, tasting once more the incomparable Marseille bouillabaisse, collecting the promised provincial recipes, checking on the well-being of the geese that provided *foie gras,* which he assured readers were not, as grisly legend had it, nailed to the floor by their feet but "are allowed to roam about the farms and grass fields of Alsace till they are seven or eight months old, kept in flocks, and well watched and tended," visiting, for the first time since his boyhood, his natal town of Meaux (he did not stay long) and spending some time in Paris with Cerrito. Finally, however, there was nothing for it but to declare the adventure ended. On May 3, 1857, he arrived back in England, never to leave it again.

His original financial arrangement with the War Office had been for expenses only. The accounts he sent in at the end of June 1855 showed payments to his private secretary, at £20 a month, £95; to a Confidential Agent at £2 10s. a week, £45; to hire of "cooks &c," £150; and to "Outfit, Hotel Expenses, Travelling Expenses for himself and staff," £309 8s. 6d. These were passed, though one civil servant considered the hire of a confidential agent "rather a questionable item." In addition, since "M. Soyer's services have been most beneficial to the Army, both in the Hospitals and in the Camp," it was suggested that he should be paid "for the period of his services at the rate of £500 a year (27s. a day) in addition to his actual expenses, and also a gratuity of six months' pay on termination of his Mission." There was no disagreement, though one civil servant "[did] not see any grounds for the . . . gratuity." However, in the end it was up to Lord Panmure; and he thought the original suggestion "reasonable"; so that was that.

This was an extremely generous offer—£500 was the annual pay of the colonel of a line infantry regiment—and it reflected real appreciation of Soyer's services. "Did we but know of its extreme importance . . . we should have paid a little more attention to Cooking in the case of Armies," wrote Florence Nightingale in 1858.[31] Soyer's priceless contribution to the British Army had been to convince it of that importance. However, his real reward—apart from the satisfaction of a job well done—was something far more precious than money; or, at least, than money in itself. After so many years as an upper servant, or at best (in the Symposium) a

---

[31]*Notes on matters affecting health, efficiency and hospital administration of the British Army,* 1858.

F. Clerk

M. Soyer was appointed in
February 1855 to enquire into
and to suggest improvements in
the culinary arrangements of
the Hospitals & Army in the East

No terms of agreement
were made besides the payment
of his actual expences, &c —
Lord Panmure's minutes on it —

M. Soyer was instructed
to draw on the Paragon in Chief
for any sums he required in
carrying out his arrangements

His

His accounts to the end of June
have just been rendered
shewing payments —

To Private Secretary at £20 a month £95 —
To Confidential Agent at £2.1/- a week £65 — } Matters in
to the of Code &c £150 — } questionable item
Outfit, Hotel Expences, Travelling expences
for himself and Staff £309.8.6
£599.8.6

It will be seen from the
accounts &c that M. Soyer expences
are chiefly on account of Travelling
and Hotel, but since his arrival
at Scutari he has been provided
with Quarters & has drawn the

---

regulated Rations for himself
and Staff

M. Soyer's services have
been most beneficial to the
Army, both in the Hospitals
and in the Camp, as will be
seen from the numerous testimonials
in & it is submitted that he
should receive pay for the period of
his services at the rate of £500 a
year (27/- a day) in addition to his
actual expences & also a gratuity of 6
months pay on the termination of his
mission —

A. Hagger

We really have no ground for refusing

tradesman, perhaps its most important function was as confirmation that the Crimea had conferred upon him a new dignity in the world's eyes.

But would it last? When he returned to England, would he revert to being "the cook"?

The answer—a qualified "yes"—was as much a comment upon Soyer himself as upon the immutability of the English class system. Twenty years of menial associations, however heartily resented, lead inevitably to menial habits of mind; and these habits Soyer, even in the Crimea, was unable to throw off. In particular, he could never overcome the compulsion to ask for references. *Soyer's Culinary Campaign* has pages of them, signed by Sir This, Lord That, Colonel the Other, each confirming the deathless value of Monsieur Soyer's contributions to the British war effort:

> Monsieur Soyer's cooking-stoves have been solely used in the Right and Left Wing Hospitals, Light Infantry Corps, during the last three months for the regimental hospital diets, for which they are admirably adapted as regards despatch, cleanliness, and economy.—G. Taylor, M.D., S Surgeon, 1st Class, 5th July 1856
>
> I had much pleasure in visiting Monsieur Soyer's field-kitchen last Monday, the 27th instant. I there saw several excellent soups made from ration meat, compressed vegetables, and other things within reach of the soldier's means, and cooked with very little fuel. I consider Monsieur Soyer is taking great pains in devoting his time and great talents to the good of our military service, especially in the field, and I wish

him every possible success and honourable reward.—James Simpson, General Commanding, Camp before Sebastopol, 31st August 1855.

Without the authentication of these stilted sentences no action, it seemed, was fully real to him, nor his own part in it wholly believable. Even Miss Nightingale, at whose side he had been through so much, was solicited for a puff.

Even in the midst of their shared travails he had always had two distinct modes with her—the businesslike, addressed to the fellow professional, and the votive, addressed to the saint—as, for example, these lines written while she was ill:

> Quitte pour quelque temps, héroine soeur du brave,
> Les soucieux rochers, cette terre d'esclave,
> Et fuis sur l'onde pure, réfuge solitaire
> Ou ton nom vénéré autant que sur terre . . .

and so forth for many stanzas, accompanied by a letter in the same overblown and worshiping style (though not, thankfully, in alexandrines).[32] But despite these aberrations (this one was preserved and later pasted into a scrapbook by Miss Nightingale's adoring sister Parthenope), they continued to work together as close colleagues through the most grueling of circumstances.

She was perhaps therefore puzzled to receive, out of the blue,

[32]In the Wellcome Collection.

alongside a businesslike missive concerning the delivery of some stoves, the following paean, written from the Hotel d'Angleterre, Pera:

26 July, 1856

> Ma chère Demoiselle, . . .
>
> *Fourteen months have passed since I had the honour of being introduced to you for the first time; I could never have imagined, having no notion, on leaving Albion's shores, of spending more than a few weeks at the Scutari hospital, whence, like a brilliant Meteor, you drew my attention to the burning skies of the East, that together we would see the end of this gigantic drama which, starting in Europe, has engulfed almost the whole world, and upon part of which you, like a beneficent angel, have ceaselessly poured your generous and consoling balm upon the dying Brave and the suffering Soldier . . .*

This apparently arbitrary effusion was followed next day by another note, in somewhat less flowery mode, enclosing an inscription she had requested for a monument to be raised at Balaklava, with a recommendation that she let Soyer have this engraved for her on a bronze plaque when he returned to Europe, rather than risk inexpert Turkish carvers spoiling the marble. He ended this letter with a sentence that cast new light on the previous day's effort:

> *A few words from you expressing your candid opinion of the humble services I was able to render in the Hospitals would infinitely oblige your very humble servant.*

Peace at last.

Miss Nightingale of course obliged:

> *I have great pleasure in bearing my testimony to the very*
> *essential usefulness of Monsieur Soyer, who, first in the General*
> *Hospitals of Scutari, and afterwards in the Camp Hospitals of*
> *the Crimea, both general and regimental, restored order where*
> *all was unavoidable confusion, as far as he was individually*
> *able,—took the soldiers' and patients' diets as they were, and*
> *converted them into wholesome and agreeable food.*

It was no more than the truth, and there can be little doubt that to
see it thus acknowledged in writing by his heroine accorded him
endless pleasure. But it—or rather, the compulsive need it fulfilled—

proved, once and for all, that equality is a mental construct and one that, however much he might crave it, Soyer would never achieve. The whole world knew of the services he had rendered; his inventiveness, his bravery, his public spirit, were attested by both his actions and his stoves; his character was established for the world to see. If ever a man had passed the point where references were necessary, Soyer was that man; if he had proved one thing, it was that his erstwhile employers were in no way his betters. But because he could never really believe it, it would never really be true.

8

Coffee

We have arrived at the end of our meal, but like our hero's life, it is not yet quite done. For no meal is complete without a cup of good coffee to round it off; and so, too, thought Soyer.

It is only in his more plebeian recipe collections that he gives any hints on coffee making—perhaps assuming that anyone working from *The Gastronomic Regenerator* or *The Modern Housewife, or Ménagère* needed no instruction from him on so basic a matter. The *Culinary Campaign* contains two. The first, for Coffee à la Zouave for a Mess of Ten Soldiers, vividly evokes camp life in that strange and unique regiment, the pride of the French army, resourceful, amoral (the baggy breeches, Mary Seacole noted ruefully, would hold vast quantities of stolen goods), and devoted to *la bonne table*. Just because they were at war, that did not mean they were going to do without decent coffee:

Put 9 pints of water into a canteen saucepan on the fire; when boiling add 7½ oz. of coffee, which forms the ration, mix them well together with a spoon or a piece of wood, leave on the fire for a few minutes longer, or until just beginning to boil. Take it off and pour on 1 pint of cold water, let the whole remain for 10 minutes or a little longer. The dregs of the coffee will fall to the bottom and your coffee will be clear. Pour it from one vessel to the other, leaving the dregs at the bottom, add your ration sugar or 2 teaspoons to the pint; if any milk is to be had make 2 pints of coffee less; add that quantity of milk to your coffee, the former may be boiled previously, and serve.

Or perhaps, being in the Crimea, the troops might prefer Turkish Coffee:

When the water is just on the boil add the coffee and sugar, give just a boil and serve. The grouts of coffee will in a few seconds fall to the bottom of the cup. The Turks wisely leave it there, I would advise every one in camp to do the same.

Doubtless these were and are highly practical hints. But as I just wanted plain coffee for two, I looked elsewhere—viz., to the "few original hints on coffee, tea, etc." to be found in the *Shilling Cookery*. In this context, it should be noted that coffee and poverty were by no means strangers: Victorian London was full of coffee stalls, used by rich and poor alike.

—— *Simplified Mode of Making Coffee* ——

Put one ounce of ground coffee in a pan, which place over the fire; keep stirring it until quite hot, but take care it does not burn; then pour over quickly a quart of boiling water, close it immediately, keep it not far from the fire, but not to simmer; then fill your cup without shaking it; or pass it through a cloth into a coffee pot, or it may be made some time previous and warmed again. The grounds can be kept and boiled for making the coffee of the next day, by which at least a quarter of an ounce is saved. The idea of warming coffee is my own, and the economy is full ten per cent.

There are of course excellent precedents for warming coffee grounds before making the actual coffee. Anyone who cooks Indian dishes will know that the spices used there are heated in exactly this way to bring out their full flavor; and tea is also improved if the pot is warmed before the leaves are put in. Soyer was a great enthusiast for warming tea in this way—his method was to put the tea leaves in the pot and then set it by the fire to warm while the water boiled.

The difficulty with coffee, in my experience, is that it almost always disappoints. The aroma is so delicious and enticing, and the taste so rarely bears any relation to it. The problem is undoubtedly one of freshness: The more recently your coffee has been roasted and ground, the more the taste will approach the aroma. Soyer's method, presumably, was intended to inject freshness by reroasting, just a little, the ground beans. Unfortunately, I found that it detracted from the aroma rather than enhancing it. This may be because long trial and error have led me to a coffee which I find almost perfect for my taste (since you ask, Cafédirect's Machu Picchu) and slightly increasing the roast in this way does not improve it. Or maybe I burned it slightly, which, as Soyer warned, is easy to do. However, his idea of good coffee is not really mine: he liked his a little bitter—"in my opinion," he writes, "a good cup of coffee cannot be made without the introduction of a little chicory"—while I prefer mine mellow; and extra roasting, unless you are very careful, increases the bitterness.

It so happens that Soyer demonstrated his method of coffee making at the home of a septuagenarian friend in "the fashionable quarter of St. Giles's"—just about where these words are being written. This was in his Ham Yard days, and this lady doubtless one of his clients there. He recounts in *Shilling Cookery* how, having taught her to cook "the ox-cheek," she and several of her friends clubbed together to invite him to a fashionable "tea," "which of course my vanity made me immediately accept." He approached it with slight trepidation, St. Giles's being London's most notorious slum, only to find when he arrived that the little parlor had been cleaned and ornamented with flowers from the neighboring garden ("the best in the world, Covent Garden") while the table held a pyramid of muffins and crumpets. Everyone clearly had a most enjoyable time stuffing themselves with these goodies, and as they ate Soyer showed them the best way to make tea, coffee, and cocoa.

However, whether or not his campfire comradeships with the *gratin* metamorphosed into genuine friendship, he was by 1857 unquestionably a respectable and respected member of society. And such a person neither lived in Soho nor socialized with old ladies in St. Giles's. Rather, he took up residence for a while in Kensington Square, and began looking for a house to buy, if not in Kensington itself, then in some other suitable part of town.

Meanwhile, he was still very weak from his Crimean experiences; and a health-giving expedition was arranged to his favorite country haunt, Virginia Water. However, when his horse arrived it seemed most unsuitable—frisky and uncontrollable. He nevertheless insisted on mounting it, but had got no farther than Holland Park Avenue when it threw him. Unfortunately, his foot caught in the stirrup, and he was dragged along for some distance before he was freed. With his usual obstinacy, however, he refused to abandon the excursion, arriving in Virginia Water late that afternoon, bruised and shaken, in a hansom cab. He did not recover for some weeks; and no sooner was he feeling a little better than a further blow hit him, when his favorite niece, Augusta, his brother Philippe's daughter, died in childbirth. The result of this accumulated hardship was that he began to cough blood, which horrified his friends, though he seemed oddly unworried by it. Indeed, it provided an excuse for his favorite indulgence, multiple medical consultations. When ill he always overdosed on doctors, consulting two or three at any one time, their visits carefully arranged to avoid embarrassing clashes.

Despite his ill health he continued to work, finishing off his Crimea memoir and taking his place as a paid-up member of the Great and the Good. In March 1858, he lectured on military cooking to a packed hall at the United Services Institute, and soon after was appointed to a committee briefed to design a movable cook-wagon for an army on the march. (Unsurprisingly, it adopted his design, first mooted in Ireland during the Famine.) Then the Emigration

Commissioners requested some new recipes for emigrant ships. Those on assisted passages were, like the troops in the Crimea, issued with salt meat rations and expected to cook for themselves; accordingly, Soyer produced a small cookery book for them, using many of the recipes he had devised for the army, and recommended that they should prepare their food in messes of eight, each group to be issued with a Scutari teapot and coffeepot and a baking-stewing pan. He was also asked to devise diets for military hospitals, and design a new kitchen for the Wellington Barracks in Birdcage Walk.

His partner in this latter enterprise was none other than Florence Nightingale. Unlike Soyer, who could never bear to remain in invalid incarceration a moment longer than was absolutely unavoidable, Miss Nightingale, similarly weakened by her Crimean experiences, had now definitively taken to her bed, where she would spend the rest of her long and productive life; but clearly, neither this nor Soyer's illness prevented their collaborating as fruitfully as ever. "My Dear Captain Galton," she wrote that April to the officer in charge,

> *Dr Sutherland desired I would further the kitchen plan for the Wellington Barracks, for which, it appears, you are waiting. So I sent up to Soyer, who is ill, for it, found it was done, sent it (with temporary directions) to Smith and Phillips in Skinner Street, and expect it back today at Soyer's. Soyer wishes it to be looked at here first, by you and Dr Sutherland and Captain Grant—and appoints Monday.*
>
> *I do not know his reason for not going at once to the place where it is to be put up. But I think that if you could find any hour between one and four on Monday, to come here, it would*

be as well to do as he wishes. Soyer gives up about the men
dining in the kitchen, and admits that it is undesirable.

The two of them were also involved in a similar scheme for the naval headquarters at Chatham, for which they proposed a copy of the Wellington kitchen plans.

Soyer had by now moved out of lodgings and sealed his new, respectable persona with the purchase of a house in St. John's Wood, where (it will be recalled) Eloise, the "Modern Housewife," had once lived at Bifrons Villa. Whether his house at 15 Marlborough Road was also double-fronted we shall never know: It no longer exists, having been razed in order to build enormous blocks of flats. But that these were substantial dwellings can be seen from their classy inhabitants and high ratable values. No. 15, belonging to Soyer, was rated at £69; Sir M. Diarmid, at no. 23, paid £95; no. 21, owned by Sir James Campwell, was rated at £110; and no. 7, owned by one Charles C. Black, was rated at an enormous £144.

At the beginning of August, he decided to visit Sydenham for a few days. Paxton's Crystal Palace had been re-erected there, and he wanted to visit its fine art exhibition, for which he had agreed to loan some of Emma's paintings. He booked in to the Paxton Hotel in Norwood, whose chef he knew and liked and which was conveniently situated "a nice walk from the Palace." He enjoyed this outing, though feeling a little tired afterward. Next day he felt relatively well in the morning, and arranged to dine with some friends, one of whom went so far as to order the dessert. However, as the day went on his condition worsened, and it was agreed he should be taken back to St. John's Wood, where after a few hours' great pain he sank gratefully into a coma. He died at eighteen minutes to ten on the night of August 5, 1858. With him were Charles Pierce, his old friend Mr. Phillips the stovemaker, and his secretary, J. R. Warren. He was forty-eight years old.

"Soyer's death is a great disaster," wrote Florence Nightingale to Captain Galton. "Others have studied cookery for the purpose of gormandizing, some for shew, but none but he for the purpose of cooking large quantities of food in the most nutritious and economic manner, for great numbers of men. He has no successor." After which, since a dead collaborator can hardly be of much use, his name vanishes from her correspondence.

He was buried, as he had requested, with Emma, sharing the tomb he had raised fourteen years before "To Her" at Kensal Green cemetery. The funeral was attended by a large number of his friends, even though the time had been rearranged at short notice, so that it took place inconveniently early in the morning. Charles Pierce delivered an oration; the other mourners were his nephew Alexis, his medical adviser Mr. Brittain, M. Comte, chef to the Duke of Cambridge, and M. Férand, chef at the Athenaeum Club. M. Simonau was there, with Emma's brother, Newton Jones; so were Soyer's estranged ex-secretary Volant, Dr. Ambler, who had saved his life in Constantinople (and whom Soyer tended in his turn at Balaklava), Lord Stratford de Redcliffe's chef, M. Rocco Vido, and many other friends and acquaintances.

The congregation did not include any of the aristocrats and generals whose friendship he had so craved and, briefly, so enjoyed. But death is no respecter of class, and he would doubtless have been gratified to know that not a stone's throw from his tomb lies that of the Duke of Cambridge himself; and that generals, lords, and

Members of Parliament are scattered freely all around the very same cemetery.

His will left Madame Soyer's pictures to the National Gallery, £50 to his great-niece Ella, the baby whose birth had killed her mother Augusta Clausen, and to his old friends Mr. Crosse and Mr. Blackwell their choice of any possessions not otherwise bequeathed. However, none of these bequests was actually made. For it transpired that, at his death, Soyer owed more than his net worth, probate being eventually granted to David Hart, who had paid off his debts following the Symposium débacle.

Evidently, things had not turned out quite as Hart had hoped when he rode to the rescue in 1851. The quid pro quo for his help had doubtless been the promise of a share in future Soyer enterprises—beginning with the Magic Stove, in which, after the death of the original partner, he took a half share. However, when the *Shilling Cookery for the People* appeared, it transpired that Soyer alone had published it and alone enjoyed its profits, while from the new Army stove no private profits whatever stood to be made. It was not even manufactured by Hart, who among other things ran an iron foundry. And in the meantime Soyer took the opportunity to put in substantial orders for wines and spirits to Mr. Hart's other business, the wine merchants Lemon Hart & Sons, his tab mounting over the years, always to be paid at some future date. So Hart took his worldly goods, while Soyer reclined, and reclines, under the figure of Faith amid the now teetering obelisks and headless angels of Kensal Green.

It will be recalled that when he buried Emma in 1842, one of the Reform Club wags had suggested that her epitaph should be

ON the 23rd day of December 18 58

Letters of Administration, with the Will and ~~Codicils thereto~~ annexed,

of all and singular the personal Estate and Effects of *Alexis*

Soyer

~~formerly of~~

and late of *No 15 Marlborough Road Saint Johns Wood in the County of Middlesex &*

deceased, who died on the *5th* day of *August* 18 58,

at *No 15 Marlborough Road aforesaid*

were granted at the Principal Registry of Her Majesty's Court of Probate

to *David Hart*

of *No 42 Trinity Square Tower Hill in the City of London Wine Merchant a Creditor of the said Deceased*

~~the Residuary Legatee named in the said Will,~~ he having been first sworn duly to administer, ~~no Executor being named in the said Will; or, the sole Executor named in the said Will having died in the lifetime of the said deceased; or, having renounced the Probate and Execution thereof~~ *Sophia Cooke Spinster and Edmund Crofts in the Will written Mr Croft the Executors named in the said Will having renounced the Probate and execution thereof and the said Sophia Cooke as the Residuary Legatee named in the said Will having also renounced Letters of Administration (with the said Will annexed) of the Personal Estate and Effects of the said Deceased.*

Effects under £ 1500

6

F. J. C. Lorford)

"Soyer Tranquille." This suggestion he had declined, but, always one to see a joke, offered, at the end of his *Culinary Campaign*, an emendation. "Soyer très heureux," runs the caption beneath a picture of his jovial self, glass in hand, bottle on the table beside him.

Happiness and death are not concepts easily reconciled—least of all in the case of Soyer, whose appetite for life, as for everything else, was so keen. But tranquil he undoubtedly lies, among the trees and ivy-clad tombs, London's roar, which he so enjoyed, blurred by the peculiar peace of deserted cemeteries, the only sound a distant mower neatening the grass around the graves.

The Soyer tomb at Kensal Green cemetery: Alexis and Emma together at last. The figure of Faith has lost an arm, but Emma's portrait remains intact.

SOYER BIBLIOGRAPHY

Almanach des Gourmands, 1803, 1825.

Askwith, Betty: *Crimean Courtship,* Salisbury, Wilts, 1985.

Brillat-Savarin, Jean-Anthelme: *The Philosopher in the Kitchen*
(*La Physiologie du goût,* Paris, 1825), tr. Anne Drayton,
Harmondsworth, 1970.

Davy, Christopher: *Architectural Precedents,* 1842.

Drummond, J. C., and Anne Wilbraham: *The Englishman's Food,*
London, 1939.

Fagan, Louis: *The Reform Club,* London, 1885.

Goldie, Sue: *A Calendar of the Letters of Florence Nightingale,*
Oxford, 1977.

Guest, Ivor: *Fanny Cerrito: The life of a romantic ballerina,* London,
1956.

Hayward, Abraham: *The Art of Dining,* London, 1852.

Heath, Sir Leopold George: *Letters from the Black Sea during the
Crimean War,* London, 1897.

Hobsbawm, Eric: *The Age of Revolution,* London, 1962.

Hobsbawm, Eric, and George Rudé: *Captain Swing,* London, 1969.

Leapman, Michael: *The World for a Shilling: How the Great Exhibition Shaped a Nation,* London, 2001.

Mawson, Michael Hargreave, ed.: *Eyewitness in the Crimea: The Crimean War Letters (1854–1856) of Lt. Col. George Frederick Dallas,* London, 2001.

Morris, Helen: *Portrait of a Chef. The Life of Alexis Soyer, Sometime Chef to the Reform Club,* Cambridge, 1938.

Olsen, Donald J.: *The Growth of Victorian London,* London, 1976.

Orléans, duc d': *Souvenirs 1810–1830,* ed. Hervé Robert, Geneva, 1993.

Ray, Elizabeth: Alexis Soyer, *Cook Extraordinary,* Lewes, 1991.

Sala, G. A.: *The Book of the Symposium, or, Soyer at Gore House,* London, 1851.

Sala, G. A.: *Things I Have Seen and People I Have Known,* in two vols., London, 1894.

Sala, G. A.: *The Life and Adventures of George Augustus Sala, written by himself,* in two vols., London, 1895.

Seacole, Mary: *Wonderful Adventures of Mrs Seacole in Many Lands,* 1857; ed. Ziggi Alexander and Audrey Dewjee, Bristol, 1984.

Somerville, Alexander: *The Whistler at the Plough,* Manchester, 1852; ed. K. D. M. Snell, London, 1989.

Soyer, Alexis: *The Gastronomic Regenerator,* London, 1846.

Soyer, Alexis: *Soyer's Charitable Cookery: or, The Poor Man's Regenerator,* London, 1847.

Soyer, Alexis: *The Modern Housewife,* or Ménagère, London, 1849.

Soyer, Alexis: *Soyer's Shilling Cookery for the People,* London, 1854.

Soyer, Alexis: *Soyer's Culinary Campaign,* London, 1857; ed. Michael Barthorp and Elizabeth Ray, Lewes, 1996.

Spang, Rebecca L.: *The Invention of the Restaurant: Paris and Modern Gastronomic Culture,* Harvard, 2000.

Straus, Ralph: *Sala: The Portrait of an Eminent Victorian,* London, 1942.

Thackeray, W. M.: *Pendennis,* London, 1849.

Thorne, Robert: "Places of refreshment in the nineteenth-century city," in *Buildings and Society,* ed. King, London, 1980.

Twicknam Park—An Outline of the History of Twickenham Park and the St Margaret's Estate, Hounslow, 1965.

Volant, F. and J. R. Warren: *Memoirs of Alexis Soyer, with Unpublished Receipts and Odds and Ends of Gastronomy,* London, 1859.

Woodham-Smith, Cecil: *The Great Hunger,* London, 1962.

Woodham-Smith, Cecil: *The Reason Why,* London, 1953.

INDEX